Making It Till Friday

A Guide to Successful Classroom Management

SECOND EDITION

Dedicated to Lib, Blakeley, Gene, David, and Amy

MAKING IT TILL FRIDAY

A Guide to Successful Classroom Management

SECOND EDITION

James D. Long
Appalachian State University

and

Virginia H. Frye
University of Tennessee

PRINCETON BOOK COMPANY, *Publishers*
Princeton, New Jersey

Sources of Cartoons
We gratefully acknowledge cartoonists
Ford Button (back cover, pages 3, 80, 134,
and 185), Martha Campbell (page 52), Clem
Scalzitti (page 105), and Bardulf Ueland
(page 17).

PREFACE

Like the first edition, the purpose of this book is to provide teachers and prospective teachers at all grade levels practical suggestions for managing their classes more effectively. Today, perhaps even more than when our original edition was published, teachers everywhere are seeking answers to increasingly difficult problems. They realize their need for special classroom managerial skills. They have learned the hard way that *spur of the moment* solutions usually do not work.

We believe there are answers to the many problems that beset teachers—even the more serious problems. Seemingly unmotivated students can be encouraged to achieve. Shy students can be helped to participate more actively in discussions. Aggressive youngsters can become more cooperative. Student defiance, vandalism, cheating, and stealing can be brought under control. Research evidence is already available to increase teacher effectiveness in managing most types of classroom difficulties. More is being learned daily. Of course, no one can guarantee 100 percent success with every problem: teachers and students differ too much in their application and response to various techniques. Armed with a variety of responses to troublesome classroom situations, teachers can move *toward* a successful career in teaching. Once teachers learn the alternative methods for dealing with problems, they are in a position to test what works best for them and their students. This book provides not one but many ways in which problems can be resolved and prevented.

Although the current edition is similar in purpose to the original, many changes have been made. Two chapters from the previous

vi MAKING IT TILL FRIDAY

edition have been combined to clarify how prompting and reinforcement go hand-in-hand to stimulate the development of desirable behaviors. Because of the importance of working closely with the home, a new chapter has been added describing ways in which school personnel can build better home-school relationships. Other chapters have been expanded and updated to reflect the most current strategies for managing behaviors related to teaching and learning.

The first chapter strives to help teachers recognize the fallacy of assuming that only "bad" teachers have problems and realize that their own difficulties cannot be solved by hiding them or by self-pity. The second chapter reveals how teachers can begin to effectuate solutions by altering their attitudes toward themselves and others. Attention is given to what experts as well as students consider valued teacher traits. The next two chapters represent the "heart" of the text, for this is where the major categories of student behaviors and ways of managing them are discussed. Chapter Three describes strategies for managing deficits in student behaviors, and solutions to problems such as truancy, shyness, and lack of interest in school tasks. Chapter Four, on managing excessive behaviors, gives tentative solutions to the problems of stealing, disruptiveness, violence, vandalism. The following two chapters cover working with the home (Chapter Five) and other school personnel (Chapter Six) to meet student needs and facilitate proper development. Chapter Six also gives special attention to meeting the needs of exceptional students. Chapter Seven describes how students can be brought to the ultimate goal in all education: self-responsibility. Chapter Eight examines the ethical and legal ramifications of classroom change strategies. The final chapter focuses on gathering all the material into a meaningful whole. It illustrates how various strategies can be combined to deal with the problems of getting students to complete assignments and of reducing defiant behaviors. Hypothetical problems are also presented in the final chapter to test the reader's ability to orchestrate the use of various alternatives for making it till Friday. While the chapters themselves are not inclusive, we believe they represent a beginning in moving away from problems to solutions—a beginning toward a new style of teaching.

J.D.L.
V.H.F.

CONTENTS

Preface   **v**

1. The Challenge: An Introduction to   **1**
   Classroom Management

   Things in Common; Hope for Teachers; Between Success and Failure; Concluding Thoughts

2. The Eye of the Beholder: **15**
   Teacher Attitudes Toward Students

   The Impact of Attitudes; Critical Attitudes; Strategies for Change; Concluding Remarks

3. A Day Late and a Page Short: **32**
   Managing Deficit Behaviors

   Prompting Desired Behaviors; Evaluating Your Approach; Reinforcing Appropriate Behaviors; Summary

4. What Will They Do Next? Managing Excessive   **67**
   Student Behaviors

   Altering Setting Events; Reinforcing Behaviors Incompatible with Disruptiveness; Using Peers as Models; Extinction; Punishment; On Reasoning with Students; School Violence; Summary and Conclusion

5. The Home Connection: Working with Parents   **103**

   Importance of Good Home and School Relationships; Developing Good Home-School Relationships; About Parents; Rights of Parents; Summary

6. They Have a Right: Meeting Exceptional Needs   **119**

Major Provisions of Public Law 94-142; Implications for Teachers; Some Problems Require Referral; When to Refer; Making Referrals for Resource Services; School Resource Specialists; School Counselor; Summary

7. I'd Rather Do It Myself: Guiding Students   **147**
     Toward Self-Management

Origins of Self-Management; Techniques of Self-Management; Concerns about Self-Management; Summary

8. Right and Wrong: Ethical and Legal Problems   **170**
     of Classroom Management

Ethical Issues: Goals of Behavior Change; Ethical Issues: Behavior Change Methodology; Legal Issues: Students' Rights; Legal Issues: Behavior Change Techniques; Legal Issues: Caution for Teachers; Legal Issues: Accountability; Summary

9. Alpha But Not Omega: Putting It All Together   **195**

General Review; Approaching Actual Problems; Concluding Remarks

Index   **210**

CHAPTER ONE

THE CHALLENGE: AN INTRODUCTION TO CLASSROOM MANAGEMENT

"I'm telling you. I'm really worried about what to do with that group. I think I've got the worst class in school. I stayed up until midnight last night planning lessons and today the class was less interested than ever. Lately I can't seem to get them enthused about anything. They spend most of their work periods talking among themselves. I have to keep after them all the time. And would you believe that Mr. Wilson caught two of *my* boys stuffing rolls of toilet paper down the commodes in the boys' restroom? And that Bobby Johnson was horsing around in the cafeteria and fell and broke his arm? I'll probably get sued for that one. Why does everything always happen to me?"

Things In Common

Are the concerns expressed by the teacher in the opening paragraph unique? Not really. To begin with, most teachers occasionally express frustration over their job. A comprehensive review (Coates & Thoresen, 1976) of studies on the incidence of anxiety among teachers suggests that teachers in general experience considerable stress, tension, or anxiety in the classroom. One study concerned with the health of teachers (Landsmann, 1978) indicates that teachers believe job-related stress is the major force affecting their health. Of course, this teacher's worries might be excessive in terms of the problems she actually experiences. Her present worry could be the expressions of an off-day or temporary depression. Or, those worries could be related to serious, long-standing personal or classroom difficulties. In either case, the teacher is not alone. Teaching poses many challenges.

While this teacher's specific problems could be different from those other teachers experience, the composite nature of her problems is not unique. Every major study on teaching shows that discipline is a principal concern of teachers: it continues to rank as the number one problem for the schools. Indeed, discipline problems of one type or another eventually touch the lives of every teacher. No one seems immune. Both men and women, rural and urban, elementary and secondary, and beginning and veteran teachers report major problems with discipline (Long & Mamola, 1978). If anything is unique, it is the mildness of this teacher's problems. While her problems—which seem to center around the motivation of students—are serious, she reports no open defiance or acts of violence from her students. Many teachers would consider her fortunate. In brief, problems, not a lack of them, are the order of the day.

Finally, this teacher's lament about everything happening to her is an understandable, not uncommon feeling. Even with national attention focused on the problems of discipline in the schools, a teacher can easily feel that his problems are more serious or that he is the only one having problems. Individuals tend to identify with what is close at hand rather than with publicized problems in a distant, unfamiliar setting. Close at hand, however, other teachers are apt to mask their problems or keep them altogether secret. Many teachers sense they can't be open about problems at a time when a surplus of teachers are looking for work. The misconception that good teachers don't have problems further inhibits teachers from advertising their difficulties. Naturally, any teacher is going to know more about what happens to himself than of the fate that befalls others. Thus, to feel occasionally that one stands alone is an unfortunate likelihood.

Hope for Teachers

With this initial attention on the anxieties and problems of teaching, you may be wondering if there is any hope for teachers. Certainly! While there is justification for concern about the presence of problems in the schools, the situation is far from hopeless. An abundance of strategies exists for helping teachers cope with the

"Teaching isn't a fun-thing anymore."

problems they encounter in teaching. Too frequently, however, teachers never get beyond identifying their problems. The teacher who was discussing her problems in the opening paragraph was doing just that: she was focusing on her troubles. Many a teacher establishes one confidant; then he and that confidant reinforce each other in complaint about their troubles. The resolution of a problem does include recognizing its existence. But teachers should avoid dwelling too long on their troubles. Becoming an effective teacher involves more than recognizing problems. It also involves examining what to do about those problems. Teachers can do much to improve their lot. For a start, teachers can recognize the control *they* exert over school problems. Next, most teachers can benefit from expanding their knowledge of existing strategies for managing problems. Third, teachers can unite with other interested persons in attacking school problems. Let's examine these possibilities in more detail.

The Teacher's Influence

A fundamental requisite to producing improvements in classroom or school-related problems is recognition by teachers of the controls they have over their own destiny. Persons who believe they are in control of their actions and the ensuing rewards and punishments possess what psychologists call an *internal locus of control* (Clark, 1976). Teachers with an internal locus of control believe that "What happens in my classroom is *largely* under my control," as opposed to "What happens in my classroom is a matter of chance" or "is a result of how students choose to behave." Researchers repeatedly affirm that an internal locus of control is an indicator of good mental health (Williams & Long, 1979). We believe it is an essential to effective classroom management. No teacher will work for improvements in student behavior as long as he believes his actions have no impact. We are not suggesting that teachers can or should control all problem behavior. Some student misbehavior is a result of normal human interactions. But teachers can markedly influence how students behave. Researchers (Madsen, Becker, Thomas, Koser & Plager, 1968; Thomas, Becker & Armstrong, 1968) have demonstrated that teachers can actually create a disruptive class by systematically increasing the amount of disapproval given to students. Other studies (Kazdin & Klock, 1973; McAllister, Stachowiak, Baer & Conderman, 1969) have shown that increased use of positive strategies (e.g., verbal and nonverbal approval of appropriate student behaviors) can reduce problem behaviors.

Unfortunately, those in education do not always accept the extent of their own influence. The home, the peer group, and the community are too frequently held responsible for problems that are amenable to change within the classroom. In one survey of public school administrators about classroom problems (Long, 1976), the administrators saw the teacher or the school as being partially responsible for less than ten percent of the reported problems. An unfavorable home background was listed as a source of problems ranging from being impolite to the teacher and tearing down a bulletin board to fighting on the school bus and disrupting academic activities. The students, the community, and the home were cited as being the cause for about ninety percent of the more than 240 classroom problems reported by the administrators. Studies among teachers (Barnes, 1963; Long & Mamola, 1978) also have found that factors related to the home were most often cited as contributing to classroom problems.

Certainly most persons would agree that a student's home life, his neighborhood, or his friends contribute to his behavior in the classroom. However, when teachers and principals make this point, they must realize that the school, too, is a part of every student's environment. If a child lacks an interest in school, can the school do nothing to remedy that circumstance? Little can be achieved by attributing all problem situations to the home, the community, or the students. Similarly, little can be achieved by trying to affix all blame on the teachers. Some problems are undoubtedly caused by the teacher, some by the home, and so on. But affixing blame is no solution. Educators who are willing to recognize their influence and who are willing to take an active role in effecting change can help students learn new and alternative behaviors *irrespective* of who caused the problem.

Expanding Personal Knowledge

Another requisite for improving the schools is recognition by teachers of the various forms of behavior problems and the ability to apply appropriate remedial and preventive techniques. Teachers nationwide, however, claim that teacher training institutions have inadequately prepared them for dealing with school disciplinary problems (Committee of the Judiciary, 1977). Typically, teachers contend that what they learned in college was too theoretical. What they seek are concrete applications of theory.

I NEVER HEARD OF IT

In an effort to get a more comprehensive view of school problems, one researcher (Duke, 1978) turned his attention to a large California high school. He interacted with the administration, faculty, and students during the course of an entire school year. Although initial observations confirmed staff reports of few student behavior problems, the researcher learned that discipline was still an important issue at school. He found that disciplinary matters accounted for much of the day-to-day activities of the school personnel. But it was not student behavior *per se* that occupied the teachers' time. The concern was largely over ways in which the teachers handled problems. Inconsistency and lack of knowledge were widespread. No more than twenty percent of the school's ninety-six teachers had tried using systematic behavior modification, teacher effectiveness training, reality therapy, or other contemporary approaches for managing discipline problems. Most of the teachers were also unfamiliar with the work of Rudolf Dreikurs and Haim Ginott. Furthermore, the teachers were not involved in in-service training related to discipline because no such courses were available. Although many of the teachers' problems were related to their handling of student behavior, Duke concluded that the teachers could not be faulted for being unaware of techniques to which they had never been introduced.

The lack of explicit attention to school disciplinary problems in many teacher preparation programs may be partially a function of the way professional educators have viewed the teaching-learning process. Doyle (1978) points out that, historically, educational psychology has stressed strategies that foster the learning of academic subject matter. The assumption seems to have been, and still is to a great extent, that the teacher who knows how to teach academics will have few classroom problems. Recent interest in child-centered psychology has also promoted the view that love of students is sufficient to maintain control of a class. Both the emphasis on learning theory and the idea that "love conquers all" have resulted in teachers studying materials that have little direct bearing on classroom management. Knowledge of learning theory and the humane treatment of students are of great importance but, in and of themselves, these approaches do not equip teachers with the specifics they need for working with students on a daily basis.

Training institutions are not entirely at fault for the lack of skill among teachers. One study (Blair, Jones & Simpson, 1975) revealed that during a given month forty percent of the 746 teachers and administrators questioned had not looked at a single professional book and fourteen percent had read no professional magazine article. This is no way for educators to expand their knowledge. But we don't want to chastize you. You have read this far and we trust you have an interest in expanding *your* knowledge. Recent developments in applied behavior analysis (behavior modification) and humanistic psychology have much to offer that is relevant to teachers. This book will draw from those two fields in offering specific techniques to help you manage your classes. While we can offer no guarantees for remedying every difficulty, those who are willing to admit they have problems, examine the reasons for those problems, and search for solutions should be able to resolve most of their difficulties. More teachers can learn to enjoy Mondays as much as (or almost as much as) Fridays.

Working with Others

Many teachers have difficulty accepting the limits of personal achievement. They equate getting any help from others with failure. While teachers do have a major responsibility for what occurs in their classes and in their school, no teacher can be the sole problem-solving agent in a classroom. Some problems are just too complex for teachers to solve alone. It simply makes good sense for the benefit of students as well as teachers that all possible resources be used in establishing a stable learning environment in the schools.

Perhaps the most important resource upon which teachers can rely to improve classroom behaviors is the students. Academic and social behaviors seem to improve almost immediately when students are actively involved in management of the classroom. For example, in a study with fifth graders (Besalel-Azrin, Azrin & Armstrong, 1977), student-reported problems decreased by seventy percent after only one month of student-oriented responsibilities and by ninety-six percent after six months. A matched group of control students showed minimal improvements until they, too, were introduced to procedures that maximized their involvement. Among other responsibilities, the students in this study assumed a large role in developing a contract for social and academic behaviors, in determining rewards for appropriate classroom behavior, and in correcting their mistakes and misbehavior by practicing the correct mode of behavior.

Other studies with special education students (Long & Williams, 1976; Lovitt & Curtiss, 1969), elementary students (White-Blackburn, Semb & Semb, 1977; Thomas, 1976), and junior high and senior high school students (Glynn, 1970; Williams & Anandam, 1977) suggest that sharing classroom management responsibilities with the students holds considerable promise for improving academic and social behaviors. Indeed, it seems doubtful that effective classroom management can exist when a teacher assumes total responsibility for it. Students need to learn that they have some responsibility for behaving appropriately. They are the ones who need to learn the academic and social skills. The role of the teacher should not be forcing students to behave. Under such conditions, students may never learn to manage their own behaviors. School, thus, becomes less meaningful for everyone.

ALL THAT GLITTERS...

An experimental study in ninth-grade English class (Arwood, Williams & Long, 1974) revealed to one group of researchers that student behavior is not always what it seems to be. In one phase of the study, the teacher precisely defined what was considered to be appropriate and inappropriate behaviors and specified what would be the consequences (rewards and punishments) for each type of behavior. The students were left out of the planning. Under the clearly specified conditions provided by the teacher, the students made improvements in their social conduct. They talked less during the teacher's lectures, appeared to be more attentive, sat straighter, and threw fewer spitwads. But they did not improve academically. Only when they were involved in the planning did they improve both socially and academically. The researchers hypothesized that when these students were excluded from decision-making processes, they simply went through the motions to earn rewards. A commitment to perform well—not just look busy—may well come only when students feel they have some control over what goes on in the classroom.

While most teachers will agree that the practice of student involvement can provide motivation to learn and can enhance enjoyment of school, the idea of student involvement raises an important question. How can teachers offer the freedom for students to participate in classroom affairs without creating havoc in the routine? The answer seems to be that students must *earn* the right to participate in managing the classroom. Teachers can begin by gradually decreasing the amount of control they exert. As students demonstrate successes, the number of choices and the amount of freedom given can be increased.

Another important resource for teachers in resolving classroom problems is the parents. While parents undoubtedly are blamed for being the source of more school problems than is justified, events taking place in the home can have a direct bearing on class behaviors. Studies (Bittle, 1977) suggest that when a teacher provides the means for parents to learn what is expected of students, the parents will help their children meet those expectations. Teachers should rid themselves of the notion that parents don't care about the activities of their children. Most parents do care. What often gets interpreted by teachers as parental indifference may be a lack of parental knowledge of what takes place in a given class. The parents may be unaware that a problem exists or they may feel they lack the skill to offer help. Even in situations in which the parents are experiencing problems at home with their children, the school is not helpless to make improvements. William Glasser (1978), a noted psychiatrist who has devoted much of his attention to helping educators solve discipline problems, says that the schools should initiate programs "where parents are specifically taught better techniques to handle their children at home and in the community." (p. 333.) Such a strategy doesn't *insure* good behavior at school because children may act differently in different settings. But maximum potentials are unlikely to be developed without a spirit of cooperation between parents and the schools. Teachers can do much to cultivate this cooperation. It rests largely with the teacher to draw upon the array of talents of the parents.

Finally, greater use of specialized school staff such as the psychologist, counselor, or nurse would go a long way toward alleviating many behavioral problems. Sometimes resource persons are perceived as rendering only one type of service and are never approached in any other way. School psychologists, for example, are often thought of as psychological examiners. Teachers who hold this limited view never seek the psychologist's assistance on problems unless the problems are related to testing. A bad experience with one resource person may also turn teachers away from using all other resource persons. Such is unfortunate. All professionals in education have much to learn from one another and much to contribute. We will go into detail in a later chapter on how teachers can work more cooperatively with other professionals. At this point, you need only to recognize that resolving school and classroom problems is a shared responsibility. No one can or should try to do everything alone.

Between Success and Failure

You may be thinking that if the steps to success are so simple, why are there so many failures? Unquestionably, there are failures. Problems persist. But many teachers are resolving a great number of problems and preventing other problems from occurring. *They are managing their classes effectively.* The successes don't come easily, however. Hard work and diligence are needed. Surprisingly, a few teachers give up too quickly. They let their honest concerns turn to despair. Recently, a young student teacher who had been working for two weeks in a first-grade classroom remorsefully asked us, "Are there some students who just can't be helped?" Although we agreed that it might be possible, we questioned the advisability of giving up on a student, especially after such a brief period. While there is no way to assure that a teacher will ultimately be successful, putting the issue of problems and how to manage them into proper perspective is a part of being successful. No teacher can get a handle on 1001 different problems. Teachers have to ask themselves what is the meaning of problems. They must also come to terms with what it means to be a successful classroom manager.

The Meaning of Classroom Management and Management Problems
    The term classroom management carries a number of different connotations. To some teachers it implies keeping order, to others having students be polite, and to still others, the elimination of all undesirable student behaviors. These restricted notions tend to inhibit any discussion of classroom management. Most teachers would like to have more than a set of strategies that make their own jobs more pleasant. They want their efforts to enrich the lives of their students. They are desirous of teaching as much as they possibly can. In essence, classroom management must reflect these desires of teachers.
    Classroom management involves more than any single approach. It consists of numerous procedures for teaching a wide range of academic and social skills as well as techniques that help teachers maintain order, instill desirable social skills, and weaken undesirable behaviors. It is still more. Classroom management includes all that teachers do to help students acquire useful skills, and the purpose is always to facilitate teaching—not merely to control or keep order. Thus, even when the focus is upon a limited aspect of management, such as weakening an undesirable behavior, the goal is to facilitate teaching other behaviors.
    A classroom management problem can be any event or behavior that persistently interferes with the acquisition of desired social and academic skills. Management problems, then, actually represent problems in learning. Either the individual has failed to learn an appropriate behavior, has learned an inappropriate behavior, or has acquired the wrong amount of a behavior (too little or too much) for a given situation. This conception of the problem is considerably broader than the common interpretation, which emphasizes control of undesirable or excessive amounts of behaviors. Of course,

classroom management entails setting upper limits on behavior, but a teacher would be wise to consider setting lower limits, too. If an individual consistently fails to interact with others, withdraws, or fails to turn in the assigned written material, does he present a problem? While such behaviors may not cause nearly the disruption created by acting out behaviors, they can constitute extremely oppositional behavior, and they do represent problems in learning.

When the purpose of classroom management is viewed as promoting instruction, and the definition of a management problem is construed as a problem in learning, teachers may be expected to ask, "What is the best way I can help this student learn what he needs to learn?" Undoubtedly, teachers will also be less inclined to make accusations, look for ways to punish, or just feel sorry about the situation they are in. Similarly, students who present problems are more likely to be perceived as persons needing assistance than as troublemakers. The way teachers look at problems, then, has a great deal to do with how they attempt to solve them.

COMMISSION OR OMISSION

Are your perceived problems in teaching related more to what students do or more to what they don't do? Some teachers are confronted with impertinence, others with a lack of student interest, and some with both. A great deal, however, may depend upon the setting in which one teaches as well as deciding if problems are a function of teaching strategies or dynamics within the students. In a survey among a group of Los Angeles teachers (King-Stoops & Meier, 1978), thirty-seven percent of those surveyed ranked a failure to motivate students as their most important problem. In other words, those teachers saw teaching competencies (i.e., ability to motivate) as more of a problem than deficiencies within the students. Lack of student respect for selves and others ranked number two.

What are the problems in your school? Your class? Is it primarily a lack of student interest? Is it impertinence? Disruptiveness? One way to find out is to log the problems that occur each day. To make sure that you don't record only disruptive acts, think also in terms of how well students interact in discussions, how well they listen, how many assignments they complete, and how many students go beyond simply completing assigned tasks. You can't orient yourself to resolving problems until you determine the nature of those problems.

What Lies Ahead

Now that you have a brief description of classroom management, you may be wondering what lies ahead in the remaining chapters. In other words, how can this book help you? Will it, for example, provide techniques that are appropriate for secondary as well as elementary teachers? Yes. Sometimes a technique that is appropriate for one age group may be inappropriate for another. Where a technique is more appropriate for one group than another, we will tell you. Often it is only the way in which a technique is applied that is different. In any event, each of the remaining chapters will in some way focus on helping teachers at every grade level to establish effective classroom management. The information is oriented toward helping you to determine your responsibility in managing various classroom activities, to expand your knowledge of techniques for motivating students and managing excessive behaviors, and to work effectively with students, parents, and colleagues in establishing better educational programs for each student. The text is more than a discussion of how to survive in the modern classroom. We hope it will also be a guide toward maximizing teachers' enjoyment of the most challenging and important of all jobs.

Concluding Thoughts

A major contention in this chapter has been that problems are an integral part of teaching. We earnestly believe that no one can interact with students all day without experiencing problems. All teachers eventually encounter students who are not learning to capacity. Most teachers also come into contact with disruptive students. Some teachers even witness severe aggression and vandalism. Teachers have to realize that problems come in a variety of shapes and sizes. The teacher who says, "I don't have any discipline problems," is certainly letting some student behaviors go unnoticed. Our focus, however, is not aimed solely at stopping problems. No book should have that as a goal. Few teachers or students are helped simply by halting unwanted behaviors. Rather, everyone benefits most when students *learn* appropriate social and academic skills. Our text, therefore, is oriented largely at *teaching* correct behaviors—not merely at *stopping* incorrect ones. We trust this is the orientation you will be seeking as you continue with your reading.

REFERENCES

Arwood, B., Williams, R. L., and Long, J. D. "The effects of behavior contracts and behavior proclamations on social conduct and academic achievement in a ninth grade English class." *Adolescence 9* (1974): 425-436.

Barnes, D. L. "An analysis of remedial activities used by elementary teachers in coping with classroom behavior problems." *The Journal of Educational Research* (1963): 544-547.

Besalel-Azrin, V., Azrin, N. H., and Armstrong, P. M. "The student-oriented classroom: A method of improving student conduct and satisfaction." *Behavior Therapy 8* (1977): 193-204.

Bittle, R. G. "Improving parent-teacher communication through recorded telephone messages." *In* K. D. O'Leary and S. G. O'Leary (eds.), *Classroom Management: The Successful Use of Behavior Modification.* 2nd ed. New York: Pergamon Press, Inc., 1977.

Blair, G. M., Jones, R. X., and Simpson, R. H. *Educational Psychology.* 4th ed. New York: Macmillan Publishing Company, Inc., 1975.

Coates, T. J. and Thoresen, C. E. "Teacher anxiety. A review with recommendations." *Review of Educational Research 46* (1976): 159-184.

Doyle, W. "Are students behaving worse than they used to behave?" *Journal of Research and Development in Education 11* (1978): 3-16.

Duke, D. L. "Adults can be discipline problems too!" *Psychology in the Schools 15* (1978): 522-528.

Glasser, W. "Disorders in our schools: Causes and remedies." *Phi Delta Kappan 59* (1978): 331-333.

Glynn, E. L. "Classroom applications of self-determined reinforcement." *Journal of Applied Behavior Analysis 3* (1970): 123-132.

Kazdin, A. E. and Kock, J. "The effects of nonverbal teacher approval on student attentive behavior." *Journal of Applied Behavior Analysis 6* (1973) 643-654.

King-Stoops, J. and Meier, W. "Teacher analysis of the discipline problem." *Phi Delta Kappan 59* (1978): 354.

Landsmann, L. "Is teaching hazardous to your health?" *Today's Education 67* (1978): 48-50.

Long, J. D. "A survey of the presumed causes and administrative actions taken for school disciplinary problems." Unpublished manuscript. Appalachian State University, 1976.

―――― and Mamola, C. "Perceived problems in teaching." Paper presented at the 2nd Annual Meeting of the Research and Development Association for Education, Alexandria, Va., November, 1978.

―――― and Williams, R. L. "The utility of self-management procedures in modifying the classroom behaviors of mentally retarded adolescents." *Adolescence 11* (1976): 29-38.

Lovitt, T. C. and Curtiss, K. "Academic response rate as a function of teacher- and self-imposed contingencies." *Journal of Applied Behavior Analysis 2* (1969): 49-53.

Madsen, C. H., Jr., Becker, W. C., Thomas, D. R., Koser, L., and Plazer, E. "An analysis of the reinforcing function of 'sit down' commands." *In* R. K. Parker, ed. *Readings in educational psychology.* Boston: Allyn and Bacon, Inc., 1968.

McAllister, L. W., Stachowiak, J. G., Baer, D. M., and Conderman, L. "The application of operant conditioning techniques in a secondary school classroom." *Journal of Applied Behavior Analysis 2* (1969): 277-285.

Thomas, D. R., Becker, W. C., and Armstrong, M. "Production and elimination of disruptive classroom behavior by systematically varying teachers' behavior." *Journal of Applied Behavior Analysis 1* (1968): 35-45.

Thomas, J. D. "Accuracy of self-assessment of on-task behavior by elementary school children." *Journal of Applied Behavior Analysis 9* (1976): 209.

U. S. Congress, Senate, Committee of the Judiciary. *Challenge for the third century: Education in a safe environment—final report on the nature and prevention of school violence and vandalism.* Washington, D. C.: Government Printing Office, 1977.

White-Blackburn, G., Semb, S., and Semb, G. "The effects of a good-behavior contract on the classroom behaviors of sixth-grade students." *Journal of Applied Behavior Analysis 10* (1977): 312.

Williams, R. L., and Anandam, K. "The effect of behavior contracting on grades." *The Journal of Educational Research 66* (1973): 230-236.

——— and Long, J. D. *Toward a self-managed life style.* 2nd ed. Boston: Houghton-Mifflin Co., 1979.

CHAPTER TWO

THE EYE OF THE BEHOLDER: TEACHER ATTITUDES TOWARD STUDENTS

"Darrel Wilson is the most impolite student I have ever had. You just wouldn't believe some of the things he says."

"Joan, I'm surprised to hear that. Darrel and I got along so well last year. He was always offering to do things for me. I wonder what his problem could be?"

Why will the same student behave appropriately for one teacher and inappropriately for another? Is it because students change so drastically from one year to the next? Certain student behaviors might be explained by developmental processes. As students enter adolescence, for example, they have a tendency to assert themselves. Other behaviors could also be a result of developmental stages. But what about students who exhibit model behavior in one class and ten minutes after a class change are misbehaving. This inconsistency cannot be explained on the basis of growth. Of course, differing interests and abilities in various subjects could be a partial explanation. Students, however, often behave differently in the same subject areas with a substitute teacher or a new teacher in the middle of the term. Can it be that much student behavior is simply a result of the way a given teacher relates to students? We think so.

The teacher is an important variable in every classroom. One teacher may view a student as a serious problem, while another teacher views the same student as interesting or, at worst, mischievous. Only by examining their own attitudes can teachers determine whether the behavior of students actually needs changing. The emphasis in this chapter is on teacher attitudes, how those attitudes affect students, and strategies for self-change. The discussion of teacher attitudes should not be interpreted as a personal indictment. Quite the contrary. Teachers who willingly examine all aspects of a problem can expect to make maximum progress toward achieving a positive classroom atmosphere.

The Impact of Attitudes

Since attitudes by definition represent feelings and emotions, many question how attitudes really affect others. The argument is often made that only the individual can be cognizant of personal feelings. True, no one can know absolutely what another is feeling, but people are not very skilled at keeping their feelings hidden. Every teacher enters the classroom with attitudes about the students, the school, the principal. The students quickly draw inferences about those attitudes based on what the teacher says and does. Words, gestures, tones, inflections, glances and innumerable other verbal and nonverbal behaviors convey significant messages. Students quickly determine if the teacher feels positive or negative toward them, is satisfied with the setting, and is getting along with others. So, it isn't the attitudes themselves that affect students: it is the inferences drawn from the behavioral manifestations of the teacher's attitudes that have the impact on classroom interpersonal relationships.

Although behaviors explain how attitudes get conveyed, a fundamental question still remains: do the behavioral expressions of attitudes actually affect how students learn? Everyone can cite a case in which students learned under a cranky teacher. Highly motivated, academic students who receive considerable support at home can probably learn despite the teacher's attitude. Such gains are exceptions and should never become a basis for concluding that attitudes have minimal impact on students. The majority of students are going to benefit both academically and socially from teachers who convey positive attitudes. Students simply behave differently for a teacher who is interested in them. They share their ideas, worries, hopes, fears, and desires with the teacher who cares. The teacher is, thus, in a better position to offer real help to the students. A teacher needs only to recall his own experiences to verify the positive changes that result from coming into contact with an adult who is concerned about others. But one need not rely on

"Elwood, we would prefer it if you stopped referring to your students as 'the enemy.'"

personal experiences alone. A number of researchers (Aspy & Roebuck, 1977; Combs, 1974; Gazda, Ashbury, Balzer, Childers & Walters, 1977) report studies that substantiate this premise. The research on teacher attitudes, of course, needs to be expanded before complete methods are available for determining which students are affected most by the variety of teacher behaviors, but the overall consensus is that teacher attitudes do markedly affect how well students learn.

SENSITIVITY—WHO NEEDS IT?

Lack of teacher sensitivity may have its most negative educational impact on those students who already feel insecure or who already are having problems in school. At least, this finding is suggested in a study among eighth grade students conducted by Dwight Webb. In Webb's study, students who were classified as insecure or as having school problems (both determined from the Mooney Problem Checklist) showed considerably more negative educational effects with teachers rated as insensitive than with teachers rated high in sensitivity. Conversely, students classified as problem-free did not appear to respond significantly differently to teachers rated as less sensitive. A sensitive teacher was defined as "one who is understanding, helpful, and concerned with individual differences among students, one who would not likely embarrass or humiliate a student in order to shape his behavior."

Another interesting outcome in Webb's study was that when the students were grouped as either "C" lane or "B" lane students, the "C" lane students were the ones who had the greatest difficulties with the less sensitive teachers. The insecure "C" lane students reported fewer school problems, more positive attitudes about their teachers, and expressed more interest in math when placed with the more sensitive teachers. The "C" lane problem-students reported feeling more secure, fewer problems, and more interest and learning in English when placed with the more sensitive teachers. The study itself is not a condemnation of task-oriented teachers. Rather, the study implies that certain students will improve their attitudes about themselves and school through contact with highly sensitive teachers. Other students may prefer a teacher whose attention is primarily to the task rather than to the individual. What is your analysis?

Critical Attitudes

To this point, we have indicated that teacher attitudes have a profound effect on student behaviors. Obviously, teachers possess many feelings about students and these get conveyed through a host of teacher behaviors. You are probably wondering what the most important of the possible teacher attitudes are. Several strategies are available for assessing critical teacher attitudes. One strategy is to examine what professionals have to say. Another is to examine student points of view. In the next few pages, we will look at teacher attitudes from both these positions.

A Professional Point of View

Carl Rogers, one of this century's most prominent psychologists, is a major spokesman among the professionals who believe that attitudes are the *major factors* controlling student learning. Rogers and his followers contend that three teacher attitudes are needed to free students to raise questions, seek answers, and become more self-directive. He says:

...such learning rests not upon the teaching skills of the teacher, not upon his scholarly knowledge of the field, not upon his curricular planning, not upon his use of audio-visual aids, not upon the programmed learning he utilizes, not upon his lectures and presentations, not upon an abundance of books, though each of these might at one time or another be utilized as an important resource. No the facilitation of significant learning rests upon certain attitudinal qualities which exist in the personal relationship between the facilitator and the learner. (Rogers, 1969, pp. 105-106)

The three teacher attitudes that Rogers has identified as sufficient conditions for the facilitation of learning are: (1) realness or genuineness, (2) acceptance, and (3) empathic understanding. Let us explore each of these in more detail.

Realness or Genuineness. Rogers describes real or genuine teachers as persons who, under appropriate conditions, are aware of their feelings. Such persons do not try to put up a facade or pretend to feel other than they do. In other words, the attitude of realness involves being honest with oneself and with others. Although realness means that teachers may occasionally admit being angry, happy, sad, bored, or excited, it is not a license to disguise how they feel by blaming others. For example, the honest teacher is more apt to say "I am upset by this arrangement" than "You students don't know how to get organized." Realness, then, means that individuals recognize personal feelings as their own—not someone else's.

DO YOU LIKE ME?

Mrs. Depaul was experiencing extremely negative feelings toward one of her students. To Mrs. Depaul, the student appeared sullen and reluctant to "go along" with the group on any potentially enjoyable class activity. Mrs. Depaul resented the student's behavior. She began to spend less time around the student, to call on her less, and became more critical of the student. The student picked up on the teacher's feelings and finally asked, "Do you like me?" Mrs. Depaul was really surprised by this question. Instead of being dishonest, something that would have been apparent anyhow, Mrs. Depaul admitted, "I have been upset by your behaviors." This honest admission led to a discussion of what was bothering Mrs. Depaul and ultimately to a new, friendlier relationship between her and the student.

If you are beginning to question the idea of being honest about your feelings, you might want to consider the alternatives. How many teachers do you know who try to hide their feelings, only to have those feelings come out in the form of sarcasm and faultfinding? In deciding whether it would be appropriate to express your feelings, you might ask: "What will be the result to myself if I do not express how I feel?"

Acceptance. To Rogers, the attitude of acceptance (sometimes referred to as prizing and trust) means that the teacher values the student's feelings, opinions, and person. This attitude reflects a kind of unconditional positive regard in which the student need not be academic, handsome, or even well-behaved in order to be appreciated. Teachers who possess the attitude of acceptance see each individual as being a person of worth. Teachers with this attitude also appreciate individual differences among students. They accept occasional apathy, differences of opinion, and lack of conformity. Rogers says that accepting teachers realize they are dealing with imperfect human beings possessing many feelings and potentials.

Acceptance should not be interpreted as meaning that one must tolerate every student behavior. Teachers would be dishonest to pretend they could accept every student act. Furthermore, students would have no standards to follow if everything they did were condoned. Teachers can tell students that certain behavior is unacceptable without rejecting them. Saying, "Bill, please don't interrupt," is quite different from exclaiming, "Bill, you don't have any manners!" The first comment is directed at behavior; the second comment implies that something is wrong with the person. We can find no justification for rejecting a student as a person. When one does so, the attitudes of prizing and accepting the student are lost. Rejecting a behavior is a more effective approach although too much rejection can show a great deal about how the student is being perceived.

Empathic Understanding. Rogers describes empathic understanding as sensitive awareness of the way education and learning appear to the student. It means the teacher actually experiences the way the student is feeling. The empathic teacher stands inside the other's shoes, so to speak, and views the world from that person's position. In this way, empathy enables the teacher to communicate an accurate understanding of what the other person is feeling.

The empathic teacher stands in sharp contrast to the one who is unable to accept honest emotional expressions from the students.

The latter may comment, "I am surprised at you" or "Don't you dare say that again." Such statements tend to cut off communication. The empathic teacher increases communication by responding to the feelings behind a student's words or actions. For example, he may comment, "Sue, you feel like you may have been mistreated," "Bill, you seem upset by the discussion," "Joe, you act as though you would rather be working on another project," or "John, you seem very concerned about your performance." These and similar statements increase open communications, correct errors in teacher comprehension, and help students recognize what they are communicating to others. Students who recognize what they are feeling may desire to change. If their feelings are never brought into the open, they may never have the opportunity for complete self-awareness. Remember that *the empathic teacher is trying to communicate an understanding of student feelings, not to judge, evaluate, justify behavior, or prohibit expression of emotions.*

A Note of Clarification. The attitudes discussed above are sometimes very difficult to display. It is questionable if anyone can ever be completely genuine, accepting, and empathic. The behavior of some students alone can make it difficult, if not impossible, for a teacher to exhibit the desired attitudes. Furthermore, Rogers himself recognizes that these qualities are rarely attained. Nonetheless, the ability to have a favorable and long-lasting influence on others will be enhanced to the extent that a teacher is able to be genuine, accepting, and empathic. Similarly, students who are accepted without reservations have no need to defend themselves. They can explore other possibilities. As their feelings are understood, they may come to be more understanding of the feelings of others. Improvements in attitudes can make a significant change in one's own life and in the lives of others.

The Students' Point of View

Students have definite ideas about the attitudes teachers can and should display. They know the types of settings in which they are happy and most likely to achieve success. Perhaps the most interesting as well as representative picture of the attitudes that students want in their teachers grew out of a radio program in the 1940s. Professor of Education Paul A. Witty (1947) suggested to officials of the "Quiz Kids" radio program that students be invited to submit a composition on "The Teacher Who Has Helped Me

Most." The officials agreed and over 14,000 pupils from grades 2-12 responded. The order of the most frequently mentioned positive traits in the compositions were: (1) cooperative, democratic attitude, (2) kindliness and consideration for the individual, (3) patience, (4) wide interests, (5) personal appearance and pleasing manner, (6) fairness and impartiality, (7) sense of humor, (8) good disposition and consistent behavior, (9) interest in pupils' problems, (10) flexibility, (11) use of recognition and praise, and (12) unusual proficiency in teaching.

The ideas of the students were surprisingly similar to what humanistic psychologists such as Rogers prescribe for an effective teaching-learning environment. What could be closer to a *real* person, for example, than teachers who are friendly, can laugh and enjoy themselves, and who get involved in a variety of activities? Similarly, what could be more accepting than teachers who recognize the worth of students and treat each pupil fairly? And how could empathy be better displayed than through the teacher who is concerned about student problems? You will also recognize that eleven items ranked higher than the teacher's proficiency in teaching, something Rogers alluded to.

A second call for compositions in 1947 in which 33,000 pupils submitted entries yielded essentially the same results. An addition to the analysis of the compositions in the second survey was an effort to determine the teacher traits that students disliked. When a student said a helpful teacher doesn't yell, scream, or holler, this was taken as an indication that teachers who do yell, scream, or holler alienate the students. The negative teacher traits that most often alienated students were: (1) bad-temper and intolerance, (2) unfairness and inclination to have favorites, (3) disinclination to show interest in the pupil and take time to help him, (4) unreasonableness in demands, (5) tendency to be gloomy and unfriendly, (6) sarcasm and inclination to use ridicule, (7) unattractive appearance, (8) impatience and inflexibility, (9) tendency to talk excessively, (10) inclination to talk down to pupils, (11) overbearance and conceit, and (12) lack of humor.

You will notice in both analyses that students responded positively to attractive teachers and negatively (by contrast) to unattractive ones. This preference does not mean students respond to physical looks alone. Analysis of the compositions shows that students value neatness and variety in dress. No teacher has to be flawless in dress or any other trait to be well received. Students typically leave room for error. They just don't like teachers whose behavior is characterized by a bad temper, unfairness, and so on. While no teacher is likely to achieve perfection, with effort most can meet the majority of student expectations. Wouldn't you agree?

"HEY KID"

Does how a teacher addresses students have anything to do with the teacher's respect for the students? John F. Check (1977) believes so and he has support for his position. Dr. Check asked students in grades 6, 10, and 12 in public and parochial schools to indicate the degree to which they objected to the use of "kid" by parents and teachers. Of the 415 students responding, seventy-six percent objected very much or to some degree to being called "kid" by their teachers. The students were more tolerant of the use of the term by parents. Dr. Check also asked parents and teachers to participate in his study. Twenty-three percent of the 205 teachers and eighteen percent of the 264 parents involved in the study felt it wrong to use the term "kid." On the other hand, when students were asked if it were wrong to call teachers by their first names, over a third of the students said it was wrong and only forty-six percent said they would do it on occasion. Can it be that students are more aware of ways to demonstrate respect than adults? Perhaps. In any event, adults are unlikely to earn respect from young people until the adults clearly show they respect the young.

Strategies for Change

After reading about the kind of attitudes psychologists and students think teachers should exhibit, you may be desirous of implementing a few changes in your attitudes toward others. A number of suggestions for making such changes are listed below. Our list is not inclusive; our interest is primarily in helping you start to change some of the behaviors that go into a variety of positive attitudes. By changing enough of the behavior that comprise attitudes, you will eventually change these attitudes. You will need to add to your list as you think of other activities related to the attitudes you are most interested in changing.

Improve Your Self-Image

Many prominent psychologists (e.g., Combs, 1974; Fromm, 1947; Rogers, 1961) have suggested that our attitudes toward others are largely dependent upon the attitudes we hold about ourselves. Indeed, attitudes toward self and others are probably inseparable.

Perhaps the first step, then, for improving our attitudes toward others is to improve the attitudes we hold about ourselves. If you are uncertain about these feelings, you might pose a few questions for yourself. For example, are your self-thoughts usually positive or negative? Do you make uplifting or derogatory remarks about yourself? Do you compare yourself favorably or unfavorably with most other people? Be honest. Even remarks that are seemingly made in jest can reveal how one actually regards oneself.

In addition to raising questions about what you think and say about yourself, you might also ask how much confidence you have in you own abilities. The way one undertakes tasks can provide clues about self-confidence. Are you hesitant or enthusiastic about accepting responsibilities? Do you generally expect to be successful or unsuccessful in your work? Do you appear calm or anxious when presenting your views to others? Are you afraid to make decisions? Having skills in a teaching area is useless unless one has the confidence to put those skills to work.

Persons with high self-esteem or self-respect tend to think and speak favorably about themselves. Altering self-thoughts and self-statements in a positive direction may change how you feel about yourself. You could begin by identifying positive thoughts that could be used to alter any of your negative feelings. Thoughts about appearance, intelligence, and relationships with others would be appropriate. Listing these thoughts on index cards and referring to them at convenient periods during each day may be a helpful strategy. Referring to oneself more positively during conversation may also have a beneficial impact on self-esteem. Of course, you want to be discreet in what you say. There is a big difference between saying, "Yes, I was pleased with my performance," and, "I did better than anyone else could possibly do." Being thought of as a braggart can create negative reactions and consequently lower feelings of self-esteem. You need to get used to thinking and speaking positively about yourself; but do not go overboard.

Accepting an honest compliment from others without down-grading self-performance can be a big step in increasing positive feelings toward oneself. People who feel negatively about themselves may eventually find that others feel the same way toward them. Changes in self-confidence can be initiated by thinking and talking more positively about personal capabilities: that success is possible, that appropriate decisions can be made, that a classroom can be effectively managed. The expectation of success is no doubt a prerequisite to actual success..

Finally, positive self-thoughts and statements may provide some immunization against the wounds that result from other people's comments and behaviors. Students can be cruel at times without even realizing it. All teachers occasionally have negative experiences. You must avoid letting those negative experiences adversely affect the way you think and act. We suggest that you focus primarily on the positive qualities that exist in oneself and in others. Remember, good things do not cease to exist when negative events occur.

BETTER ATTITUDES THROUGH BETTER THINKING

Can teachers improve their self-esteem by altering what they say to themselves? A study by James Hannum and two of his colleagues suggests that teachers can improve how they feel about themselves. Hannum and his colleagues asked three elementary teachers who had complained of being excessively critical of themselves to alter their self-thoughts. The experiment began with the teachers using wrist counters to record their positive and negative self-thoughts during a specified hour each day. Positive self-thoughts included such thoughts as "I'm patient with children," while negative self-thoughts were thoughts like "I'm just too old for teaching." Subsequently, the teachers tried increasing the number of positive self-thoughts by cuing themselves to think a positive self-thought every time they engaged in a high probability behavior such as looking at the clock. All three teachers were successful: positive self-thoughts increased along with a decrease in negative self-thoughts. Not only did their thinking change, but two of the three teachers reported feeling much more positively toward themselves. They said the experiment was among the most significant events in their lives. Unfortunately, the changes in feelings failed to produce immediate changes in the way the teachers responded to students. A follow-up interview, however, indicated that positive overt behavior changes had occurred.

Closely related to the idea that you should think and speak positively about yourself is the need for you to recognize your achievements. We have found that many times people with low self-esteem and self-confidence completely forget about their past achievements. In new situations they fear they will fail or in some way prove inadequate. These people have undoubtedly had successful experiences in the past but the negative experiences have made the most lasting impressions. As a means of focusing on successful experiences, it may be helpful to make a list of all the positive things that have happened and to review that list periodically. One teacher reported to us that she occasionally rereads all the positive notes she has received from her students over the years. She commented that when others can value her so much she just has to feel better about herself. Everyone has had some success. Do not forget to recognize your own.

Listen to Others

Listening to others can be an especially helpful procedure for changing attitudes toward others; it permits one to learn more about what others really think and feel. Listening also communicates to others that one is interested in them and what they have to say which makes them more receptive. Unfortunately, most of us do more talking than listening. Bellack and others (1966), for instance, concluded from their studies of interactions between teachers and students that teachers account for seventy percent of all talking in a class. Adams and Biddle (1970) found that teachers were the center of attention in over eighty percent of class conversations. Having a captive audience probably has a lot to do with the amount of talking teachers do. Naturally, teachers can never hope to learn about others by doing all the talking.

To improve your own listening ability, you might record the amount of time you spend talking and listening to others. A stopwatch could be used for documentation. Our college students who have done this have generally been surprised by the amount of talking they do. If you should try the strategy and obtain similar results, you might enlist the aid of a friend to give you listening cues and provide feedback on the quality of your listening.

Obviously, listening to others involves more than passive toleration of what others are saying. Paraphrasing and commenting directly on what others have said lets them know that you are listening carefully. Paraphrasing also permits clarification of any misunderstanding on your part. A good way to begin a paraphrase is "You think..." or "You are suggesting..." Paraphrasing, however, should be more than a mere parroting of what others have said. Effective listeners communicate that they have heard more than words. When you discern that others are happy, sad, frustrated, angry, and so on, this understanding should be communicated. An appropriate comment might be, "You feel let down by..." "You can't make up your mind about..." "You are strongly in favor of..." Listening, then, means that the listener is tuned in to the verbal and nonverbal expressions of others and, by being tuned in, much is learned about the needs, desires, hopes, and frustrations of other persons. Such knowledge is a step in changing attitudes. Often the more one learns about other people, the more they are appreciated.

How much listening are you doing? Do you put aside what you are doing when others want to talk? Do you avoid interrupting others? Do you comment on what others say or do you switch conversations to what you want to talk about? Are you attentive to the feelings that words and nonverbal behaviors convey? Do you really hear what others are saying or do you spend your listening time thinking of what you wish to say next?

Look for Positive Qualities in Others

Occasionally, a teacher may realize that he always reacts negatively to certain students. Such a situation may arise when he is confronted with highly disruptive students, who often appear to be more disorderly than they actually are. It is not uncommon to hear teachers say, "He never does *anything* right." No student is totally bad, however. Even the most disruptive students usually exhibit twenty-five to fifty percent appropriate behavior (Williams & Anandam, 1973). The commendable qualities that exist in every person must be recognized. Otherwise, one may never be able to develop positive attitudes toward some individuals.

To help focus on the positive qualities in others, you might try talking informally with your students. Desirable times for talking may be during lunch hours, before or after school, or at school social functions. These settings offer unique opportunities for getting to know more about students' interests, special talents, and needs. We frequently find that informal conversations give us much more positive attitudes toward students than can be acquired through classroom discussions alone. But we do have a word of caution. A few students may reject initial efforts to get to know them better. More than one try is often needed to convince these students of your interest in them. Teachers who take the time to talk with students will usually find that students have positive qualities overlooked in the classroom.

Respond More Positively to Others

At least a part of our attitudes toward others is a function of how others respond to us. Research in classroom settings (Graubard,

Rosenburg & Miller, 1971; Polvistok & Greer, 1977; Sherman & Cormier, 1974) has shown that student behavior has a predictable influence on teacher behavior. The evidence from these studies indicates that when students behave appropriately (e.g., are attentive, follow directions, are less critical of the teacher), the teacher is more positive (e.g., praising). Conversely, when students are disruptive of learning activities, the teacher is more critical and reprimanding. You may realize from your own school experiences how students can affect the teacher. We certainly can. We have seen teachers in tears run from the classroom because of things the students said and did. It is very difficult for anyone to enjoy teaching and to have positive attitudes toward students who are responding negatively.

An important question, then, is how to get students to respond positively toward you. The answer seems to lie in a deliberate increase of positive responses toward the students. The principle of reciprocal liking appears to exist in most human relationships. That is, others like us to about the extent that we like them. Students respond more positively when responses to them have been positive.

Put Misbehavior in
Perspective

Much of students' misbehavior is unrelated to their real feelings about the teacher. Problems at home or with peers, disappointments over a performance, or any number of other frustrations could lead students to misbehave. Even when a student openly expresses a dislike for the teacher, it may be the position the teacher holds—not the teacher—that is disliked. Teachers must, therefore, avoid taking misbehavior as a personal affront. A more productive approach, in terms of increasing favorable student and teacher attitudes in the classroom, is to view the misbehavior as a problem that can be remedied, and develop a behavior-change strategy. Establishing a dialogue with the offending students and observing their behavior may reveal the sources of the problem and suggest possible solutions. By putting the behavior of students in an objective perspective, you increase the likelihood of responding more positively to the students.

Cultivate Interests Outside
of School

Many teachers report that having interests outside of school facilitates the development and maintenance of positive attitudes toward others. We agree completely. We have found that we are most productive and agreeable when looking forward to a game of tennis or a night on the town. After engaging in enjoyable events, we seem to appreciate our work and other people even more. If you look around at persons who respond most positively to others, you will probably find that they engage in many different happiness-producing activities.

Do not misunderstand us. We are not saying that work is an unenjoyable experience; most of us derive much satisfaction from our work. But people need outlets from the occasional frustrations of their work. A teacher who relies solely on students and colleagues for friendship may feel resentful if the students and colleagues fail to be totally committed to the relationship. Attitudes toward self and others can suffer. Our belief is that one should not rely upon work for every satisfaction. If you have not already done so, we suggest that you identify a number of activities that might prove enjoyable to you (for example, reading, listening to music, tennis, golf, swimming, hiking, jogging, gardening, crafts, or similar activities). Establishing a time each day or week for participating in these leisure activities helps to insure that one does not become too busy for relaxation.

I'LL GET AROUND TO IT TOMORROW

Sue was always a hard worker who planned to find time for recreation whenever she got "caught up." In college she kept postponing developing any hobbies because she wanted to devote most of her time to studying. She frequently vowed that as soon as she graduated she would start enjoying herself. After graduation, Sue found that her teaching job was just as engrossing as her studies had been. So she continued to put off recreation until the summers. But in the summers Sue found herself taking graduate classes and preparing for school to reopen.

One day just as Sue entered the teachers' lounge she heard a teacher talking about retirement. The teacher commented, "When I retire I think I'll take up golf. I've always thought I'd enjoy that." Sue knew then that she was not alone. She wondered how many persons were putting off "fun" until a later date. She wondered if she would even make it till retirement. She resolved at that moment to make recreation an integral part of her life. Today she is enrolled in an after-school recreation program and is learning to play tennis. Tomorrow, who knows?

Be Willing to Admit Mistakes

Perhaps nothing is more reflective of genuineness than a willingness to admit some human frailties. Admitting mistakes is not easy. A mystique seems to have grown up around teachers. Many persons act as though teachers are supposed to be paragons of virtue. Given this assumption, you could have a difficult time saying, "I was in error," "I goofed," "You are right," or "Please accept my apology." People who can never be wrong may be faced with the problem of having to distort circumstances so as to place themselves in a positive light. Those who can admit mistakes have no need to distort reality. They can see themselves and others in clearer perspective. Furthermore, teachers who can admit weaknesses are more likely to make it easy for students to admit mistakes and seek ways of improving. Shortcomings should not be a primary focus, but one should be able to accept one's own humanness. The realization that one has weaknesses may be prerequisite to admitting mistakes.

Concluding Remarks

Although this chapter has emphasized the importance of teacher attitudes, you still may wonder how successful you can be in improving these attitudes. You also may question Rogers' contention that certain teacher attitudes are sufficient to promote learning. We certainly feel that you can alter your present behaviors. What you are today is largely a function of your past experiences. What you are tomorrow just as surely will be a function of the things you experience today. We strongly oppose taking the "I'm just that way" philosophy. You can arrange today's experiences so that tomorrow you will more closely approximate what you would like to be. We also doubt if your attitudes alone, even though improved, will be sufficient to maximize student learning. Other techniques for preventing and controlling classroom problems may also be necessary, perhaps because of our inability to achieve essential attitudes. Perhaps our use of other techniques is necessary because attitudes alone are not the only determinants of classroom behavior. In any case, we do not plan to ask you to rely solely on your personal charms. In succeeding chapters, a variety of strategies that can be used in conjunction with improved teacher attitudes will be discussed. By combining positive attitudes with other classroom management skills, learning may be made more pleasant for both students and teachers.

REFERENCES

Adams, R. and Biddle, B. *Realities of teaching: Explorations with video tape.* New York: Holt, Rinehart and Winston, 1970.

Aspy, D. N. and Roebuck, R. N. *Kids don't learn from people they don't like.* Human Resource Development Press, 1977.

Bellack, A., Kliebard, H., Hyman, R., and Smith, F. *The language of the classroom.* New York: Teachers College Press, 1966.

Check, J. F. "Respect—a two-way street." *Physical Educator 34* (1977): 122-124.

Combs, A. W. et al. *The professional education of teachers.* 2nd ed. Boston: Allyn and Bacon, Inc. 1974.

Fromm, E. *Man for himself.* New York: Holt, Rinehart and Winston, 1947.

Gazda, G. M., Asbury, F. R., Balzer, F. J., Childers, W. C., and Walters, R. P. *Human relations development: A manual for educators.* 2nd ed. Boston: Allyn and Bacon, Inc., 1977.

Graubard, P. S., Rosenburg, H., and Miller, M. B. "Student applications of behavior modification to teachers and environments or ecological approaches to social deviancy." *In* E. A. Ramp and B. L. Hopkins, eds. *A new direction for education: Behavior analysis 1971.* Lawrence, Kansas: Support and Development Center for Follow Through, 1971.

Hannum, J. W., Thoresen, C. E., and Hubbard, D. R., Jr. "A behavioral study of self-esteem with elementary teachers." *In* M. J. Mahoney and C. E. Thoresen, eds. *Self-control: Power to the person.* Monterey, California: Brooks/Cole Publishing Company, 1974.

Polvistok, S. R. and Greer, R. D. "Remediation of mutually aversive interactions between a problem student and four teachers by training the student in reinforcement techniques." *Journal of Applied Behavior Analysis 10* (1977): 707-716.

Rogers, C. R. *Freedom to learn.* Columbus, Ohio: Charles E. Merrill Publishing Company, 1969.

_____ *On becoming a person.* Boston: Houghton-Mifflin Company, 1961.

Sherman, T. M. and Cormier, W. H. "An investigation of the influence of student behavior on teacher behavior." *Journal of Applied Behavior Analysis 7* (1974): 11-21.

Webb, D. "Teacher-sensitivity: Affective impact on students." *In* T. B. Roberts, ed. *Four psychologies applied to education.* New York: Schenkman Publishing Company, 1975.

Williams, R. L. and Anandam, K. *Cooperative classroom management.* Columbus, Ohio: Charles E. Merrill Publishing Company, 1973.

Witty, P. A. "The teacher who has helped me most." *Elementary English 26* (1947).

CHAPTER THREE

A DAY LATE AND A PAGE SHORT: MANAGING DEFICIT BEHAVIORS

"You know, Betty, I feel sorry for Bill. He just stood around at the class party. I never saw him speak to anyone. I wish he'd interact more with the other students. He's really a very nice boy."

Bill's problem is not uncommon. Many students stand on the sidelines watching others enjoy themselves. To us, the bystanders appear to be naturally shy and withdrawn, while in reality they simply may have never learned how to interact appropriately with others. The chances are that many "shy" persons would like to participate more actively—they just don't know how.

Shy students are not alone in their problems. Many more students have never learned what fun school can really be. These students would rather be at home or in the streets than at school. Still other students don't know what it is like to attend fully to their lessons, complete an assignment by themselves, or finish a task on time. All of these students share something in common. They exhibit deficient amounts of valued behaviors. Such deficits in behavior create special difficulties for teachers. First, a low level or absence of a behavior is much less noticeable than an excess of a behavior. Teachers can get so involved with class clowns, for example, that they forget about students who seldom contribute to discussions. Similarly, the frequently absent student may be forgotten as the teacher tries to cope with the disruptiveness of those in attendance. Secondly, the management of deficits in behavior requires that the teacher exercise great care in selecting remedial strategies. Such behaviors as attendance and attentiveness need to be strengthened rather than suppressed. The teacher must seek ways of prompting and reinforcing the wanted behaviors. Easier strategies of applying punishment must be avoided. To punish students for a failure to exhibit a desired behavior would only lessen the probability of achieving what is wanted. The thrust of this chapter, therefore, is to demonstrate how teachers can prompt and reinforce desired behaviors. Although the focus of the chapter is on resolving one major category of problems (deficient amounts of behavior), the reader will recognize that strengthening desired behaviors is a primary means of preventing other types of problems. Teachers who can generate more of what they desire from students are less likely to be plagued by the presence of what they don't want.

Prompting Desired Behaviors

The first step toward increasing the probability that students will exhibit wanted behaviors is to set the stage for those desirable behaviors. That is, teachers must arrange circumstances so as to prompt wanted actions rather than expecting *all* students to exhibit desired behavior on their own. There are any number of ways of indicating to students what behaviors are expected. These include: letting students know the rules, giving clear and simple instructions, making the setting conducive to learning, providing appropriate academic activities, and modeling desired behaviors.

THE RICH GET RICHER

Are students who are slow, unattractive, and socially disadvantaged afforded fewer learning opportunities than their classroom counterparts? Clare Burstall's review (1978) of research on the influence of teacher behaviors on their pupils indicates this is the case. Burstall suggests that a principle similar to that mentioned in the gospel according to Saint Matthew is operating in the classroom: that those who have in abundance shall receive while those with less will lose even what they have. Evidence cited by Burstall to illustrate her point includes research showing that good readers are called on to read more often than poor readers, that those who are more capable academically are given more opportunity to be the teacher's helper and to be in charge of classroom and playground activities than less capable students, that high achievers get more chance to comment in class discussions than low achievers, and that the misbehavior of attractive students is more likely to get overlooked than the same behavior by unattractive students. It seems that the very students who need to be given opportunities to read, to lead, to interact, and to receive rewards for desirable behaviors are the ones least apt to receive them. Obviously, quite different actions must be taken if those who already have learning deficits are to be helped. What is your thinking?

Let Students Know the Rules

Classroom Rules. The establishment of class rules can serve as a means of prompting and guiding desired student behaviors. All teachers have certain general ideas about what students should or should not do. But these expectations are not always clearly understood by the students. We teachers sometimes assume that students come into classes knowing the rules of the game. This assumption is more likely to be made as students get older. However, teachers vary in what they expect from students. Different situations also call for different behaviors. These differences can create confusion for students. Too often students complain that they learn about the teacher's rules for conduct by unwittingly violating those rules. Students are not clairvoyant. They need to know what is expected so they can adjust their behaviors accordingly.

Although class rules can help prevent problems, the approach used to develop and make the rules known to students can easily influence the results obtained. For example, a long list of regulations can give students the impression that the teacher is more interested in increasing restrictions than in promoting learning. A better approach is to keep the list to a minimum. Perhaps you might initiate only those rules that are needed to keep your students from interfering with others' learning. We know one very effective high school teacher who claims to have only two rules: (1) You are to listen when I or any student speaks to the class, and (2) You are to work so as not to disturb others. His approach is simple but effective.

A class discussion might be a good starting point in developing classroom rules. Involving students in decision-making is especially important at the secondary school level. However, even very young students can provide some ideas as to what makes a good or bad class. A modified form of the strategies presented by Taba (1966) for teaching cognitive skills could be used for conducting a class discussion to generate workable ideas for classroom rules. Initially, the procedure involves giving students a *focus* question (e.g., "What do you consider to be appropriate or inappropriate behavior in the classroom?"). After a student has responded, an extended or a related question (e.g., "Why do you feel that throwing erasers in the classroom is not appropriate?") is asked. Students should be encouraged to explain and support their statements. For example, the teacher might say, "John, you state that we do not need a rule about coming to class on time. Give me some reasons why you think the class would operate better if we did not have such a rule." Predictions (cause and effect) as to classroom behavior if suggested ideas are or are not implemented should also be elicited. Students may have divergent opinions on some suggestions. All students should be encouraged to participate in the discussion and to defend their own beliefs about proposed rules (e.g., "David, what do you think about the rule proposed by Jerry?"). The discussion should be structured to generate student-developed rules that are acceptable to the teacher as well as the students.

REMEMBER WHEN?

Can you recall from your student days school rules that set teachers and students at odds with one another: rules that focused on matters unrelated to learning, rules without any reasons behind them except *because*, rules that made the school seem out of touch with the times? We can. We recall when students were allowed to take only one sip of water at the water fountain (Can you top that one?); when boys were *required* to wear belts; when girls were forbidden to wear jeans, strapless dresses, and dresses with string straps; when sunglasses could not be worn at school without a doctor's prescription; and when a boy with hair over his ears would be sent home. Today such rules make us smile. "Back then," however, the rules were sources of much unnecessary irritation. A few rules were more than irritating; they were unconscionable. We recall when married students and pregnant students were forbidden to attend school.

Have things changed since our school days? Or are some of today's rules just as ridiculous, just as likely to be stumbling blocks to the process of education?

Madsen and Madsen (1974) provided suggestions that may serve as additional guides for establishing classroom rules. These points seem especially appropriate for elementary school classes:

1. Involve the class in making the rules.
2. Keep the rules short and to the point.
3. Phrase rules, where possible, in a positive way. ("Sit quietly while working," instead of "Don't talk to your neighbors.")
4. Remind the class of the rules at times *other* than when someone has misbehaved.
5. Make different sets of rules for varied activities.
6. Let children know when different rules apply (work-play).

7. Post rules in a conspicuous place and review regularly.
8. Keep a sheet on your desk and record the number of times you review rules with class.

Letting students know what is expected of them is critical to establishing effective classroom discipline, but one would be unjustified in assuming that rules *per se* will prevent all behavior problems. Teachers who feel that rules are ends in themselves usually become disillusioned when rules prove ineffective. Whether a student will be influenced by a rule depends largely upon what happens following compliance with or violation of rules. In at least one study, researchers (Madsen, Becker & Thomas, 1968) found that rules alone had no appreciable effect on inappropriate behaviors. However, marked improvements occurred when rules were paired with teacher praise for appropriate behaviors and ignoring of minor inappropriate acts. The discussions in subsequent chapters should further clarify the importance of praising students for doing what is expected of them.

School rules and policies. In addition to classroom rules, it is important that students be cognizant of school regulations and policies that have a direct bearing on their conduct. Are certain school rooms off limits at certain times during the day? Is smoking permitted on school grounds? How many absences or times tardy are allowed before an attendance teacher is consulted? Questions of school policy are especially important for secondary school students. Discussing the regulations with students and posting a copy in the classroom to allow for continued reference may be helpful in reducing the number of rule infractions. Providing each student with a small handbook or xeroxed copy of school policy is also recommended. Taking the time to discuss the policies during class periods will provide an opportunity to stress the positive aspects of the policies, thus increasing the probability that the desired behavior will occur. A discussion period will also allow students to vent any feelings they might have toward certain restrictions. In cases where rules are felt to be unfair or unnecessary, students can be helped to work within the school structure to effect a satisfactory change.

ALLOWING STUDENTS TO USE THE LIBRARY BEFORE SCHOOL

One of the school policies at P.S. 34 involved hours when the library was open to students. The rule prohibited students from using the library before and after regular school hours. The library was open only when Mrs. Flynn, the librarian, could supervise. Students continually expressed dissatisfaction with this policy, stating that they were unable to complete assigned research during the school hours. In addition, many students rode school buses that dropped them at school thirty to forty-five minutes before the first period. This waiting time was felt to be wasted.

Mrs. Scott, in discussing school regulations with her students, found strong dissatisfaction with the library rule. She suggested that the students formulate a positive, workable alternative to be presented to the student council. The recommendation eventually made by Mrs. Scott's students suggested that students be recruited and trained as library staff members and that parent volunteers be solicited to supervise the library for one half hour before and after school. Students would be allowed to use the library during these times after obtaining a pass from the teacher who was on bus duty for the day. The procedure was eventually worked out with the librarian, principal, and student council members with the added stipulation that misbehavior in the library would result in suspension of before- and after-school library privileges for two weeks. Student input about this school rule resulted in a decrease in grumbling about "not having a chance to use the library" and in an increase in the number of reports handed in on time.

Students often learn school rules by experience. That is, they may break a rule before they are aware of its existence. Questions of school policy should not be ignored by the classroom teacher. A frank discussion with students is recommended.

Give Clear Instructions

Closely related to the suggestions about making rules explicit is the need to give clear instructions to students. Rules can provide a general guide as to what is expected in the classroom, but a rule cannot be initiated every time students are to perform a task. Providing clear and simple instructions can sometimes eliminate the need for elaborate behavior management programs. We have known teachers who set up elaborate systems for managing students when a simpler approach would have been to tell the students, "This is what I want you to do...." Simple approaches should be tested before initiating more complicated techniques.

Clear, simple instructions are fundamental to prompting desired behaviors. Lovitt and Smith (1972) indicate that teachers deliver several hundred instructions a day. They note that some students perform inadequately because the instructions have not been given precisely and consistently. For example, telling a student, "Improve

UNCLEAR INSTRUCTIONS	CLEAR INSTRUCTIONS
1. Come in early in the morning and finish your chemistry test.	Come in at 7:45 a.m. and finish your chemistry test.
2. Show more team spirit.	Cooperate with team members by allowing other players to score rather than always attempting to run the ball. Show you are a team member by cheering other players on.
3. Make the school proud of you.	During the band competition sit quietly while other bands are playing: do not boo or yell; follow all instructions from your chaperons, and play your best during the concert. Be a good winner by not boasting and ribbing other bands, or be a good loser by congratulating the winning band.
4. Show you have some responsibility.	Demonstrate responsibility by completing your homework assignments without being reminded.
5. Show you have some manners during lunch.	Use your napkin. Keep your elbows off the table. Chew your food before swallowing. Swallow your food before talking.
6. Don't take too long in the bathroom.	You have five minutes to go to the bathroom before you board the bus.
7. Don't be so immature.	Spitwads are not to be thrown during Alegbra II class. Note passing is not allowed during class discussions.
8. Don't get too far from the building during recess.	Stay on the asphalt area during recess. Stay inside the fence during recess.

your work," "Give more thought to the issue," or "Think before you act" are too broad to prompt desired behaviors. These instructions may only result in students becoming frustrated and, perhaps, disruptive. A more instructive comment would be, "John, your writing could be improved by giving more examples for each of the points you mentioned in your theme," "Jane, what do you think about including . . . position in your debate?" "Bill, why don't you check the correctness of your work by performing the reverse operation . . . before you hand in your test?" Taking the time to be precise has the added advantage of letting students know that a teacher really cares about their work. Perhaps examining how the instructions on page 38 were made more specific will further assist you in evaluating the kind of instructions you give.

In addition to preciseness, you will want to provide consistency in giving routine instructions so that students can be sure about what they are to do. Changing the wording or emphasis of instructions can create unneeded problems. One way to improve both the precision and consistency of your instructions is to ask students for feedback about how well points are being communicated. In working with slower students, it may be helpful to ask them to explain what they have been instructed to do. This technique often clears up sources of miscommunication. A teacher should also give instructions only when students are paying attention.

Make the Setting Conducive to Learning

Physical surroundings are cues for different kinds of behaviors. For example, you may have noticed that a certain student will work diligently when placed with one group of students but behave disruptively when placed anywhere near another group; that when desks are aligned in rows, students often fail to interact freely during group discussions; that the time of day for presenting materials of differing difficulty levels has an influence on how well students pay attention. Numerous other environmental stimuli such as lighting, temperature, and decor of the room can become the occasion for various student responses.

Part of the teacher's efforts in managing a classroom should, thus, be aimed at arranging the setting in such a way that desired student behaviors are triggered. This is not necessarily a difficult process. A first step is to identify the conditions that seem to increase appropriate behavior and then insure their presence on future occasions. Making certain that each child can see the chalkboard, spending some time improving the physical appearance of the room, developing strategies for moving students from class to class or to different locations in the classroom, and controlling the number of interruptions from outside sources, to name just a few, can serve to prompt the kinds of behaviors desired by teachers. The point is that conditions in the classroom can make a substantial difference in how students behave.

A LITTLE ELBOW ROOM, PLEASE!

Is it a good idea to bring students close together for demonstrations, reading sessions, and the like? That depends on how close the students come to one another. Teachers have long seen that placing students in too crowded conditions generates pushing, shoving, and fighting. However, the teacher's desire to have students see material often leads him to ask students to "huddle around a little closer." Unfortunately, research indicates that crowding students not only increases aggressiveness but also markedly reduces attention to the teacher and the material. Krantz and Risley (1977), for example, found that asking kindergarten students to crowd around a teacher's demonstrations resulted in far less attention to the teacher and material and much more disruptiveness. It is possible that students who must compete for limited space are too concerned about their "personal space" to be attentive to lessons. Making sure that students have some elbow room, then, seems necessary if students are to be brought close together for a lesson.

Provide Appropriate Materials

As axiomatic as it may seem, another principal means for prompting desired student behaviors is the provision of academic work at appropriate levels of difficulty. Teachers sometimes talk about poor attention span, restlessness, and lack of interest as though students were predisposed to those behaviors. It is more self-assuring to think that students have the problem than to believe that the class itself is boring or unexciting. The truth is that some students do misbehave because they have become bored with the lesson activities. Lessons that are too easy, repetitious, and routine can easily lead students to seek other things to do. Conversely, work can also be too difficult. Some students may give up and misbehave simply to avoid undertaking tasks that they know are far beyond their present skills. Students may feel that they can "save face" by being disruptive rather than undertaking and failing at impossible tasks. At least, a disruptive student can say, "I could have done it if I had really wanted to." Apparently, desired behaviors cannot be prompted by asking the same thing of all students.

BOB TRIED BUT JUST COULDN'T QUITE DO IT

Bob was repeating a required high school course in biology. He seemed interested in the work at first. He even told Mr. McGalliard , his biology teacher, that he really planned to try hard this year. Bob brought his book to class every day during the first grading period. He appeared to listen intently to the lectures and created no disturbances. But he performed miserably on the exams. Eventually, he began to show less interest. He started teasing the girls who sat close to him, and soon was a constant source of disruption. One day Mr. McGalliard asked him to read a short passage from the text. Bob slammed the book closed and stormed from the class.

Later, when Mr. McGalliard went through Bob's school record, he discovered that Bob was a very poor reader. Mr. McGalliard immediately changed the text that Bob was using. He also started giving oral exams to Bob and other students who were having similar problems. Bob's work slowly improved and by the end of the term he had earned a D for the course.

Not all stories have an ending even as happy as the one above. Providing stimulus materials at appropriate difficulty levels for every student is a major task. You may never completely achieve the degree of success that you seek. Continuous evaluation, planning, and flexibility are required. We know of no easy way the task can be achieved. But we do have a few suggestions that may prove helpful in guiding your efforts.

Evaluate present skill levels. Before instructional plans are developed, the skill levels at which each student is working ought to be determined. If a class is large, an adequate educational diagnosis may require several days. However, the evaluation period will eliminate time lost from starting students on skill levels that are much above or below current levels of functioning. Subsequent classroom management problems may, thus, be prevented.

You will find that many commercial tests, and those that you develop, can be administered to the entire class at the same time. Other tests, such as reading instruments, may need to be administered individually. Sometimes a handicapped student may require individual testing. With planning, however, even teachers of large classes should be able to include some individual testing in their evaluation period. Students who are not actively involved in the diagnostic process at any given time can be involved in other planned activities. For example, short encyclopedia reports, bulletin boards related to selected topics, art, reading, and independent study to be followed by short class discussions are activities that can be instructive and exciting enough to maintain the interest of most students. A great deal of useful information regarding work habits and ability to work cooperatively with others may also be gleaned from these less formal activities. And, while our suggestions may require a few hectic days for you, formal instruction in content areas is likely to be enhanced as a result of the preliminary diagnostic process.

Consider the use of programmed materials. After you have completed the preliminary diagnosis, you will undoubtedly have to do some planning to take care of individual differences among students. Seldom will every student in your class possess the same skills. One of the most useful strategies for dealing with individual differences involves using programmed materials. They present information in small steps, progress from easy to more difficult, demand active participation from the students by requiring an overt response (usually a written response to a question), and offer feedback on performances. Such materials permit students to work at their own pace and almost assure the students of success. Published programmed materials are currently available for practically every subject. It would be unrealistic, however, to assume that the majority of teachers have a variety of programmed materials available to them for use in the classroom. A growing number of teachers have, therefore, become involved in developing their own individualized programs. Teacher-made programs typically include (1) identification of the concepts, skills, or values that students are to learn, (2) objectives that state how the students must demonstrate mastery of the material, (3) provision of a variety of activities from which students can select to reach the objectives, (4) pretests that determine who really needs to study the materials, (5) directions regarding how to proceed, (6) posttests to determine how well the objectives have been attained, and (7) enrichment activities for students who desire further exploration on the unit of study.

You have probably surmised that you would not be able to sit down over a weekend and prepare programmed materials for your classes. Much more effort is required. You might find it beneficial to attend a summer workshop on developing individual programs. Such workshops usually allow time for participants to begin developing materials for use in their classes. Or, you could suggest an in-service training course for your school. Some teachers have found that the best way to proceed with the development of individualized materials is to join forces with their colleagues and prepare the materials together. Although the task will be time-consuming, you will be able to reach far more students once you have developed individual programs on a range of topics. You can also use the materials more than once.

Consider skills grouping. Providing appropriate materials does not mean that you must work with only one student at a time. Another possibility for meeting individual differences is to arrange for skills grouping in your classes. The skills groups can vary depending upon student interests, needs, and readiness to undertake the tasks. Be assured that we are not advocating the establishment of permanent groups. That approach is unacceptable because no two students are going to have identical abilities for every task. As new activities are initiated, students with different skill levels should be grouped according to their differences. The composition of such groups should remain flexible so that students can move freely in and out of different groups as specific skills are mastered. For example, if the class is mathematics, a student might move to a group studying division of fractions only after achieving success with multiplication of fractions. As you can see, flexibility in grouping necessitates considerable planning for the teacher, but the strategy insures that students are presented with appropriate assignments. The work is hard, but the alternative of failing to plan for individual differences is failure for some students.

Use variety in teaching. While the provision of appropriate materials can have a major impact on student behaviors, doing the same thing day in and day out can present problems. The following case illustrates what can happen with too much repetition.

WHY CAN'T WE ...?

Mr. Copeland and Mrs. Shoemaker both taught French II classes. Mrs. Shoemaker had taught for several years and had her lessons for the year well outlined. Vocabulary lists, grammar worksheets, selections from the textbooks, and drill in pronunciation formed the mainstay of her teaching activities. One day she overheard several students in her class say that students in Mr. Copeland's class had more fun. She overlooked the comments, feeling that French was a serious subject.

Mary Jane eventually got up enough courage to ask in class why the students were never allowed to do anything different. Mrs. Shoemaker decided to look at her lesson plans objectively to see whether she could vary the way she taught the material. She met Mr. Copeland in the teachers' lounge later in the day and asked what techniques he was using that prompted so many positive student comments. She learned that Mr. Copeland devoted at least one day a week to teaching vocabulary and grammar in a unique way. For example, students made up crossword puzzles using French words and then exchanged puzzles with other students. Or they developed and acted out short scenes in French. Mrs. Shoemaker began to realize that she was relying too heavily on lessons she had used for years and that her lessons contained very little variety. She and Mr. Copeland decided to spend time together planning new activities for teaching French II.

No set of materials or teaching approach *per se* is sufficient to maintain the interests of students indefinitely. Having a variety of materials and methods is probably the best way to maintain maximum interest in school activities. As a matter of fact, Kounin (1970) found that variety and challenge in seatwork were significantly related to students' behavior in a learning setting. The use of movies, discussion groups, academic games, and group competition may serve as viable breaks from the routine, and prove to be useful learning activities in and of themselves.

Consider student interests. The importance of student interests should be included in any discussion of providing appropriate materials. One's efforts may prove fruitless if students have no interest in what is offered to them. The common lament, "These students have no interest in learning," probably is not entirely true. The students may only be disinterested in studying what the teacher has in mind. A number of things can be done to combat this seeming lack of interest. First, and possibly the most important, students can be given some choice. There is some data (Davis, 1971; McEwen, 1972) to show that students' choice of activities produces higher achievement levels than teacher choice of activities. Students at all age levels can be given some choice even if that choice is nothing more than selecting between two possibilities. Second, student interest in activities can often be heightened by the way the materials are introduced. Indicating how a topic is relevant to a student's occupational goals, presenting seldom recognized and stimulating thoughts, behaving enthusiastically, and associating the materials with other events known to be interesting to the students could have an impact on how interested the students become. Third, students' existing interests can be used to involve them in academics. Suppose a teacher knows that a student has an interest in automobiles. That student could be asked to read about racing, to study how the automobile has contributed to society, to report on the occupations related to the automobile, and to investigate how geometric designs are involved in automobile engineering. The student's interest could trigger appropriate academic endeavors in any number of disciplines. Students do not lack interest. However, their interests are often overlooked in prompting other behaviors.

THIS SHOULD INTEREST YOU

Research indicates that student interest and freedom from misbehavior is directly related to the teacher's skill in keeping students alert. Kounin (1970) found that *group alerting*, that is, keeping nonreciting students involved and on their toes, is significantly related to freedom from deviancy. Kounin observed that group alerting might be achieved by maintaining suspense about who is going to be called on, calling on different students frequently, creating interest in what is going to be asked (e.g., "This might fool you"), letting nonperformers know they may be called on in connection with what someone else has said, and introducing novel ideas into recitations. Kounin also noticed that holding students responsible for tasks going on during recitations is related to work involvement and freedom from deviancy. How predictable are you regarding who will be called on? Do you wait until a question is asked before identifying who is to respond? Once a student has been called on, can he expect to be overlooked on subsequent questions? Are your questions of a yes-no variety or do they stimulate thought and encourage discussions? Do you circulate and check the work of those who do not respond? Who does most of the talking in your class? How much attention have you given to keeping students on their toes and a part of the learning experience?

Model Desired Behaviors

Another procedure that can be exceedingly helpful in prompting desired student behavior is the planned use of role modeling. Individuals acquire much of their behavior by copying or imitating the behavior of others (models). This learning process is usually called role modeling or imitation. As a teacher, you have probably observed and imitated behaviors exhibited by your former teachers. You may have developed some good and bad teaching behaviors through imitation without even realizing that you were imitating others. Public school teachers may sometimes utilize the same strategies that were used by their college professors. The teaching styles that worked in college, however, may be totally inappropriate for a public school setting. Students, too, are constantly learning through imitation. They undoubtedly imitate more of their teacher's behavior than is expected. And they, too, can be acquiring some desirable and undesirable behaviors. With some forethought, modeling can be used advantageously.

There are several important ways in which modeling can be used to influence student behaviors and possibly prevent many classroom management problems. One tactic involves focusing attention on appropriate models in the class. For example, commenting that Joe and Bill are working together nicely allows students to see firsthand what is expected. Since this tactic is especially helpful in reducing disruptive behaviors, it will be discussed in more detail in Chapter Four. Our attention in this section will be devoted to the effects a teacher's behaviors can have on students.

Modeling critical behaviors. Suppose you scurry about the classroom, chatter constantly, and frequently find yourself yelling at the students. What influence will exhibiting such behaviors have on how your students react toward each other, how much self-control they demonstrate, or how they respond to learning situations? Suppose, on the other hand, that you begin walking about the room more slowly, stop chattering so much, speak softly, call students by name, and respond to them in more positive ways. How will these behaviors affect students? A teacher reported these conditions to Wesley Becker and his colleagues (Becker, Engelman & Thomas, 1975), and noticed a dramatic improvement in student behaviors soon after she began setting a calmer example herself. You can probably think of numerous other teacher behaviors that serve as examples for the students to copy. Teachers who are enthusiastic, who demonstrate good work habits, and who are themselves polite and friendly quickly come to mind. Punitive teachers also have their effects. In fact, the extensive research efforts of Albert Bandura and his co-workers (1963 and 1969) clearly demonstrate that the behaviors of adult models have a pervasive influence on the way students behave.

MR. NORRIS CAN'T UNDERSTAND TODAY'S YOUTHS

Mr. Norris spends considerable time in the teachers' lounge discussing what has gone wrong with the youths of today. He generally concludes that students don't know what hard work means. According to him students have it soft. He believes that today's students are much less productive than the students of his era.

Observation of Mr. Norris's own behaviors reveal that he seldom takes school work home with him. He frequently plans his own work or relaxes while students are given something to keep them busy. When asked to help with extracurricular activities, Mr. Norris usually has to decline because he "has to be out of town that night." Do you wonder why Mr. Norris's students seem so unproductive?

You may be thinking that no teacher can exemplify every worthy virtue. They cannot. Teachers are human, and, like everyone else, they have their faults. Nonetheless, teachers should not expect much success in getting students to exhibit behaviors that they themselves do not exhibit. A unique study by Bryan and Walbek (1970) illustrates the need for consistency between what individuals preach and what they practice. These experimenters exposed children to one of several types of models. Some children heard a model advocate giving a portion of his game winnings to charity. The model made no donation, however. Other children heard the model complain about giving, but the model did make a donation. The children's experimental opportunities to give a portion of their game winnings was influenced by what the models *did*, not what the models *said*. "Do what I say, not what I do" is simply an unworkable admonition. Teachers who are perplexed about why students behave as they do will surely want to examine their own behaviors for clues. A teacher is not expected to be perfect, but those behaviors desired from students should be modeled.

Crucial variables. A number of variables can influence how effective a teacher will be in getting students to imitate modeled behaviors. First, students are influenced by the perceived status or prestige of the model. Students are more apt to imitate someone who has status than someone who has not. Thorough preparation, demonstrated expertise on a particular topic, activities undertaken during and after school, friendliness, and a host of other behaviors could affect how much status or prestige students attribute to the teacher. Second, perceived similarity between the teacher and students can greatly enhance the modeling process. This does not mean one should dress like the students, wear their hair styles, or hang out with them. Students can see through superficial attempts at trying to be "just one of the gang." Admitting mistakes, requesting assistance from others, and laughing together with students at a funny story could reflect a similarity between a teacher and students. Students need to know that teachers are human and not paragons of virtue who share little in common with others.

Third, personal attitudes toward students may influence whether one is imitated. Feshback (1967), for example, has pointed out that students are more prone to imitate teachers who respond positively than those who respond negatively to incorrect responses. If students have been accustomed to negative approaches, one probably should avoid coming on too fast with positive techniques. Gradual changes would be better. Finally, students are most likely to imitate behaviors that can be demonstrated in a clear and simple fashion. Trying to shoot over the heads of students or to impress them with new-found knowledge is not only poor teaching, but reduces the possibility of influencing students in other ways. Being a good example requires conscious effort on the part of every teacher. However, most teachers possess the necessary skills to model desired behaviors.

Evaluating Your Approach

We have now discussed a number of techniques for prompting desired student behavior. The sample evaluation form on pages 50-51 summarizes our suggestions for using these techniques. The form is designed to provide data as to how the strategies are implemented and how well they work in the classroom. You may want to use our form for evaluating use of the strategies in your classroom. Or you may wish to develop your own evaluation form.

Reinforcing Appropriate Behaviors

To this point, our discussion has focused on procedures for initiating appropriate student behavior. The provision of rules, giving clear and simple instructions, making the setting conducive to learning, providing appropriate academic materials, and modeling were suggested as ways for prompting desired behaviors. As mentioned earlier, however, whether students will be guided by a rule depends largely upon what happens *after* they have displayed desired responses. The long-range effects of other prompts is also a function of what happens following the students' behavior. Students will not indefinitely continue following instructions, behaving appropriately in the classroom, or imitating a teacher's behavior unless their actions produce meaningful consequences. Psychologists have long cautioned that only those behaviors that produce pleasant consequences (positive reinforcers) tend to be repeated, whereas behaviors that have no noticeable effect on the environment are discontinued. In other words, persons continue performing both appropriate and inappropriate behaviors because of the consequences produced by those behaviors.

Make Desired Behavior Pay

The appropriate behaviors that a teacher would like to increase in the classroom are sometimes unintentionally discouraged. At the same time, inappropriate behaviors may begin to occur with distressing frequency. What happens to produce such clearly undesirable changes in students' behavior? An analysis of the events occurring in the classroom may reveal that the contingencies have been reversed. That is, the appropriate behaviors fail to receive a payoff, while the inappropriate behaviors are rewarded.

ASKING PERMISSION TO SPEAK

Mrs. Carter began preparation for a unit examination in her fifth grade American History class with a brief review. Most of the students had spent the previous week reading and working on projects related to their study and were well prepared for the test. The first question resulted in many students' raising their hands for permission to speak. However, before she could recognize one of these students, Max blurted out the answer. After commenting on the correctness of Max's answer, Mrs. Carter moved to the next question. Again several hands waved frantically in the air, but Jim quickly called out the answer. Mrs. Carter commended Jim for his excellent answer and praised the class as a whole for being so well prepared. She then continued the review by asking a third question. This time few hands went up. Instead, several students began to answer the question immediately. At this point, Mrs. Carter attempted to restore order by admonishing the students to remember the class rule: Raise your hand and be recognized before speaking out in class.

Unfortunately, the classroom example described above is not atypical. All of us at one time or another have probably observed a similar situation. What went wrong in this classroom? Something obviously happened to change the behavior of the students so that a classroom rule was disobeyed. The fifth graders would probably answer very simply, "If I raise my hand, I won't get to answer." In more technical terms, the teacher failed to reinforce desired behavior.

EVALUATION FORM FOR PROMPTING DESIRED BEHAVIORS

Strategy	Application Did you remember to:	Results		Recommendations
		Yes	No	
A. Let the students know the rules	1. keep rules to a minimum? 2. involve students in making the rules? 3. make different rules for different occasions? 4. state rules positively? 5. review the rules periodically? 6. give students a copy of the rules? 7. post a copy of the rules?			
B. Give clear instructions	1. avoid vague terminology? 2. specify precise behaviors? 3. maintain consistency in giving routine instructions?			
C. Make the setting conducive to learning	1. arrange student groups, seating arrangements, and time of presenting various materials so as to facilitate appropriate behaviors? 2. look for and change conditions that seem to serve as cues for inappropriate behaviors (e.g., lighting, temperature)? 3. make certain that each student can see the chalkboard? 4. consider ways of improving the physical appearance of the room? 5. develop a plan to allow for smooth transition from one activity to			

D. Provide appropriate materials

1. evaluate present skill levels of your students?
2. consider using programmed materials to individualize instructions?
3. consider developing your own programmed materials to individualize instruction?
4. consider flexible skills grouping?
5. reevaluate and reassess students to groups as skill levels change?
6. use a variety of materials?
7. use a variety of teaching methods?
8. use teaching materials and activities that are related to student interests?

E. Model desired behaviors

1. demonstrate behaviors in a clear and simple fashion?
2. behave positively toward the students?
3. refrain from acting in an aggressive manner?
4. occasionally volunteer to assist with activities that students especially enjoy?
5. demonstrate special areas of expertise for the students?
6. demonstrate an interest and concern for the students?

"To tell you the truth, Dad, for a quarter an A, it's hardly worth the effort."

Appropriate behaviors occur frequently in every classroom. Students *do* remember to raise their hands before speaking. They *do* remember to bring their books to class. They *do* remember to complete their homework. But teachers sometimes forget how important it is to reinforce the behaviors they expect from students. Good behavior is often taken for granted. You may have given up on an idea, become totally discouraged, or struck out at someone because nobody seemed to notice how hard you were working. "What's the use?" or "Nobody cares" are familiar refrains. Students react the same way. The appropriate behaviors that teachers initiate in students must pay off or the behaviors will diminish. A key, then, to preventing many classroom management problems is to make appropriate behavior pay.

Select An Effective Reinforcer

The term reinforcer has been used several times in the preceding discussion. Psychologists use the term to refer to any stimulus or event that strengthens behavior. We are concerned with positive

TABLE 4—1

POTENTIAL REINFORCERS FOR CLASSROOM USE

Social Reinforcers	Activity Reinforcers	Tangible Reinforcers [1]	Token Reinforcers	Feedback Reinforcers
Teacher praise	Spelling contests	Consumables	Points	Knowledge of results
"Correct."	Choosing a seat in	M&Ms	Checkmarks	
"Very good."	the cafeteria	Cereal pieces	Grades	
"I'm pleased	Choosing a seat in	Raisins	Poker Chips	
with you."	the classroom	Cokes	Money [2]	
"Excellent idea."	Being a line leader	Crackerjacks		
"Good job."	Going to library			
"You're doing	Working on	Inexpensive toys		
well."	special projects	Marbles		
	Talking to others	Balloons		
Nonverbal approval	Arranging a	Award buttons		
Smile	bulletin board	Baseball cards		
Hug	Answering doors and	Puzzles		
Wink	taking messages	Comics		
Pat on shoulder	Being a group leader	Magazines		
Nod	Class parties			
	Athletic contests			
Being asked for	Movies			
one's opinion	Field trips			
	Being teacher's helper			
Recognition	Free time for			
	reading, games or			
	other events			
	Access to play area or			
	special area in classroom			

[1] Tangible reinforcers are often used with special education students. These reinforcers may also be necessary in regular classrooms when students are not amenable to change through other approaches.

[2] May be provided by parents and used as a reinforcer in implementing change programs in the school.

reinforcers, which are those events or items that strengthen (maintain or increase) the behaviors that they follow. Examples, for most people, include money, candy, good grades, and praise. The terms reward, payoff, and positive consequences are sometimes used in the place of the more technical term, positive reinforcer. In this chapter, these four terms may be used interchangeably.

At this point, you may be thinking that teachers often use positive reinforcers but still are unable to strengthen the desired behaviors of some students. You have undoubtedly heard teachers say, "I have tried everything with that student and nothing seems to work." Or, you may have heard teachers exclaim, "There is really nothing to positive reinforcement. It simply doesn't work." In many instances, the items or events used as payoffs may be reinforcing *only* to the *teacher*. The student may be turned off completely by what the teacher perceives as a reward. The fact that some events may be non-reinforcing to students can account for many of the "failures" in getting students to continue behaving in desired ways.

The most accurate way to determine whether an item will serve as a reinforcer is to present it following a behavior and observe its effect on the behavior. Remember, the presentation of a positive reinforcer will increase the frequency of the behavior that it follows. Presenting a potential reinforcer and observing its effects on behavior may not be the most efficient method of identifying reinforcers for classroom use, however. Time and effort may be saved in trying to improve classroom management if *potential* reinforcers are identified prior to implementing any new programs. One useful method for determining items that may serve as positive reinforcers in the classroom involves observation of the students. What activities do they engage in when they have free time? What books do they read? What games do they play? It is apparent that all students do not choose to engage in the same activity. One student may eat a snack; another may read a book. *Events that are reinforcing to one student may not be reinforcing to another.* Given a choice, the student will engage in the activity that is reinforcing to him. Observation of students during free time periods should, thus, provide useful clues regarding potential reinforcers.

A second method for determining items that may serve as positive payoffs involves asking the students. The most direct method often turns out to be the easiest and most effective one. A class discussion can identify reinforcers that the teacher has failed to consider. Textbooks and articles dealing with classroom management may also yield ideas for possible rewards. Talks with other teachers can add additional possibilities. The potential reinforcers listed in Table 4-1 offer some ideas for the classroom teacher. You might try adding to our list.

Using Teacher Attention as a Payoff

Perhaps the most natural and readily available payoff for appropriate student behavior is teacher attention. A word of praise, a pat on the back, a smile, a friendly glance, or a wink can drastically improve relationships within a classroom and go a long way in minimizing classroom management problems. In fact, teacher approval has been widely used in reducing a variety of problems with elementary (O'Leary & O'Leary, 1977) and junior high and senior high school students (Long & Williams, 1973). Teacher approval has the apparent advantage of taking little time and effort. Certainly no more time or effort is involved in catching students being "good" than in catching them being "bad." But the systematic use of teacher attention is not quite as simple as it may appear. First, all students do not respond in the same way to teacher approval. Second, some teachers are unaccustomed to the systematic use of attention, especially in using their approval in meaningful ways.

Student reactions. Teachers are occasionally surprised when their approval proves ineffective with certain students. Most students have learned to value praise and other forms of social approval because their parents coupled attention, praise, and smiles with food, warmth, comfort, and other important reinforcers. Some youngsters have had the misfortune of never having affection paired with things typically associated with a wholesome home environment. Such students may fail initially to respond in expected ways. The situation can be remedied, however, by repeatedly pairing approval with other known reinforcers. For example, a teacher might comment, "Bill, because you have been working so hard on your math assignment, you can line up first for lunch." Eventually, by preceding known reinforcers (e.g., special privileges) with teacher approval, approval should become a potent influence on student behavior.

Students may also respond atypically if the teacher's approval generates ridicule from peers. Public accolades occasionally result in students' being called teacher's pets. Praise under such circumstances only creates problems for the teacher and the students. The use of nonconspicuous approval may constitute a better strategy. Comments on homework assignments, gestures, winks, and private comments may be just what is needed to help the student continue behaving appropriately. Most students relish approval when it is judiciously administered, but careful consideration should be given to how students react to your choice of verbal comments and nonverbal approval. Hugs and physical closeness, for example, may prove beneficial with elementary students, yet be disastrous with junior high students. Obviously, discretion should be used in selecting and administering approval.

Offering meaningful approval. Indiscriminate use of approval can conceivably produce an increase in unwanted behaviors. Students can also be turned off by the way approval is offered, especially if they interpret the praise as phony or insincere. A teacher can be totally honest in wanting only to recognize the accomplishments of students and yet be perceived as manipulative or artificial. For these reasons, we are offering the following suggestions (Williams & Anandam, 1973) for giving praise in an authentic and meaningful way:

1. Praise significant behaviors. Students know when they have worked hard on a task and they know when they have expended little effort. Few students will welcome being praised on trivial matters. Of course, what is significant or trivial may vary from student to student. By observing students' work and by listening to them, a teacher should soon be able to offer some meaningful praise to *every* student.

2. Be precise. Generally, the more specific the praise, the more reinforcing it will be. A student can be told that something is "great" or "very good" without much effort. Indicating what is particularly liked requires greater thought and attention. Perhaps that is why specific praise is more valued and less apt to be deemed insincere. Pinpoint the exact behavior that is being approved. "I liked your painting because ..." "You got nine of ten problems correct; that's good work." "Your question about ... raises some interesting issues."

3. Consider how you praise. A teacher can be so lavish in administering approval that what is said is minimized. Coming on too strong represents a common mistake in using praise. One need not be grandiloquent. A wiser strategy is simply to make the approval commensurate with the student's actual performance. A student can be told that he is working hard or that he did his assignment correctly without going to

extremes in praising and without comparing his work with others'. Some of the most effective teachers are those who remain calm in recognizing the accomplishments of their students.

4. Avoid redundancy. Students can get tired of hearing a single word or phrase. They may also doubt the sincerity of a teacher who repeatedly uses only one form of approval. Try identifying and using many different words, phrases, gestures, facial expressions, and forms of contact for conveying approval. With practice, a teacher can become proficient in expressing approval in new ways.

5. Develop consistency between verbal and nonverbal behavior. The impact of verbal comments can be readily diminished by nonverbal actions. For example, telling a student "that's good work," while attending to something else, will not be nearly as effective as examining the work, looking at the student, and smiling while the approval is being given. Eye contact, closeness, attention, tone of voice, facial expression, and body movements tell students as much as words. Words are useless when nonverbal behaviors contradict what is being said.

6. Be consistent. Students need to know what they can expect. When students realize that they can depend upon a teacher to recognize and appreciate their efforts, the teacher is on the way to becoming an important influence in their lives.

7. Try a gradual approach. Abruptly increasing the amount of approval administered can make a teacher appear awkward or insincere. Students may interpret the change as an indication that they can behave any way they choose. Give them a chance to adjust to the new approach. Approval can be increased as they increase their achievements. Other rewards can also be used in order to avoid overdoing verbal approval.

Expressing approval is a basic means of reinforcing appropriate student behaviors. What is approved, how precise the approval is, the style, the choice of words, the consistency between verbal and nonverbal behaviors, the consistency in giving approval, and the frequency of approval can all add to or detract from the influence of the teacher. Effort in recognizing and controlling these factors should greatly enhance the overall effectiveness of approval both in strengthening desirable behaviors and in preventing classroom management problems. The benefits are numerous. The task is a relatively easy one for most teachers.

"I TRIED IT—IT DIDN'T WORK"

While correctly expressing approval is a must, nothing works unless it is given a fair chance. An eighth grade teacher who was skeptical about the value of approval recently told us that he had "tried" approval with his students but that it didn't work. After observing in his classroom we learned that he was using approval far less frequently than he thought. In fact, he was using almost twice as much disapproval as approval. This teacher's "natural" use of approval and disapproval is fairly typical. Research in ten junior high teachers' classrooms (Thomas, Presland, Grant & Glynn, 1978) revealed that the teachers as a group used almost three times as much disapproval (.58 disapproving comments per minute during observation) as approval (.20 approval comments per minute during observation). Earlier research (White, 1975) with teachers in grades 1-12 yielded similar results. It seems that many teachers aren't giving approval a chance to work. They expect good behavior without paying for it. How much approval are you *actually* using? How much disapproval? If you are frequently catching students being good, can you improve upon the way in which you offer approval?

Using Other Reinforcers

Teacher approval, of course, is only one of many potential reinforcers available in the classroom. Any of the types of potential reinforcers identified earlier could strengthen desired student behavior. Asking students for their opinions, holding up an idea for further discussion, and giving students feedback about a performance can serve as potent reinforcers. Even tokens (e.g., points, poker chips) with the use of back-up reinforcers (e.g., free time privileges, consumables) may be used if less complicated and more natural classroom approaches prove ineffective. Items that serve as reinforcers may vary, depending upon the students and the situation. As mentioned earlier, the only way a teacher can be certain as to whether something is reinforcing is to assess its effects on the students. Different ideas can be tested to determine what works best in a particular classroom. It may be found that a combination of teacher approval, feedback, tangibles, and activity reinforcers is more helpful than the use of any single technique. Seldom will any one technique have the same impact on everyone. Through careful selection of reinforcers, teachers can help each student develop desired academic and social skills.

While care in selecting a reinforcer can be a critical element in strengthening the appropriate behaviors that students exhibit, careful attention must also be given to the way in which reinforcers are used. Indiscriminate use of positive reinforcement will seldom produce intended results. Fortunately, a number of well-known educators and psychologists (e.g., Kazdin, 1975; Krumboltz & Krumboltz, 1972; Piper, 1974; Wilson & Williams, 1973) have provided practical suggestions regarding the use of positive reinforcers. So let us turn now to the most frequently suggested strategies for using positive reinforcement to best advantage.

1. Specify the target behaviors. Very little information is conveyed to students if the behaviors desired by teachers are defined in general terms. Precisely specifying desired behaviors has the advantage of bringing into focus for students *and* teacher exactly what is expected and required. Miscommunication is less likely to occur if the behaviors are defined in terms that allow them to be counted. Telling John that he should do a better job in spelling provides little direction regarding desired behavior change. Telling him that after studying Lesson Five he should be able to spell fifteen out of twenty words correctly on the weekly unit exam conveys exact information concerning the desired goal.

2. Deliver contingent reinforcement. Once the target behaviors have been clearly defined, reinforcers should be delivered only *after* the behavior has been exhibited. The promises "I'll finish this after I . . ." and "I'll do it later" are often heard by classroom teachers. Teachers who acquiesce to these requests may be repaid by students failing to complete their work on schedule. Most teachers prefer not to appear cold and hardhearted. So they often reason, "What will it hurt if the student fails to complete the work just this once?" But a teacher's well-intentioned failure to make the reward contingent upon the appropriate behavior could easily result in students being "taught" undesirable behaviors.

3. Provide an immediate payoff. Many students, especially younger or slower ones, may lack the ability to delay gratification for very long. Thus, the promise of reinforcement in the future is insufficient to generate behavior change. When a reinforcer (e.g., attendance at a later ballgame) cannot be delivered immediately following the desired response due to unavailability of the reinforcer, other reinforcers such as points, stars, or check marks can be used to bridge the gap between the behavior and the payoff.

4. New behaviors should be reinforced more frequently than established behaviors. When teaching new behaviors, it is desirable to reinforce them as frequently as possible in order to strengthen them and make them more likely to occur. Once behavior become more established, teachers can reinforce less frequently. For example, a truant student who has returned to school should be recognized for his attendance until attendance becomes a well-established part of his behavior. Subsequently, you can deliver reinforcement intermittently every three days or so instead of daily.

5. Reward behavior consistently. Students may become confused and disillusioned when a teacher is indiscriminate in the types of behaviors that are reinforced. Responding to appropriate behavior only on certain days (when you feel good) will seldom result in effective classroom management. Consistency in implementing a behavior change plan must be maintained.

YOU CAN'T TEACH THEM IF THEY DON'T ATTEND

Truancy and tardiness are problems of epidemic proportion. Every school has students who are social and academic underachievers because they attend school infrequently. Teachers certainly can't teach and students can't learn when students stay home, cut class, or come late. Punishing students for nonattendance, however, may never solve the problem. Such action merely makes students enjoy school even less. Students need positive reasons for wanting to attend. Although external reinforcement for attendance should never become the sole reason for attendance, some students have to be "encouraged" to attend school before they can develop other reasons for coming.

One school found an effective means of encouraging attendance (Barber & Kagey, 1977). The school, composed of grades 1-3, markedly improved school attendance by making attendance at a monthly party contingent on school attendance. Students received daily attendance stars and thus could earn the right to join all or part of a school party dependent on the in-school attendance. The more the students attended school, the more game rooms (up to four) they could visit on party day and the longer they could stay at the party (up to one hour). During the four months in which the program was being monitored, improvement in school attendance ranged from 3.97 to 6.07 percent over preceding years. A one-percent increase was equivalent to forty-five composite days of student attendance. Neither a party that was not dependent on school attendance nor the daily stars on a chart were nearly as effective in improving attendance as the daily stars *and* contingent party. Giving students a *good* reason for attending school does seem to make a difference. Can you think of other positive ways to encourage school attendance?

More Difficult Situations

What has been said thus far is most applicable to students who readily display the behaviors desired by teachers. The teacher sets the stage (i.e., establishes class rules) for desirable beahvior, the student engages in correct behavior, and the teacher immediately provides a reward to stengthen the student's appropriate response. A few students may seldom emit the exact behaviors teachers want. And prompts *alone* may be insufficient for getting these students to exhibit the desired behaviors. Thus, the teacher may encounter difficulty in planning reinforcement for students who possess few of the social and academic skills that can earn rewards. However, a technique for enhancing the behavior of these students has been developed. Essentially, the procedure involves looking for and reinforcing crude approximations of desired behavior. Gradually, more complex behaviors are required and rewarded until the terminal goal is reached.

Rewarding successive approximations of a terminal goal rather than requiring its entire mastery before the reinforcer is delivered allows for individual differences among students. The procedure involving rewarding small increments of behavior change has been called "shaping." New behaviors can be created even though the one that the student can originally perform is only marginally related to the terminal goal. The first response to be reinforced may resemble the final goal or it may include only a small component of the terminal response. By reinforcing small steps toward the terminal response, that is, by requiring responses that are increasingly similar to the final goal before giving a reinforcer, the desired behavior is gradually achieved. Responses that do not approximate the terminal goal are not reinforced and thus are extinguished.

Strengthening Academic Response. The shaping procedure is often used in teaching academic behaviors. Consider the method for teaching a child to print his name. For kindergarteners and very slow students whose skills are limited to drawing a circle, a square, and a roughly drawn man, printing may be a formidable task. The task can appear more manageable if it is broken down into small steps that allow for frequent feedback and reinforcement. At the beginning, a child's name is printed on ruled paper and the child is given the opportunity to trace over it many times. When the child is able to trace accurately the letters of his name, he must more closely approximate the desired behavior by tracing letters that have been only faintly printed on the paper. Again, mastery of this step must be achieved before progressing to the next step, i.e., tracing the name over dotted lines. Cues are eliminated until the final goal of printing the name without prompts is achieved. The terminal goal is attained by beginning with a crude approximation of the desired response and gradually requiring more complex components of the terminal behavior. Prompting the response increases the probability that it will occur; "fading" the cues by gradual elimination increases the likelihood of a more independent response. In applied situations, fading and shaping procedures are often used simultaneously (Piper, 1974).

Strengthening Social Behavior. The use of the shaping procedure is not limited to developing academic responses. Social behaviors, such as talking to others or volunteering in class, are also amenable to change using this process. An often overlooked classroom problem is the shy, withdrawn student who fails to participate in group discussions and who is seldom selected by peers to be included in group activities. With the more outgoing students clamoring for attention, that student may receive little or no reinforcement. Because the shy student usually does not volunteer to participate in class activites or group games, it may be necessary to use a shaping procedure in order to develop self-initiated participation.

In shaping behavior toward a terminal goal of volunteering to talk during class discussions, the first behavior to be reinforced should be one that has an element of the desired response. For example, looking at the teacher when a question is asked during a class discussion may initially be rewarded. It is important that the reinforcers be carefully chosen. Asking the student to answer the question may result in further withdrawal. Instead, a comment, such as, "I'm pleased to see that you are interested in the discussion," may be more effective. Continuing to reinforce only attending behavior will not result in the establishment of the final goal, however. The next step will require rewarding a behavior that more closely approximates self-initiated participation. Raising a hand to answer when a question is asked represents a second step toward volunteering, and should be reinforced. After the student begins answering direct questions, reinforcers can be delivered for comments that are not direct answers to questions, e.g., "I'm pleased that you are sharing your thoughts on this matter." The shaping procedure should be continued until the student reaches the desired degree of participation in the classroom.

Reinforcement, of course, is a reciprocal process. As shy students become more outgoing, they receive more reinforcers and, as a result, increase their participation. They also deliver more reinforcers, thus increasing the probability that others will be interested in interacting with them. The teacher can further prompt social interaction by arranging classroom activities that will require cooperative effort. Choosing an activity that a shy student can perform well, and naming that student as group leader, may also facilitate the process. If, for example, a shy student is proficient in art, his group might be assigned responsibility for advertising a class play. Most students like to have a "winner on their team." In dealing with shy students, the points to remember are simple: prompt the behavior, and reinforce small steps toward the terminal goal.

In contrast to shy, withdrawn students, hyperactive students are seldom or, more accurately, never overlooked. "He is like a whirlwind," "She never sits still for one minute," "She keeps the other children upset," "He's driving me up the wall" are comments that are often used to describe the child who is constantly talking and on the go in the classroom. Even though the behavior may rarely occur, hyperactive students can sit down, however. They can look at books. They never talk one hundred percent of the time. In other words, the desired behaviors are in the repertoire of the child, but they are seldom performed.

To minimize hyperactive behavior, use of a shaping procedure is essential and the steps must be small. If the terminal goal is to have the student sit without talking and look at a book for fifteen minutes, even one minute of the desired behavior may be too much to require initially. Perhaps thirty seconds would be more realistic. When the student has learned to sit still for thirty seconds, the length of time required before a reinforcer is delivered can be lengthened. It is better to go slowly with the process. A very gradual increase in the sitting and attending time required for a reward will increase the probability of success. The reinforcer for a hyperactive student will also need to be carefully chosen. Teacher praise and attention alone may be insufficient reinforcement. A tangible reward such as candy may also be required.

Summary

Teachers are generally confronted with two broad categories of problems. One is deficient amounts of desired student behaviors and the other is excessive amounts of undesirable student behaviors. In the case of deficient behaviors, teachers must seek ways of motivating students. This chapter has been largely devoted to describing ways that teachers can motivate students and, thereby, manage their classes more effectively. The following chapter will describe ways of managing student excesses.

Specifically, this chapter has included information on how to (1) prompt students to exhibit wanted behaviors, and (2) strengthen desired behaviors once they occur. The discussion on prompting desired behaviors has emphasized procedures that could be used in initiating desired student behaviors. The procedures discussed included letting students know the rules, giving clear instructions, making the setting conducive to learning, providing appropriate materials, and modeling desired behaviors. These procedures were presented as starting points, not ends in themselves. The section on strengthening desired behaviors stressed the importance of rewarding desired student actions as well as the conditions under which reinforcement should be delivered. Methods for selecting reinforcers were discussed and a number of potential classroom reinforcers were identified. Teacher attention was suggested as a viable reinforcer for most students. The possible reactions of different students, ideas for offering meaningful teacher approval, and alternative reinforcers were also explored. We pointed out that positive reinforcement that is applied indiscriminately will seldom produce the desired results. Guidelines for using all forms of positive reinforcement were presented. Strategies for strengthening the academic and social skills of students who seldom spontaneously emit desired responses was also covered.

Throughout the chapter the theme has been that increasing what is *wanted* from students, rather than focusing primarily on what is *not wanted*, can exert a powerful influence on the emotional climate in the classroom. A positive approach is contagious. Classroom management problems are minimized when the teacher looks for and cultivates what is best in each student.

REFERENCES

Bandura, A. *Principles of behavior modification.* New York: Holt, Rinehart and Winston, 1969.

Bandura, A. and Walters, R. H. *Social learning and personality development.* New York: Holt, Rinehart and Winston, 1963.

Barber, R. M. and Kagey, J. R. "Modification of school attendance for an elementary population." *Journal of Applied Behavior Analysis 10* (1977): 41-48.

Becker, W. C., Englemann, S., and Thomas, D. R. *Teaching I: Classroom management.* Chicago: Science Research Associates, 1975.

Bryan, J. H. and Walbek, N. H. "Preaching and practicing generosity: Children's actions and reactions." *Child Development 41* (1970): 329-353.

Burstall, C. "The Matthew effect in the classroom." *Educational Research 21* (1978): 19-25.

Davis, M. *Some effects of having one remedial student.* Paper presented at the 3rd Annual Kansas Conference on Behavior Analysis in Education, Lawrence, May, 1972.

Feshback, N. D. "Effects of teacher reinforcement style upon children's imitation and preferences." *Proceedings of the 75th Annual Convention of the American Psychological Association 2* (1967): 281-282.

Kazdin, A. E. *Behavior modification in applied settings.* Homewood, Ill.: The Dorsey Press, 1975.

Kounin, J. S. *Discipline and group management in classrooms.* New York: Holt, Rinehart and Winston, 1970.

Krantz, P. and Risley, T. R. "Behavioral ecology in the classroom." *In* K. D. O'Leary and S. G. O'Leary, eds. *Classroom management: The successful use of behavior modification,* 2nd ed. New York: Pergamon Press, Inc., 1977.

Krumboltz, J. D. and Krumboltz, H. B. *Changing children's behavior.* Englewood Cliffs, N. J.: Prentice-Hall, 1972.

Long, J. D. and Williams, R. L. *Classroom management with adolescents.* New York: MSS Educational Publishing Company, Inc., 1973.

Lovitt, T. C. and Smith, J. O. "Effects of instructions on an individual's verbal behavior." *Exceptional Children 38* (1972): 685-693.

Madsen, C. H., Jr., Becker, W. C., and Thomas, D. R. "Rules, praise, and ignoring: Elements of elementary classroom control." *Journal of*

Applied Behavior Analysis 1 (1968): 139-150.

Madsen, C. H., Jr. and Madsen, C. K. *Teaching/Discipline: A positive approach for educational development*, 2nd ed. Boston: Allyn and Bacon, Inc., 1974.

McEwen, J. H. "An examination of the effects of manipulating setting events on the behavior and academic achievement of secondary school students." Ed.D. diss., The University of Tennessee, 1972.

O'Leary, K. D. and O'Leary, S. G. *Classroom management: The successful use of behavior modification*. New York: Pergamon Press, Inc., 1977.

Piper, T. *Classroom management and behavior objectives*. Belmont: Lear Siegler, Inc./Fearon Publishers, 1974.

Taba, H. *Teaching strategies and cognitive functioning in elementary school children*. (Cooperative Research Project No. 2404. United States Department of Health, Education, and Welfare). California: San Francisco State College, 1966.

Thomas, J. D., Presland, I. E., Grant, M. D., and Glynn, T. L. "Natural rates of teacher approval and disapproval in grade-7 classrooms." *Journal of Applied Behavior Analysis 11* (1978): 91-94.

White, M. A. "Natural rates of teacher approval and disapproval in the classroom." *Journal of Applied Behavior Analysis 8* (1975): 367-372.

Williams, R. L. and Anandam, K. *Cooperative classroom management*. Columbus, Ohio: Charles E. Merrill Publishing Co., 1973.

Wilson, H. D. and Williams, R. L. *Before the geraniums die: A primer for classroom management*. New York: MSS Information Corporation, 1973.

CHAPTER FOUR

WHAT WILL THEY DO NEXT? MANAGING EXCESSIVE STUDENT BEHAVIORS

"I can't believe it! What are those students going to do next?" Do these words sound familiar? Well, they are. Almost every teacher is faced at one time or another with highly unpredictable, surprising student behaviors. Generally, these "unbelievable" actions are disruptive in nature. Fighting, arguing, disobedience, shouting, clowning around, and a host of other overt acts that distract attention and interrupt learning activities could be classified as disruptive. Occasionally, surprising behaviors are more private in nature, but they, too, usually fall into a category of excessive acts that cannot be tolerated in a school setting. This chapter, therefore, focuses on strategies for managing disruptiveness and other forms of unwanted student excesses.

You will notice that some of the strategies used in prompting and reinforcing desired student behaviors can also be used to manage *unwanted* acts. The basic difference in managing desirable and undesirable behaviors is that positive strategies alone are recommended for encouraging desired behaviors, whereas managing unwanted behaviors may legitimately involve some forms of *punishment* as well as the use of positive techniques. Thus, this chapter will consider a number of positive as well as punitive alternatives for eliminating and reducing excessive student behaviors. The positive strategies include: altering setting events, reinforcing behaviors incompatible with disruptiveness, using peers as models, and extinction. The punitive strategies include: soft reprimands, time out, response cost, and overcorrection. A special section is also included on dealing with violence in the schools.

Altering Setting Events

Before you try more complicated strategies, you undoubtedly will want to think about possible changes in setting events (i.e., stimuli) that could reduce disruptive behaviors in your classroom. This strategy is one of the quickest and simplest ways of reducing problems. Its use involves only the identification and alteration of the events that seem to stimulate the undesirable behavior. The changes need not be drastic in order to be effective. Sometimes a very small change is all that is required to resolve a problem, e. g., temporarily separating two talkative students. Similarly, reducing the distance between yourself and a misbehaving student, changing the materials students are using, or altering the classroom routine may produce desired changes in behavior.

In making any changes, you will want to create as little fanfare as possible. Too much attention to a problem could instigate more of a disturbance than the one you hope to eliminate. For example, in separating two misbehaving students, you might quietly comment to the students involved, "I think it would be best for you to be seated in different areas today. That way both of you can get more accomplished." There is no reason to dwell on the misbehavior. Likewise, in moving closer to a misbehaving student, you should avoid any threatening gestures or statements that could generate a more serious problem. The idea is to let the misbehaving student know you are aware of the misbehavior and desire a change. Closer proximity paired with a nod toward the student's work should be sufficient in many instances. Changing texts or altering the routine can also be achieved without a lot of commotion from the teacher.

DEFUSING TENSE SITUATIONS

Mr. Carpenter was a seventh-grade teacher who especially disliked aggressive behaviors. He could not tolerate one student bullying another. Whenever he saw any such sign of aggression, he was quick to step in and admonish the aggressor. Mr. Carpenter's approach often generated more problems than it solved. The admonished student usually tried to get even with the other student during recess. And sometimes Mr. Carpenter made errors about who was at fault. Errors on his part typically led to disagreements and backtalk from wrongly accused students.

Mr. Carpenter realized something was wrong with his approach. He knew that temporarily separating talkative students was a useful way of reducing disturbances. So, he thought about how he could use changes in setting events to defuse situations among students. Mr. Carpenter decided that when he saw friction building between two students, he would remove one of the students from the setting. To avoid calling unnecessary attention to the problem, he simply would ask one of the students to run an errand or perform a chore for him. This tactic allowed both students time to "cool off" and precluded the need for either to get even. Since repeated aggressive acts by any given student were infrequent, Mr. Carpenter did not have to worry about reinforcing aggression by letting a student perform a favor for him.

You have probably recognized that changing setting events is an effective deterrent to less serious disturbances or the spread of minor problems. But whenever the changes you make to prevent or solve an existing problem, the strategy can be effective in reducing disturbances.

One thing to remember in making changes in setting events is that a problem may reappear once you return to the original condition (e.g., when talkative students return to their regular seats). For that reason, you may need to combine stimulus changes with other strategies. For example, after you make a change in setting events, you could reinforce the appearance of desired behaviors. Some experimenting should help you determine what works best for you and your students.

Reinforcing Behaviors Incompatible with Disruptiveness

Another strategy for reducing a disruptive behavior is to reinforce behavior incompatible with that response. When one behavior is incompatible with another, the two cannot occur simultaneously. For example, a student cannot be aggressive and cooperative at the same time any more than he can simultaneously talk and listen, agree and disagree, stand and sit, or be tardy and on time. So, once you have identified the behaviors you want reduced, your task is to strengthen the opposite of those behaviors. Strengthening an incompatible behavior will lead automatically to a reduction in the other behavior. Unfortunately, teachers sometimes get so involved in dealing directly with disruptive behavior that they forget about strategies that will resolve problems indirectly.

Although the reinforcement of incompatible behavior sounds easy (and often is), several factors that could pose problems deserve

EVALUATION CHECKLIST FOR ALTERING SETTING EVENTS

Did you remember to:	Yes	No	Results and Recommendations
1. look for environmental factors that might be changed, e.g.:			
A. seating arrangements?			
B. proximity to chalkboard?			
C. proximity to teacher's desk?			
D. lighting?			
E. textbooks?			
F. other classroom materials?			
G. classroom routine (roll-taking, administrative duties)?			
H. method of lesson presentation?			
I. other?			
2. make changes quietly in order not to create a greater distrubance?			
3. combine the use of altering setting events with other strategies?			

careful consideration. First, a few students may exhibit only minimal amounts of the behaviors you wish to strengthen. An aggressive student, for instance, may engage in few cooperative acts. In such instances, you would need to shape the desired behavior, that is, you would need initially to reinforce any sign of cooperation. The requirements for reinforcement would then be increased gradually as you moved toward the terminal goal—greater cooperation and less aggression. Second, in strengthening incompatible behaviors you must use reinforcers that are meaningful to the students, otherwise you will have little success in producing wanted changes. What is reinforcing to some students could have minimal influence on others. Social attention (e.g., praise) may be adequate for some students. For others, you may have to rely upon tangibles, tokens, and activities. The key to success, however, will depend largely upon making the desired behaviors pay off for the students. You cannot get what is not paid for.

A general application. A study by Allyon and Roberts (1974) clearly demonstrates the benefits of reinforcing incompatible behaviors. These researchers were interested in reducing negative behaviors among five of the most disruptive students in a large fifth-grade reading class (thirty-eight students). The average level of such behavior among the most disruptive students was thirty-four percent, while these students' correct responses on daily reading assignments was below fifty percent. The disruptions included such acts as running, walking around the room, loud talking, noise-making, and a variety of other overt acts. Instead of trying to reduce these behaviors directly through punishment and other means, a token economy was established. The system enabled students to earn points for completing academic assignments. Students could earn two points for eighty percent accuracy on an assignment and five points for 100 percent accuracy. The points could be cashed in daily or weekly for a variety of backup reinforcers. For example, two points would buy fifteen minutes access to a game room or ten minutes of extra recess. Reduced detention, becoming an assistant teacher, and having free time to work on a bulletin board were a few of the other backup reinforcers that could be purchased.

The results were highly encouraging. By the end of the study, the average rate of accuracy on academic performances for the five most disruptive students rose to about eighty-five percent. Although no direct effort had been made to reduce disruptiveness, the average rate of disruptive behavior fell to about five percent. Apparently, the kinds of behaviors being reinforced were incompatible with disruptiveness. Students were reportedly heard making such remarks as, "Shut up, I'm trying to do my work," and "Quit bugging me, can't you see I'm reading?"

Using Peers as Models

Modeling, like positive reinforcement, is a strategy that has broad applications in the classroom. Chapter Three showed how the strategy could be used to prompt desired student behavior, emphasizing ways in which the teacher could serve as a model. In this section, you will briefly examine how modeling can be used to reduce unwanted responses. Emphasis here will be on pointing out appropriate models among the students.

You undoubtedly realize that students learn much of their behavior simply by observing and imitating that of their peers. Your realization of this fact can be helpful because you can draw attention to the kinds of behavior worthy of imitation. Suppose that John and Frank are talking when they should be working on a classroom assignment. Instead of calling attention to their disruptive behavior, you might choose to let them hear you tell Bill, "I'm glad to see you working so quietly on your assignment. Keep up the good work." Your approving comment will enable John and Frank to see the kind of behavior that produces approval. This strategy is especially useful since you need not wait for the misbehaving students to exhibit praiseworthy responses; you can identify and direct attention to the appropriate behavior being exhibited by someone else. Of course, you want to be certain to reinforce the disruptive student or students should they elect to imitate the desired behavior. Broden et al. (1970), in fact, have found that reinforcing the attending behavior of one student increased not only that behavior but also that of a disruptive student in an adjacent seat. It is hoped that you will also obtain changes in disruptive behaviors by drawing attention to the appropriate behavior of others.

INAPPROPRIATE USE OF A MODEL

Mrs. Morris, a tenth-grade English teacher, was an avid reader. She eagerly consumed practically every new book on the market; a best-seller never escaped her attention. She loved to discuss the books she read with the students. The problem was that only one of Mrs. Morris' students, Steve, enjoyed reading as much as she. Mrs. Morris found herself directing more of her attention toward Steve. She would comment, "I'll bet Steve has read this book. Why not let him give his views." Invariably, he had read the book. Steve became the sole student whom Mrs. Morris wanted others to emulate. She often used him as an example and said more than once, "I wish more of you could be like Steve." How do you think others felt about Steve? About Mrs. Morris? How did Steve feel?

You no doubt recognized from the preceding example the major problem of using students as role models: students can become jealous when a classmate is held up as an example and becomes the exclusive recipient of teacher attention. That student may then be labeled as "teacher's pet" and receive considerable ridicule from others. You can avoid such an occurrence by occasionally using every student as a role model. Even the most disruptive student will exhibit some behavior worthy of recognition. Also, by drawing attention to appropriate behavior of models, you can avoid making comparisons with other students. Saying, "I wish others could be like..." can only generate jealousy and resentment. A better strategy is to call attention to the desired behavior without putting others down. It is sufficient to say, "I like the way John is..."

Successful use of models, however, will depend on more than the appropriate recognition of desirable behaviors. As you will recall from Chapter Three, the teacher who is prestigious, in some way similar to the students, positive in treatment of students, and who presents tasks in an uncomplicated manner is likely to be frequently imitated. The same is generally true with student models. Students who have status with observers, are similar to the observers (e.g., in age, sex, background, or interests), and who obtain positive results from their behavior are more likely to be imitated than models who lack status, are dissimilar, and do not get reinforced for their behavior. You will recognize from the above comments that the consequences for imitating the behavior of a model are also of critical importance. Unless an individual is positively reinforced for imitative behavior, that behavior is unlikely to persist for very long. Your use of student examples will have to be closely tied to your use of positive reinforcement. A combination of the two strategies should vastly improve class behavior.

Extinction

You learned in Chapter Three that the use of reinforcement strengthens behavior and, thus, increases the probability of the behavior's recurrence. It was also mentioned that both desirable and undesirable behaviors can be strengthened by the payoff they produce. The reverse is also true. Behaviors strengthened by reinforcement can be weakened when reinforcement is withheld. The strategy of withholding reinforcement is called *extinction*. While many possible reinforcers can be withheld to alter different responses, attention is the one generally withheld to weaken undesirable behavior in classroom settings. Our discussion of extinction will, therefore, focus on how behaviors can be weakened by withholding social attention.

Withholding Teacher Attention

Teachers are sometimes heard to comment, "That student is just misbehaving to get my attention." Such a statement indicates that they are aware of the pervasive influence of their attention. Unfortunately, teachers frequently continue to deliver exactly what the student is trying to produce—teacher attention. In other words, they recognize what the student is trying to get with misbehavior, but then fail to do what is needed to produce change. Students will continue to emit responses that pay off. And the payoff in terms of attention need not be positive. Students who do not get attention for desired behaviors may find any form of attention to be reinforcing. Besides, being fussed at might help a student get out of doing an assignment, gain the attention of peers, or let him know he has irritated the teacher. Students can make a game out of getting the teacher mad.

An interesting study (Madsen, Becker, Thomas, Koser & Plager, 1968) supporting the value of withholding attention for excessive amounts of unwanted behaviors showed that the more teachers told students to sit down, the more the students stood up. In that classroom, students were receiving little attention for sitting and working; the attention for standing, although in the form of reprimands, served to reinforce out-of-seat behavior. When teachers stopped telling the students to sit down and started praising sitting and working, the students spent more time doing so. Other studies have demonstrated that withholding attention can be a helpful addition to reducing argumentative statements (Hall et al., 1971), tantrums (Zimmerman & Zimmerman, 1962), hyperactivity (Patterson, 1965), aggression (Brown & Elliot, 1965), and disruptiveness (Becker, Madsen, Arnold & Thomas, 1967; Kazdin, 1973). Seldom, however, is withholding of adult attention the sole strategy for producing behavioral changes. Praise or other reinforcers for desired behaviors are typically paired with the withholding of attention for undesirable behavior. In fact, studies (e.g., Madsen, Backer & Thomas, 1968) have indicated that merely ignoring inappropriate behavior without the use of other strategies could lead to increases in inappropriate behavior. Nonetheless, the literature clearly suggests that teachers should avoid "catching" students in every deviant act. To do so would only serve to increase misbehavior. Overlooking some problems is part of successful classroom management.

Apparently, teachers cannot ignore every deviant act that occurs in the classroom. To avoid giving attention to some responses would be catastrophic. If students might injure themselves or others, for example, the teacher should respond quickly. If disruptive responses occur repeatedly, teachers cannot simply turn their heads and expect the problem to disappear. We shall discuss further ways in which serious, frequently occurring problems can be managed. The point now is that certain behaviors can be overlooked in order to weaken them and diminish their immediate impact. For example, students who snap their fingers to get the teacher's attention, or call out answers without raising their hand can be ignored. If the teacher recognizes only students who raise their hand, *everyone* may soon get the idea of what is required. No big issue will have been created and no unnecessary embarrassment will have resulted for the students. Similarly, teachers can avoid responding when students occasionally make a "cute" remark or an argumentative statement. Walking away will let the student know the teacher does not have to get in the last word. Furthermore, the student will have been deprived of an opportunity to practice becoming a better arguer. Whining, pouting, complaining, and excessive verbalizing are other student behaviors that could easily be put on extinction. Students will eventually stop emitting behaviors that do not pay off. Life will also be more pleasant for the teacher who realizes that a 100 percent detection rate on misbehavior is unnecessary for establishing effective classroom management.

SEEKING ATTENTION
Billy was a third grader who had lots of things to tell his teacher,

Mrs. Martin. Whenever he saw anything wrong in the classroom, he would call her aside to let her know what was happening. He usually made at least twenty to thirty trips to her desk every day to keep her informed. He made other visits to ask for special help and to find out "exactly" what he was supposed to be doing. Any hurt also sent him clamoring for Mrs. Martin. She was so exasperated from the special attention given to Billy that she seldom gave Billy any attention when he was cooperating with others, working on his assignments, or simply minding his own business. What would you recommend?

Withholding attention for undesirable behavior has broad applications in the classroom. But certain factors should be considered if the strategy is to be properly used. First, teachers must remain consistent in what they will and will not attend to. Ignoring a behavior one day and calling attention to it the next will strengthen, rather than weaken, it. Students will learn that the payoff will eventually be delivered if they are persistent enough. A good tactic for teachers would be to list the behaviors they will reinforce as well as those to be ignored. Having clear objectives should produce greater consistency. Second, teachers should be prepared for a possible increase in undesirable behavior when attention for those behaviors is withheld. Individuals who have been accustomed to getting something for their misbehavior will probably "try harder" when the payoffs are no longer forthcoming. However, if reinforcement is available for other responses, students will soon learn which behaviors pay off. Third, teachers should realize that withholding their attention will weaken undesirable behavior only if *their attention* is the actual reinforcer for the undesirable behavior. It may well be that other events are maintaining the unwanted behaviors. The real test comes from consistently withholding attention and evaluating the results. In many instances, a teacher might ignore student behaviors only to have those behaviors reinforced by a student's peers. Ignoring the "class clowns," for instance, would be ineffective as long as classmates laugh and otherwise support undesirable antics. Because peers can provide attention for behaviors the teacher may be trying to extinguish, we need to take a look at how teachers might enlist the help of students.

Obtaining the Cooperation of Peers

Most teachers would agree that peer attention is a powerful influence in the development of both desirable and undesirable student behavior, but teachers have sometimes been remiss in mobilizing peer attention. Perhaps the conception that teachers *alone* should manage class affairs has hindered seeking the support of students. Nonetheless, for those who desire the cooperation of students, several possibilities exist for getting students to use their attention in ways that benefit others.

First, teachers can plan classroom discussions to help students recognize the importance of peer attention. During class discussions, teachers might ask, "Why do some students break class rules although it only seems to get them into trouble? What would happen if no one paid attention when individuals engaged in disruptive activities? How can classmates help one another make greater academic progress?" At least a few, if not all, students will surmise that peer attention often sustains undesirable acts, that peers withholding their attention could weaken those behaviors, and that peer approval for appropriate behaviors could have favorable impact on the entire class. Periodic discussions could very well sharpen everyone's understanding of why people behave as they do. Some disruptive youngsters might alter their own behaviors after they see what is sustaining their actions. Further, teachers could use these discussions to solicit the cooperation of students.

It would probably be best for teachers to avoid having discussions about disruptiveness immediately following an unpleasant classroom incident. There is no reason to embarrass anyone. A better strategy would be to select a time when no disruptive acts have recently occurred. Possibly, discussions could be held when class rules are being established, or, if the teacher has a time set aside for discussing class activities with students, that time would be appropriate. Establishing a cooperative planning time, or setting aside a time (for example, every grading period) to discuss student and teacher concerns would be an appropriate step for teachers at any grade level.

Another possibility for obtaining peer cooperation in ignoring inappropriate behaviors would be initially to seek support from those students who appear to have the most potential for influencing others. Solomon and Wahler (1973) conducted an experiment that demonstrated the utility of this approach. They selected peer "therapists" who had shown a willingness to cooperate with adults and who were also popular with their sixth-grade classmates. They received training from videotape in spotting desirable and problem behaviors. They also heard explanations about extinction and reinforcement procedures. They were asked later to ignore problem behaviors among disruptive classmates and to respond positively to desirable behaviors. The results were encouraging. During experimental conditions, the "therapists" gave less attention to problem behavior. Those behaviors among disruptive classmates decreased substantially. The peers were not as successful in responding positively to desirable behaviors. Perhaps longer periods of training were required for responding positively than merely for ignoring others' actions. But the study showed that teachers can get selected students to help produce needed changes. This tactic might be required in classes where the teacher cannot rely upon the help of all students. The support of larger numbers of students could be sought after the teacher has achieved success with selected groups.

Whether teachers are working with an entire class or with a small group, an effort should be made to reinforce students for judiciously using their attention. Teacher approval would be a potential reinforcer for most students. Special privileges, tangibles, or tokens might also be considered. Long and Williams (1973) have demonstrated, too, that group rewards are useful in getting students to attend appropriately to the behavior of others. When a reward is contingent upon the desirable behavior of *every* student, peers are reluctant to support undesirable behaviors. However, if teachers choose to use group rewards, they should be sure that every student can perform the expected behaviors. Furthermore, if one or two students fail to respond to group payoffs, the strategy should be altered so that all the others are not continuously deprived of privileges.

Evaluating Your Use of Reinforcement Techniques

Reinforcement techniques represent effective methods for reducing disruptive behavior in the classroom. The evaluation checklist on page 79 can be useful in determining whether the techniques have been properly implemented.

Punishment

Although the positive strategies previously described can have far-reaching effects on student behaviors, situations may arise occasionally when punishment is required to suppress an undesirable behavior immediately. A student who may do harm to

EVALUATION CHECKLIST FOR REINFORCEMENT TECHNIQUES TO REDUCE INAPPROPRIATE BEHAVIOR

Did you remember to:	Yes	No	Results and Recommendations
1. focus on behavior you would like to increase by:			
A. identifying behaviors that are incompatible with inappropriate behavior?			
B. reinforcing the behaviors that are incompatible with the inappropriate behaviors?			
C. shaping the desired behaviors by initially reinforcing approximations of the terminal goal behavior?			
2. use peers as models appropriately by:			
A. directing attention to desired behavior through comments to students who exhibit the behavior?			
B. occasionally using every student as a role model?			
C. avoiding making comparisons between students?			
D. combining reinforcement of appropriate behavior with peer modeling?			
3. withhold attention from inappropriate behaviors?			
4. remain consistent in the behaviors you reinforce?			
5. determine whether teacher or peer attention is maintaining the inappropriate behavior?			
6. reduce peer attention to inappropriate behavior by:			
A. talking with the students about the importance of ignoring inappropriate behavior?			
B. identifying potentially influential students who will cooperate in ignoring peer deviancy?			
C. reinforcing students for ignoring inappropriate behaviors?			

"It's my new motivational teaching tool."

himself or others requires immediate attention. Similarly, if a student has failed to respond to positive strategies, the teacher cannot indefinitely overlook repeated instances of misbehavior. Action is required to keep the student and others from assuming that the undesirable behavior is permissible. But even in isolated cases necessitating the use of punishment, the type of punishment must be carefully selected and used with discretion. Otherwise, the teacher could create more problems than the punishment would resolve.

Types of Punishment

Many persons think of only one form of punishment when the need for quick action arises—an aversive or negative stimulus to the "culprit." This is typically referred to as "type 1" punishment. Paddlings and harsh criticism (e.g., loud reprimands, criticism directed at the person) qualify as aversive for *most* students and, thus, their use would be examples of type 1 punishment.

A MISTAKEN "PUNISHER"

Mr. Edwards relied heavily upon corporal punishment in disciplining boys in his eighth-grade class. It was not uncommon for him to line up five or six boys and give every one of them a "good thrashing." The boys would howl, rub their behinds, and generally "horse around" before and after each took his licks. Mr. Edwards noticed that the boys did not really seem to mind the paddlings. Oddly enough, they seemed to enjoy them. He also noticed that the paddlings were ineffective in changing the boys' behaviors. One day after lunch, he accidentally discovered why the paddlings were so ineffective. The boys were lined up trading licks. They were making a game of being able to take hard licks with a wooden paddle. One student even commented, "You can't even hit as hard as Mr. Edwards." He realized that what appeared to be punishment was not punishing at all for these boys. He resolved to try something else.

The preceding example may be atypical, but occasionally teachers will use what they think is a harsh punisher only to find that their perceptions do not fit the students' perceptions. Real punishers suppress behaviors. Although paddlings, harsh criticism, and similar acts may temporarily suppress unwanted behaviors for most students, we must still caution against their use for several reasons. First, these punishers generally place the teacher in the role of an aggressive model. Teachers who manage their frustrations by physically (or verbally) striking out at students run the risk of teaching students to deal with their frustrations in a similar fashion. It is indeed paradoxical that a teacher would try to suppress fighting among students through the use of corporal punishment. Second, these punishers may generate any number of emotional reactions from the students. For example, students may counterattack. We do not know how many personal assaults on teachers actually follow teacher's attacks on students. Perhaps none. Nevertheless, assaults on teachers and vandalism in the schools are a great concern for teachers. One can only speculate why students attack teachers and return to school at night to break windows, set fires, and write on school walls. Part of the answer may be because of the kind of punishment that students received. Physical punishment and harsh criticism may have just the opposite emotional influence on some students. Some students may feel so threatened and intimidated that they are afraid to do much of anything. Furthermore, the more timid students who observe others being punished may become so upset that they become less productive. Other students may simply choose to remain at home. Much of the absenteeism and tardiness in the schools could be an effort to avoid the aversive tactics used at school.

Third, the choice of physical punishment or a similar approach could become so upsetting to the teacher that he cannot function for the rest of the day (or longer). "This hurts me worse than you" is frequently more than hollow verbiage. Finally, physical punishment and harsh criticism do little to engender a love of learning. For these and other reasons (e.g., legal problems), teachers are well-advised to look for other means of suppressing unwanted behaviors.

An alternative to type 1 punishment consists of withdrawing positive reinforcers.[1] This approach is known as "type 2" punishment. Examples are: (1) *time out,* the temporary removal of the opportunity for any reinforcement; (2) *response cost,* the withdrawal of reinforcing consequences such as tokens, free time, or special privileges; and (3) *overcorrection,*[2] removal of probable sources of reinforcement when disruptors are required to correct their disruptions immediately. The use of type 2 punishers is generally more acceptable to teachers because they minimize the likelihood of adverse side effects. For example, they eliminate placing before students an aggressive model to imitate. Counterattacks should also be less likely, since no aversive stimulus is presented to the students. Indeed, the overall strategy of removing positive reinforcers should minimize the adverse emotional reaction associated with the use of certain type 1 punishers. No form of punishment is entirely pleasant, however, and if it were, students would be unaffected by its use. The idea is to let students know their inappropriate behaviors do not pay, without, at the same time, turning students against school. Rather than remove all the unpleasantness of punishment, teachers should concentrate on how to use properly the punishers they select. Inappropriate use of any tactic can create problems. Let us look now at a few major guidelines that may help you use punishment more judiciously.

---

[1] You will recognize a fine distinction between extinction and type 2 punishment. Extinction means that, when an undesirable behavior occurs, reinforcers are simply withheld for that behavior. Type 2 punishment occurs when a reinforcer is actually *taken away,* that is, the person being punished gives up something of value. For example, in time out, the disruptor is taken away (all potential reinforcers are given up) and in response cost the person forfeits token, privileges, etc.

[2] We have chosen to classify overcorrection as a type 2 punisher because the strategy involves potential forfeitures of reinforcers. One could argue, however, that correction of disturbances is the application of an aversive stimulus. You can choose how you view overcorrection after you have had a chance to study the strategy later in the chapter.

The Effective Use of Punishment

In Chapter Three, we discussed a number of factors that influence the effective use of positive reinforcement. Similar factors influence the effective use of punishment. First, behaviors that may result in punishment should be clearly specified. As we have suggested previously, students sometimes unwittingly get themselves into trouble. They break a rule and then are told about the rule. Letting students know what is appropriate and inappropriate should reduce the necessity for using punishment. Most students will behave appropriately if they know what is expected of them. Furthermore, clearly specifying which behaviors will result in punishment can be extremely helpful to the teacher. Teachers who know which actions they plan to take with different behaviors should be less likely to punish indiscriminately. Certain behaviors, although undesirable, and perhaps very irritating to teachers, should never be punished. For example, shyness and timidity suggest that students need help in acquiring desired responses. Students should not be punished for these responses.

Second, once the behaviors that lead to punishment have been identified, punishment should be delivered contingent upon the occurrence of *those* behaviors. When delivering the punishment, the teacher should tell misbehaving students what they are being punished for so they can see the contingent relationship between the undesirable behavior and its consequences. Before the teacher delivers punishment, however, he will want to issue at least one warning. The warning itself could reduce the need for punishment. But, if the warning is insufficient, punishment should be forthcoming. Students who learn that certain behaviors lead to punishment may be willing to forego engaging in those behaviors.

Third, punishment should closely follow the undesirable behavior. Delay in delivering punishment could result in the misbehaving student's failure to see the relationship between the undesirable behavior and its consequences. Research (Walter, Parker & Cane, 1965) has also shown that punishment that is introduced early in a response sequence (e.g., when the misbehavior is just beginning) is more effective than punishment introduced later in a response sequence. Waiting until misbehavior has spread to others before action is taken may also increase the necessity for using punishment with others.

Fourth, we mentioned in the previous chapter that the establishment of a new response is facilitated when the response is reinforced each time it occurs. Suppression of a response calls for punishment *each* time the response occurs. Behaviors that reliably produce punishment are less likely to be emitted than behaviors that produce reinforcement. Fifth, a point closely related to the preceding one is the need for teachers to be consistent in what they do. The teacher who overlooks a behavior one day and punishes the same behavior the next may only confuse students. Similarly, the teacher who is inconsistent in following through on threats may cause students to conclude, "She is only bluffing," or "He won't do anything to you." Sixth, the amount of intensity of punishment can influence the effectiveness of punishment (Parker & Walters, 1967; Solomon, 1964). Generally speaking, the more intense the punishment, the longer-lasting the effect. This does not mean that teachers should use *extremely* aversive strategies. Mildly aversive stimuli may be sufficiently intense to suppress undesirable classroom behaviors. Only punishers that are sufficiently aversive to suppress the unwanted behaviors are needed. Finally, as with positive reinforcers, the teacher must realize that what is punishing to one student may not be punishing to another student or even the same student every time it is used. Students can become satiated with a punisher the same way they can with a given reward. This fact is yet another reason to preclude ever using any single approach.

Now that we have established these general guidelines, let us look at a few of the specific punishers that seem most appropriate for classroom teachers.

Soft Reprimands

One form of type 1 punishment that appears effective in reducing disruptive behavior without producing adverse side effects is the use of soft reprimands. Several studies (O'Leary & Becker, 1968; O'Leary, Kaufman, Kass & Drabman, 1970) show that soft reprimands, audible only to the misbehaving student, are more effective than loud reprimands in reducing disruptive classroom behaviors. O'Leary et al. (1970) note that soft reprimands have at least three advantages over loud ones. First, they do not call the attention of the entire class to the misbehavior. You will recall from earlier discussions that too much attention to inappropriate behavior could serve as a reinforcer for that behavior. Second, since soft reprimands may be different from what disruptive youngsters customarily receive at home or at school, they should be less likely to trigger emotional reactions. A youngster who receives harsh treatment at home is certainly entitled to different treatment from teachers. Third, soft reprimands may represent an acceptable alternative for teachers. We know of *no* teachers who never disapprove of student behavior. We know of many teachers, though, who wish they had explored alternative ways of expressing their disapproval. Soft reprimands are surely superior to sarcasm and shouts.

DID I SAY THAT

Mrs. Craven's first graders sometimes got too noisy with their work. To quiet them, she would try talking louder than the students. She got so accustomed to talking over the students that she did not even realize how loudly she was talking. Sometimes she practically shouted orders to the students. She did not even consider what she was saying.

One day as part of an assignment for a graduate class she was taking, Mrs. Craven made a recording of her own teaching. She could not believe what she heard. She was shouting, "Please get quiet!" "Get back to work!" "Don't you know better than that?" Fortunately, after making the discovery about herself, Mrs. Craven decided she wanted to respond differently to her students.

As with all punitive strategies, soft reprimands must be used cautiously. Teachers must be careful about how frequently they use reprimands. The need to rely heavily on any form of disapproval suggests something is fundamentally wrong. Perhaps the instructional program needs revision, or the teacher may need to examine whether students are being reinforced for desirable behaviors. Teachers must also be cautious about *what* is being reprimanded. Disapproval should always be directed at behavior. The students themselves should never be the targets of disapproval. Personal attacks on the students can lower their self-concept. Comments such as, "Don't you have any respect for the rights of others?" or "I should have expected that from you," make unneeded implications about the *person*. Furthermore, affronts on the students are frequently associated with counterattacks. Most students can accept mild reproof for their behavior, but few students appreciate statements that go beyond what is needed to correct misbehavior. We should also caution against overdwelling on misbehavior. A soft reprimand that is short and to the point will be better received than a long oration. Reprimands that involve bringing up every past iniquity will overburden the students as well as unnecessarily take up class time. Stick with present offenses. Finally, we should point out that soft reprimands are most applicable when teachers can move freely about the class. Occasions may arise when teachers cannot immediately move close enough to a student to deliver a soft reprimand. In those instances, teachers can respond mildly (rather than shouting), direct disapproval at the behavior, and be brief in stating what is wrong and what should be done about it. Adhering to the guidelines provided earlier in the chapter for using punishment also will facilitate the appropriate use of soft reprimands.

Time Out

Another mild form of punishment that is especially suited for reducing disruptive behavior of kindergarten and elementary students is the time-out procedure. The procedure typically involves removing the misbehaving student from the classroom for a brief period of time—five or ten minutes. One study (White, Nelson & Johnson, 1972) found that time out as brief as one minute could be effective in reducing disruptiveness. The duration of time out is probably much less important in controlling misbehavior than the student's temporary loss of an opportunity to receive reinforcement for misdeeds. The student who is no longer in a setting to receive peer and teacher attention should be less inclined to engage in disruptive acts. At times, the tactic will also give the teacher, as well as the student, a chance to cool off.

The usefulness of time out is illustrated in a study by LeBlanc, Busby, and Thomson (1974). The subject of the study was a four-year-old boy enrolled in a preschool class with fifteen other children. He frequently made physical attacks on other children, called them names, and made demands to "Give me that" or "Shut up." Before time out was begun, the teachers repeatedly tried controlling the child by admonishing him for his aggression. This proved ineffective. Two types of time out were then implemented. The first step consisted of removing the youngster from the play area and placing him in a "time-out chair." If he refused to go to the chair or left it before a minute was up without first obtaining permission, he was sent to a time-out room. The time-out strategies were used first in dealing with the physical attacks, then with the name calling, and finally with the inappropriate demands on other children. Each time the time-out strategies were used with one of the aggressive behaviors, the behavior declined immediately to near zero. Soon, only the time-out chair was needed and eventually that was no longer required.

In order for time out to be effective, several conditions must be present. First, the classroom from which the student is removed must be reinforcing. If the classroom is itself aversive, then it would be nonpunitive to remove the misbehaving student. The student might even consider time out to be the lesser of two evils. Second, the setting used for time out must be devoid of opportunities for reinforcement. Placing a student in a busy hallway, for example, would be unsuitable. Too much opportunity exists in the hall for the student to talk with others or obtain other reinforcements. The principal's office, nurse's room, and similar settings would be unacceptable for similar reasons. A more likely time-out area would be an empty room adjacent to the classroom. Teachers sometimes turn a cloak room into a time-out area. Other teachers have found that a portable partition placed in the back of the class is suitable. Any area that is selected should be well-lighted and well-ventilated. Time out is *not* intended to frighten the student. You will also want to remember that it should be of short duration. Ten minutes might be considered an upper limit to exclude a student from the class. Occasionally, even less time is required. You could try going to the student after a few minutes to ask if he is ready to return to the class and behave appropriately. This approach could reduce the amount of time the student is out of class. While a long stay from the class might do the teacher some good, students do not learn appropriate behavior by being excluded from activities. Further, when a student returns to class, the exile should end; the student should be reinforced for appropriate behaviors.

Although the preceding conditions can help make time out effective, you should be prepared for several potential problems in its use. You will need to be prepared for the occasional student who refuses to go to the time-out area. Under such circumstances, you will need to remain calm or else you could create more commotion than the student. Calmly reminding the student of the predetermined rule that X behavior leads to time out should be sufficient with most students. A few students may require more persuasion. You may have to ask the principal to escort the student to time out, or a conference with the student's parents may be required. A tactic for reducing potential difficulties with students might be to give students a greater role in imposing time out on themselves. One study (Pease & Tyler, 1979), for example, revealed that student self-regulation of time-out duration was as effective in controlling the disruptive behavior of learning-disabled and behavior problem students as teacher-imposed time out. Of course, regardless of how you use time out, parents should be made aware of the strategies that you are using to manage disruptions. Surreptitious use of time out could lead to problems. Let parents know what you expect and how you plan to manage problems. Get their suggestions. Used infrequently and properly, time out can be an innocuous way of managing problem behaviors. Parents will probably agree once they know what you are doing and what you are trying to achieve.

Response Cost

A third alternative to harsh punishment is response cost. This strategy is particularly suited to classes where token economies or special privileges are being used to enhance desired behaviors. Since rewards are being given for desired behaviors, fines and loss of privileges (costs) can readily be used to weaken unwanted behaviors. In fact, combining both rewards and response cost may assist students to learn more quickly that appropriate behaviors pay, while inappropriate ones do not. However, you will want to avoid relying so heavily upon response cost that students are reluctant to engage in any behavior for fear it will cost them.

I EARNED FIFTY DOLLARS
AT SCHOOL TODAY

Mr. Padgett, a general business teacher, had read about token economies and the use of response cost, but he was skeptical of their usefulness. He decided to give tokens a try only after other strategies had failed to get students interested in his class. Disruptive behaviors were so frequent that he was even considering quitting.

Mr. Padgett began by having a student committee design and duplicate "money" to be used as tokens. He held a class discussion to determine how much should be paid for appropriate behaviors, lost for inappropriate behaviors, and how the money could be spent. The students (and Mr. Padgett) agreed that money could be earned for attendance, being on time, having appropriate materials, assignments completed (amount depended on accuracy), special projects, and participating in daily lesson activities. Fines (response cost) were imposed for disruptive behaviors such as loud talking, fighting, and destruction of school materials. Any earnings could be used to purchase free time, special privileges, and leadership roles in the class. The students rotated the responsibility for helping Mr. Padgett maintain accurate payroll records. He was surprised at the way students got involved in class activities. Grades improved and disruptive behaviors declined appreciably.

To use response cost effectively, you will need to limit the use of the procedure to highly disruptive behaviors. Imposing a fine or loss of privilege for every misdeed would generate unnecessary anxiety. Students must be free to make mistakes. Also, the price for engaging in an undesirable behavior should be reasonable. A student who has worked diligently all period to earn ten tokens should not lose his entire earnings because of a single inappropriate act. Loss of one or two tokens might be sufficient to inhibit the behavior. Whatever is withdrawn need only be costly enough to reduce the behavior in question. One group of researchers (Hall, Axelrod, Foundopoulos, Shellman, Campbell & Cranston, 1972) found that merely by taking back colored slips of paper with the student's name on them each time he cried or complained, those behaviors were reduced. We should caution, however, that what is withdrawn should not be a privilege to which students are entitled by student policy. Witholding recess is a popular tactic in elementary schools, but this constitutes a misuse of response cost. The action is also illegal in many states. A better technique is to establish special rewards or privileges (e.g., free time) that are separate from the regular school activities. These can then be temporarily withheld whenever students fail to perform appropriately.

TO CATCH A THIEF

Should teachers spend time trying to determine who steals? Or, is reducing stealing a more productive route? We prefer arranging conditions so that students *choose* to be honest. (Of course, when detection for stealing is high or when stealing is more difficult, stealing will decline.)

One group of researchers (Switzer, Deal & Bailey, 1977) experimented with an approach that offers promise in reducing school thefts. Their approach involved both group rewards and group response cost. During one phase of this experiment, students in three second-grade classes received ten extra minutes of free time following their snack if nothing had been stolen (*reward*). If something were stolen, the teacher left the room to permit return of the item. Return of the stolen item meant students could talk quietly, as usual, during snack, whereas nonreturn of the item meant all students must sit quietly during the snack (*response cost*). The program proved highly successful. In one class thirty-seven items had been stolen during an eleven-day period when the only control for stealing was a teacher lecture. However, during the reward and response cost phase of the study, only two items were stolen and one of those was returned. Similar results occurred in the other class.

You will recognize that this approach brings peer pressure to certain individuals to conform to class expectations. Also, the entire class may suffer (cost) when a single individual refuses to behave as expected. The teacher should be alert to the effects of group rewards and punishment procedures and take precautions so no one is hurt by undue pressure and so an entire group does not suffer needlessly because of one person. The approach, however, does offer an alternative to playing detective. It is easy to get overly zealous in trying to identify a thief. The current strategy emphasizes reduction of stealing—not punishment *per se*. Other alternatives might include keeping valuables under lock and key, not leaving valuables unattended, and having class monitors when you are absent from the room.

While response cost is an easy technique to use, it has its perils. Students may become upset when a privilege is withheld. You, of course, should remain calm about emotional reactions. A good strategy is to ignore the response and continue with classroom activities. Being fair in imposing the penalties with all misbehaving students will reduce complaints and emotional reactions. Indicating how students can redeem themselves may also prove helpful. You should also consider that a response such as, "Hell! Penalize me again and see if I care," could be a signal that the student does indeed care about being penalized. If not, why the reaction? A second problem may arise when a student is repeatedly fined for a misbehavior. Some students may try to see how many tokens or privileges they can lose. This problem can be averted by setting an upper limit on the number of times response cost will be imposed before more severe actions are taken.

Overcorrection

A mildly punitive strategy tested by Foxx and Azrin (1972) holds considerable promise for reducing disruptive behaviors. The strategy requires that disruptive individuals restore the environment to a better condition than existed before their disruptiveness. Thus, the procedure is called overcorrection or restitution. Foxx and Azrin's initial use of the strategy eliminated several disruptive-aggressive behaviors of one brain-damaged and two mentally-retarded patients. For example, one of the patients frequently damaged furniture by throwing and overturning beds, tables, and chairs. Disapproval of the actions and having the patient set right the overturned furniture were ineffective in reducing the undesirable behavior. When the overcorrection procedure was begun, the patient was required not only to restore the overturned furniture to its correct position, but to straighten and clean all other furniture in the ward. Overcorrection resulted in an immediate reduction in the undesirable behavior and completely eliminated the long-standing behavior within twelve weeks.

Subsequent use of the strategy (Azrin & Wesolowksi, 1974) proved effective in eliminating stealing among retarded adults. Overcorrection applied to stealing consisted of having the offender return more than was actually taken from the victim. If the offender stole food (e.g., a candy bar), he had to return the food plus an identical item. The prior simple correction procedure of having him return the stolen property was unsuccessful in reducing thievery. Once the stealing began costing the thief, however, it quickly ended. The overcorrection strategy also reversed the typical condition in which the victim is the one who suffers.

Overcorrection has also been used in treating autistic behaviors (Azrin, Kaplan & Foxx, 1973) and bedwetting (Azrin, Sneed & Foxx, 1973), and in toilet training (Foxx & Azrin, 1973). To date, the strategy remains untested in the schools, but one can think of numerous situations to which it might be applied. For example, the strategy could be used with the student who carves on school desks, tears down a bulletin board, throws food in the cafeteria, litters the school grounds, or creates a mess in the classroom. In all of these instances, the student could be asked to put the environment in a better condition than existed before the misbehavior. The student who carves on a desk could be asked to sand that desk, plus one or more desks. The litterer could be asked to pick up more debris than he threw down.

Overcorrection offers several major advantages. First, the strategy has the potential for teaching desirable behavior by requiring the disruptive individual to improve the environment. He can then see the results of appropriate behavior. Other forms of punishment lack this benefit. Second, the strategy permits individuals to make amends for any damages they have caused. Overcorrection would permit them to set the situation straight. Overcorrection is unique in that people get a chance to improve the environment, and, thus, can begin to feel good about taking appropriate actions. Any bad relations between the disrupter and the educator should improve as the problem situation is overcorrected. Preliminary use of overcorrection also suggests that the strategy produces quick, permanent changes in behavior. Harsh punishment is certainly uncalled for when one has the opportunity of using overcorrection.

Although overcorrection has considerable promise for reducing misbehaviors, use of the strategy could pose problems for the classroom teacher. Requiring a student to correct more than actual damage done may be misunderstood by some administrators and parents. We would suggest that all parties concerned (parents, student, and administrators) be involved before the strategy is used. Also, teachers will need to withhold approval during overcorrection lest a student misbehave in order to receive praise for correcting the misdeed. As with all procedures—positive and punitive—discretion is required if one is to be successful.

A Final Note of Caution

The forms of punishment previously described may temporarily control certain disruptive behaviors, but in order to be effective, the techniques must be implemented properly. The checklist on pages 94-95 summarizes our guidelines for use of the punishment techniques described in this chapter.

Even if you follow every precaution in using punishment, you must realize that punishment *per se* is not a solution. Punishment teaches youngsters only what they should *not* do. It has never been an effective way of teaching what should be done. Positive strategies are needed to strengthen desire behaviors. At most, punishment should serve only to suppress behaviors long enough so that positive strategies can be implemented to strengthen desired responses. Even then, punishment is justified only in cases of repeated misconduct and for extreme misbehavior. Other uses of punishment would be insensitive to the well-being of both the user and the recipient. The individual who frequently uses punishment runs the risk of being reinforced for punishing others. If the punishment works, the user may become reluctant to explore other alternatives. Perhaps this is the greatest danger punishment holds for teachers. On the other hand, the recipient of nothing but punishment will become bewildered about what is correct behavior. That person may do little wrong, but will surely do little right. Being punished, but not rewarded, is a fate to which few of us aspire. We, therefore, caution that punishment be used infrequently. It can never be a substitute for all the positive things that constitute effective classroom management.

On Reasoning With Students

Some teachers contend that much classroom misbehavior can be controlled by reasoning with the student. If what these teachers mean by reasoning with the students is that students are involved in decision-making processes, then we agree. Many problems can be averted and others resolved by involving students in decisions about what is expected at school and what the consequences for different behaviors will be. The aim of using any positive or punitive strategy should be helping students better their own behaviors. (We will provide details in Chapter Seven on how teachers can move students toward self-management.) But, if reasoning with students means that the teachers will try to discover the reasons behind a student's behavior by delving into the student's past, then we disagree. This is not to say the past is unimportant. Students are inflenced by their background. Knowledge of a student's home life or neighborhood experiences may give you ideas about what will work with a student. But too much emphasis on the past can be detrimental. Sometimes teachers will excuse repeated misconduct because of knowledge of a student's past history. They may comment, "With his background, he's lucky to be doing that well." Often students will learn they can use stories about their upbringing to "justify" misbehavior and to keep from learning new behavior.

What we are saying is that you could let reasoning or an attempt to understand students get out of hand. Teachers need not ask, "Why did you do that?" for every disruptive act. Students may be unaware of why they behave as they do. Some students may give logical-sounding reasons that actually have minimal influence on their classroom behaviors. Students behave appropriately or misbehave because those behaviors are reinforced. Our previous discussions should provide ways in which you can make desirable behaviors more reinforcing while minimizing the payoffs for undesirable behavior. By all means, involve your students. Let them help make choices regarding rewards and punishment for various behaviors. But use your knowledge of students in selecting appropriate activities and do not permit reasoning to keep you from helping students make needed changes.

School Violence

No form of student excessive behavior is more on the general public's mind today than episodes of school violence. Teachers, too, have a great stake in the matter. Though the problem has no simple

EVALUATION CHECKLIST FOR USE OF PUNISHMENT

Did you remember to:	Yes	No	Results and Recommendations

1. follow the general guidelines for using punishment by:
    A. clearly specifying the behaviors that will result in punishment?
    B. delivering punishment contingent on the specified behaviors?
    C. delivering the punishment immediately following the specified behavior?
    D. punishing each occurrence of the specified behavior?
    E. being consistent in punishing the same behaviors?
2. use soft reprimands properly by:
    A. delivering reprimands only when you are able to move close to a student?
    B. avoiding berating the entire class?
    C. avoiding nagging?
    D. delivering infrequent disapproval?
    E. disapproving current behavior rather than behavior that occurred earlier?
3. use time out appropriately by:
    A. determining whether classroom events are maintaining the inappropriate behavior?
    B. primarily limiting use of time out to younger students?
    C. providing a time-out place devoid of opportunities for reinforcement?
    D. making sure the time-out period is of short duration?
    E. remaining calm in taking			

EVALUATION CHECKLIST FOR USE OF PUNISHMENT
(continued)

Did you remember to:	Yes	No	Results and Recommendations
students to the time-out place?			
F. welcoming the student into the class after time out?			
G. letting administrators and parents know of plans to use time out?			
4. use response cost properly by:			
A. limiting its use to highly disruptive students?			
B. making sure that what is withdrawn is not something that students are entitled to as a basic right?			
C. setting a reasonable price as the cost for inappropriate behavior?			
D. setting an upper limit on the number of times response cost will be imposed before more severe actions are taken?			
E. remaining calm while implementing the procedure?			
5. use overcorrection appropriately by:			
A. notifying administrators and parents prior to using this technique?			
B. determining whether the inappropriate behavior has resulted in damage that can be amended?			
C. determining what can be done to amend and improve the situation?			
D. withholding your attention during overcorrection so students will not misbehave to receive the attention during implementation of the technique?			

solution, it is just too grave to sidestep and we would be irresponsible to overlook it. However, there are hints from government reports (National Institute of Education, 1978) that the upsurge of violence in the past few years has leveled off and may be declining. Still, the situation remains catastrophic for anyone who has been the victim of violence. The continued presence of violence at any level is more than we prefer.

The National Institute of Education estimates reveal that, during any given month, some 5,200 secondary-school teachers (1%) are physically attacked (most not seriously, although 1,000 do require medical attention), and some 130,000 (12%) have an item of $1 or more in value stolen from them. About 282,000 secondary students (1%) report being attacked (most receive only minor injuries) during any school month, and 2.4 million secondary students (11%) have something stolen from them. Also, during any month, some 24,000 of the nation's 84,000 public schools report an act of vandalism. The average cost of vandalism is $81 per act. The chances, then, are about one in 200 that a secondary teacher will be attacked in a given month or about one in 84 of having something stolen from him. Secondary students have about one chance in 80 of being attacked and about one chance in nine of having something stolen. The risk of being victimized is much greater in the northeastern and western states than in the north central and southern states, and is greatest in junior-high schools in large communities. While the chances for any given individual being victimized are statistically low, anyone can see the situation is far from satisfactory.

Acts of violence *per se* constitute only a part of the story of the crisis in our schools. *Fear of violence* is much greater. No one can teach and no one can learn effectively when fear is present. The nationwide surveys of the National Institute of Education reveal, among other things, that:

—20% of the students said they were afraid of being hurt or bothered at school at least sometimes.

—4%, or around 800,000, stayed home from school in the previous month because they were afraid.

—12% of the secondary-school teachers said they hesitated to confront misbehaving students because of fear.

—Almost half (48%) of the teachers reported that some students had insulted them or made obscene gestures at them in the last month.

With the situation as it is, you may be thinking that teachers really can't do very much to prevent school crime. You may be reasoning that home life and social institutions must be altered before the problem can become more manageable. Perhaps. Improved relations in the home, affirmative programs by police and in the courts, and increased funding for youth-oriented recreation and rehabilitation could alleviate numerous difficulties. But teachers *can* reduce school problems. They can defuse many explosive situations merely by increasing their managerial skills. Don't misunderstand us. All acts of violence are not a function of teacher ineptness. Sensitive, well-trained teachers can make inroads toward reaching troubled youths as well as avert violent acts that are a direct result of unresponsiveness to student needs. Nevertheless, thorough preparation is no guarantee that a teacher or student will never be assaulted or robbed. Unprovoked attacks do occur. No approach offers absolute protection against harm. Teachers can only apply the best of what is known with the realization that a problem may still arise.

MAKING A MOUNTAIN OUT OF A MOLEHILL

Have you ever known a playground fight that did not draw a crowd? Neither have we. There is something about cursing and hitting that gets everyone's attention. Typically, though, the spectators don't get directly involved except to urge on the fight. "Don't take *that*" or "You got in a good lick" or "Let him have it" are common crowd exhortations. Such was the case at a large junior-high school when two of the ninth graders were going at it strenuously. A well-respected teacher saw the crowd and heard all the commotion. He worked his way through the students, telling those he knew (and expected to obey him) to go about their business. The crowd slowly grew smaller. When he finally reached the combatants, he persuaded them to sit down and talk about their problem. This seemed to have been an adequate remedy at the moment.

Unfortunately, later in the day, the principal learned about the incident and decided on an additional course of action. He tried to round up everyone who had been in the crowd (to get all the details) and give them a lecture on the dangers of aggression. He got emotional and so did the students. What earlier had been only a minor incident quickly escalated into a school riot. We are not saying that students should never discuss the hazards of aggression. They should. But discussions are best conducted in small groups under controlled conditions. Typically, when a fight occurs, only those persons most directly involved should discuss that specific incident. The problem should be isolated—not expanded. What are your views on managing school fights? How would you disperse a crowd?

We believe that much of what has already been discussed in this and preceding chapters can increase teacher effectiveness for coping with hard-core problems. More will be said in subsequent chapters about working with the home and other resource persons to effectuate change in student behaviors. A subsequent chapter (Chapter Seven) also describes how to assist students toward greater responsibility for their own actions. We believe these approaches can *help* resolve difficult problems. As a matter of fact, positive relationships do exist between the approaches we have discussed and low incidence of school violence. For example, among the findings of the National Institute of Education was evidence that violence is lower in:

—Schools where students rate the classroom as well-disciplined, where rules are strictly enforced, and where the principal is considered strict.

—Schools where students consider school discipline as being fairly administered.

—Schools where students say that classes teach them what they want to learn.

—Schools where students believe they can influence what happens in their lives by their efforts, rather than feeling that things happen to them which they cannot control.

All of the above characteristics are variables that can be directly manipulated by school personnel. Teachers and principals can initiate actions to solve problems. They can be firm without being authoritarian. They can participate in plans to improve home relationships. They can cooperate with police to improve school security. Teachers can also become active in professional organizations aimed at better informing the public of school problems and school needs. Furthermore, teachers can enroll in courses that prepare them for managing school disruptiveness and coping with job-related stress. The list could go on and on. The point is that a solution orientation can work for teachers. We honestly believe that teachers can *safely* make it till Friday—every Friday of a long career.

Summary and Conclusion

Sometimes teachers are perplexed over the need to deal immediately with disruptive behaviors. They can think of few, if any, alternative ways of controlling misbehavior. Even when they do come up with an idea, too often it takes the form of punishment. This chapter has emphasized a number of positive strategies for managing disruptive classroom behaviors. Altering setting events, reinforcing incompatible behaviors, modeling, and extinction were discussed as possible alternatives to punishment. It is hoped that our review of these strategies will help you reduce the necessity for dealing punitively with students every time quick action is required. We recognize, of course, that no teacher ever has managed a class (and probably never can) without occasionally resorting to punishment. Hostile student acts that could result in personal injury and repeated misconduct often necessitate the use of punishment. So, rather than deny that punishment is used or pretend that teachers can rely solely on positive approaches, this chapter has focused on ways that punishment can be used more humanely and judiciously. Types of punishers were identified along with a discussion of the potential side effects of using harsh punishment. Guidelines for the effective use of punishment also were provided. Soft reprimands, time out, response cost, and overcorrection were suggested as mildly punitive strategies that seemed most acceptable for classroom use. Caution was advised even for using these forms of punishment lest you become dependent on temporary solutions rather than seek productive ways for teaching desired behaviors. The chapter concluded by stating that students can be involved in classroom decisions without dwelling on why they behave as they do.

After reading about all the alternatives for managing disruptive behaviors, you may be wondering, "Which ones should I use?" Perhaps all of them. No strategy by itself is likely to be effective with every student. Your decision to select a particular approach may be governed by your own likes and dislikes, school policy, parental responses, or by student response to positive strategies. Perhaps you have even involved students in selecting consequences for inappropriate actions. It is unlikely that you would ever rely solely on one approach. You may make changes in setting events while using modeling and reinforcement of incompatible behaviors. You might also simultaneously be ignoring inappropriate acts. Further, you would never use punishment by itself. Once you have suppressed an undesirable response with punishment, you should certainly seize that opportunity to use positive means for teaching what you want. Your knowledge of alternatives merely increases the possibility that you can respond appropriately to student misbehavior. Certainly, you are better off being somewhat perplexed over having appropriate choices than wondering, "Is there anything that can be done for this student?" Different strategies are at your disposal. Try them and make note of what works for you and your students.

REFERENCES

Ayllon, T. "Intensive treatment of psychotic behavior by stimulus satiation and food reinforcement." *Behavior Research and Therapy 1* (1963): 53-61.

Ayllon, T. and Roberts, D. "Eliminating discipline problems by strengthening academic performance." *Journal of Applied Behavior Analysis 7* (1974): 71-76.

Azrin, N. H., Kaplan, S. J., and Foxx, R. M. "Autism reversal: Eliminating stereotyped self-stimulation of retarded individuals." *American Journal of Mental Deficiency 78* (1973): 241-248.

Azrin, N. H., Sneed, T. J., and Foxx, R. M. "Dry bed: A rapid method of eliminating bedwetting (enuresis) of the retarded." *Behavior Research and Therapy 11* (1973): 427-434.

Azrin, N. H. and Wesolowski, M. D. "Theft reversal: An overcorrection procedure for eliminating stealing by retarded persons." *Journal of Applied Behavior Analysis 7* (1974): 577-581.

Becker, W. C., Madsen, C. H., Arnold, C. R., and Thomas, D. R. "The contingent use of teacher attention and praising in reducing classroom behavior problems." *Journal of Special Education I* (1967): 287-307.

Broden, M., Bruce, C., Mitchell, M. A., Carter, V., and Hall, R. V. "Effects of teacher attention on attending behavior of two boys at adjacent desks." *Journal of Applied Behavior Analysis 3* (1970): 199-203.

Brown, P. and Elliot, R. "Control of aggression in a nursery school class." *Journal of Experimental Child Psychology 2* (1965): 102-107.

Foxx, R. M. and Azrin, N. H. "Dry pants: A rapid method of toilet training children." *Behavior Research and Therapy 11* (1973): 435-442.

Foxx, R. M. and Azrin, N. H. "Restitution: A method of eliminating aggressive-disruptive behavior of mentally retarded and brain-damaged patients." *Behavior Research and Therapy 10* (1972): 15-27.

Hall, R. V., Axelrod, S., Foundopoulos, M., Shellman, J., Campbell, R. A., and Cranston, S. S. "The effective use of punishment to modify behavior in the classroom." *In* K. D. and S. G. O'Leary, eds. *Classroom Management: The Successful Use of Behavior Modification.* New York: Pergamon Press, Inc., 1972.

Hall, R. V., Fox, R., Willard, D., Goldsmith, L., Emerson, M., Owen, M., Davis, F., and Porcia, E. "The teacher as observer and experimenter in the modification of disputing and talking out behaviors." *Journal of Applied Behavior Analysis 4* (1971): 141-149.

Kazdin, A. E. "The effect of vicarious reinforcement on attentive behavior in the classroom." *Journal of Applied Behavior Analysis 6* (1973): 71-78.

LeBlanc, J. M., Busby, H. H., and Thomson, C. L. "The functions of time-out for changing the aggressive behaviors of a preschool child; a multiple-baseline analysis." *In* R. Ulrich, T. Stachnik, and J. Mabry, eds. *Controls of Human Behavior: Behavior Modification in Education.* Glenview, Ill.: Scott, Foresman and Company, 1974.

Long, J. D. and Williams, R. L. "The comparative effectiveness of group and individually contingent free time with inner-city junior high school students." *Journal of Applied Behavior Analysis 6* (1973): 465-474.

Madsen, C. H., Becker, W. C., and Thomas, D. R. "Rules, praise, and ignoring: Elements of elementary classroom control." *Journal of Applied Behavior Analysis 1* (1968): 139-150.

Madsen, C. H., Jr., Becker, W. C., Thomas, D. R., Koser, L., and Plager, E. "An analysis of the reinforcing function of 'sit down' commands." *In* R. K. Parker, ed. *Readings in Educational Psychology.* Boston: Allyn and Bacon, 1968.

The National Institute of Education. U. S. Department of Health, Education and Welfare. *Violent Schools—Safe Schools: The Safe School Study Report to Congress.* Volume I (1978).

O'Leary, K. D. and Becker, W. C. "The effects of the intensity of a teacher's reprimands on children's behavior." *Journal of School Psychology 7* (1968): 8-11.

O'Leary, K. D., Kaufman, K. F., Kass, R., and Drabman, R. "The effects of loud and soft reprimands on the behavior of disruptive students." *Exceptional Children 37* (1970): 145-155.

Parker, R. D. and Walter, R. H. "Some factors influencing the efficacy of punishment training for inducing response inhibition." *Monographs of the Society for Research in Child Development, 32*(1) (1967).

Patterson, G. R. "An application of conditioning techniques to the control of a hyperactive child." *In* L. P. Ullmann and L. Krasner, eds. *Case Studies in Behavior Modification.* New York: Holt, Rinehart and Winston, 1965.

Pease, G. A. and Tyler, O. T., Jr. "Self-regulation of timeout duration in the modification of disruptive classroom behavior." *Psychology in the Schools 16* (1979): 101-105.

Solomon, R. L. "Punishment." *American Psychologist 19* (1964): 239-253.

Solomon, R. W. and Wahler, R. G. "Peer reinforcement control of classroom problem behavior." *Journal of Applied Behavior Analysis 6*(1) (1973): 49-56.

Switzer, E. B., Deal, T. E. and Bailey, J. S. "The reduction of stealing in second graders using a group contingency." *Journal of Applied Behavior Analysis 10* (1977): 267-272.

Walters, R. H., Parker, R. D., and Cane, V. A. "Timing of punishment and the observation of consequences to others as determinants of response inhibition." *Journal of Experimental Child Psychology 2* (1965): 10-30.

White, G. D., Nielson, G., and Johnson, S. M. "Timeout duration and the suppression of deviant behavior in children." *Journal of Applied Behavior Analysis 5* (1972): 111-120.

Zimmerman, E. H. and Zimmerman, J. "The alteration of behavior in a special classroom situation." *Journal of the Experimental Analysis of Behavior 5* (1962): 59-60.

CHAPTER FIVE

THE HOME CONNECTION: WORKING WITH PARENTS

"Mrs. Smith sent a note to school by Katy saying that she wants me to call her. I wonder if she is upset about something?"

"I don't know about Mrs. Smith. But as a teacher, I find coping with *parents* as well as students almost too much to ask!"

Previous chapters have dealt with techniques which may be used to manage students' behavior in the classroom. Sometimes, however, your effectiveness in creating an optimal learning atmosphere and in maintaining appropriate student behaviors may be influenced by factors outside the classroom. Specifically, the relationship between school and home can enhance or undermine teachers' efforts in both instruction and discipline. The purpose of this chapter is to examine ways of working with parents which may be helpful in developing and maintaining a high level of cooperation between the home and the school.

Importance of Good Home and School Relationships

Expending the effort to develop good relationships between the home and school can be expected to pay positive returns. Research during the last decade has shown that home and community influences are vitally linked to student success (Mattox & Rich, 1977). Thus, it is important that these influences be cultivated and directed toward maximal student development.

A cooperative working relationship between parents and teachers does not just happen. It requires planning, a willingness to listen to parents and to spend the time required to develop mutual goals. Above all, it requires mutual respect. One's attitude toward parents' roles in school affairs influences the outcome of any attempts to develop cooperative relationships.

Teachers and other school officials are in a position to lead parent involvement in a positive direction from which many benefits can accrue. First, the effectiveness of the educational process can be maximized. Parents who are aware of a teacher's goals for their child can reinforce the development of these goals at home. Although the specific intervention strategies which produce increased achievement are difficult to identify, most families respond with interest to involvement in the educational process when the home activities that are used are practical, specific, and centered on mastering basic skill objectives (Mattox & Rich, 1977). Actually having parents participate in student learning activities through a "hands-on" workshop has also been suggested as a means of increasing parent involvement (Carbo, 1978).

USING PARENTS AS TEACHERS

During the 1974-1975 academic year, the Home and School Institute of Washington, D. C., (Mattox and Rich, 1977) studied the effects on student achievement in reading and math of sending home a series of Home Learning Lab Activities for parent use with their child. Two hundred eighteen first-grade children participated in the Home Education Learning Program with the study population drawn from inner city and suburban areas. The study involved treatment and control classes. The "treatment" was eight short, easy activities that were written "recipe style" for parents to follow. The activity instruction sheet included the name of the activity, a statement of purpose for the activity, a list of materials needed, instructions on how to perform the activity, instructions on the amount of time to spend on the activity, and an evaluation procedure. For example, parents might be given instructions on how to teach the letters of the alphabet by using cooked spaghetti to shape the letters. An activity was sent home once every two weeks for a period of sixteen weeks. The following results were obtained:

1. A significant rise in reading achievement.
2. Willing participation by the families.
3. No extra costs and little time aside from the initial training of the teachers.

We are not suggesting that you attempt to develop home

programs for all of your students. Some students, however, may need additional practice in selected areas and generalization of learning may be an added benefit when they are given the opportunity to use different materials and to practice the skills in a variety of settings. Parents can be important members of the educational team when the value of their contributions is recognized and incorporated into the educational planning.

Increased cooperation between the home and school can also result in fewer disciplinary problems. Parents who are cognizant of and agree with a teacher's goals for their child can be expected to value the educational process and to communicate these values to their children. Community pride, enthusiasm, and commitment to the school can be increased. Conversely, when parents are left out of the educational process, little commitment to the school and misunderstanding of goals will be engendered. Contacting parents only when problems arise with a child is hardly conducive to the development of optimal cooperation between the home and school. When parents have negative feelings about their child's school or teacher, these feelings are often communicated to the child who may then act out the feelings by vandalizing or creating disturbances in the classroom.

"Tommy's bad behavior wouldn't be so intolerable if it weren't for his perfect attendance."

SEND A "HAPPY GRAM"!

Mr. Brown, a sixth-grade teacher, gradually became aware that his feelings toward his son's teacher were not always positive. When he analyzed the reasons for this, he realized that he was invariably contacted by the teacher when his son misbehaved. He was sure that his son also displayed some behaviors that were worthy of note but he was never told when this was the case. He decided that he would like to have the parents of his students think more positively of him than he did of his son's teacher. He developed a schedule to insure that every parent would receive a "Happy Gram" once a month to tell them about some accomplishment of their child. After he began the "Happy Gram" procedure, he found that student behaviors worthy of a "Happy Gram" began to increase. Not only did the parents appear positive toward him and the school, the students in his class also seemed to develop a more positive attitude.

Next, cooperation between the home and school may lead to decreased absenteeism. Having a child attend school regularly can become more important when parents are aware of and committed to the educational goals for the child. As both parents and students become more involved in the educational process, the importance of school assumes a greater role.

Finally, job satisfaction of teachers may be increased as a result of positive relationships between the home and the school. Certainly nothing builds one's ego more than to have a parent say, "I never really knew until now how much the school is trying to do for my child," or, "I really feel good about Tim's school experience. I think he is getting a good education." There may be little difference in academic programs between two adjacent school systems but parent attitudes toward the systems can be significantly different. When parents are enthusiastic about a school program, teachers usually feel that their efforts are being recognized and, consequently, their enthusiasm also increases.

Developing Good Home-School Relationships

Work With Administrators

The philosophy of school administrators concerning parent involvement in school affairs is usually communicated to teachers and principals working in the system. The prevailing philosophy is exemplified by the approach these individuals take toward such involvement. When an effort is made at the system level to create positive home and community understanding of the system's goals and activities, additional follow-through at the local school level can have a tremendous impact in further cementing good relationships.

Local schools are often identified with the principal. These administrators influence the extent to which teachers tend to work at developing community-school ties. They can provide a major source of support for both parents and teachers when home-school problems are encountered. When your efforts to resolve problems are unproductive, you may find that seeking the viewpoint of the principal provides needed insights for coping with a problem. However, all parent-teacher problems should not be brought to the principal. Teachers should make every effort to resolve personal difficulties with parents before involving a third party.

Principals can often insure that teachers receive guidance and training in techniques for working with parents although you may find it necessary to request this instruction before such a program is included on the in-service calendar. Be specific about what you would like to have included in an in-service session. Many teachers would welcome suggestions concerning ways to create effective parent involvement or may need guidance concerning problem situations that may arise with parents. Such situations can be extremely intimidating if one has had no experience or training in this area. Teachers need to know beforehand how to defuse rather than escalate a hostile situation. Unfortunately, the need for in-service education in the area of parent-teacher relationships is often overlooked until an unfortunate incident occurs.

Principals are usually responsible for developing the yearly calendar at their school. If time is not allotted for parent conferences, you may want to discuss with your principal the benefits of including time for this important activity. Too often, conferences are held on an emergency basis only for those children who are having problems. Usually, the conferences are scheduled before or after school hours. When all meetings with parents must be made outside of regular school hours, it is not surprising that many teachers have limited contact and knowledge of their students' home life. Teachers may feel more charitable about spending time after hours meeting parents when some regular school time can also be devoted to this endeavor. Scheduled conference days also provide time for parents of children who are performing well and who have no identified problems.

A school open house provides an efficient way of making parents aware of general classroom goals and activities. If an open house is not on your school calendar, discussing the benefits of such a program with the principal, especially if you offer assistance in organizing the event, may be helpful in getting this program added. An open house allows the school to put its best foot forward and show what students and teachers are doing. The open house should be a time for displaying the accomplishments of all students and discussing plans and goals for the year. It is not a time for comparing students or for conferences about individual children.

Attendance at school open houses and at individual parent-teacher conferences can often be increased by providing baby-sitting services. More intensive parent involvement, including work in the schools, can also be increased when child care is provided (Brady, 1977; Johnson, 1977). Junior- and senior-high school students may be recruited to serve as sitters under the supervision of a teacher, the school secretary, a resource person, or other responsible adult. For parents of young children, this can be a tremendous service.

BRINGING PARENTS TOGETHER

Bellanca (1978) suggests that active parent involvement can be developed through three activities: "Parents Together Night," the goal-setting conference, and operation follow-through. The "Parents Together Night" is a two-hour group session which includes introductory activities designed to help parents feel at ease. Each subject area and expectations for performance are discussed and parents are given a Parent Responsibility Packet containing materials to help them become more involved in their children's learning. Prior to closing the meeting, followup activities are clarified, parents are invited to browse through the learning center, and a conference appointment is made.

The goal-setting conference is a thirty-minute meeting of parents, teacher, and child. Each person establishes his own priorities for learning, common goals and priorities are agreed upon, and each person's responsibilities are described and discussed.

Operation follow-through embodies a work report logged by the child and sent home weekly, phone contacts as needed, positive notes to parents twice monthly, and notes with report cards.

Administrators should be kept informed of special projects, interesting units, and special events that are being planned. With administrative support, timely newspaper articles, radio interviews, and public affairs television programs can be used to create public awareness of the continuing educational program. Parental interest can be increased through a well-planned public relations program. In developing such a program, it is important that day-to-day school life be given regular attention. Parents lose interest quickly when only the "stars" of a class receive publicity unless, of course, they happen to be the stars' parents. Certainly, positive news about the goals and accomplishments of the school can help to support the frequent request for additional taxes to support the school program.

Emphasize Teacher Involvement

The key to a strong relationship between the home and the school remains with teachers. What can you do to promote positive involvement? Commonly, the primary contacts teachers have with parents come through conferences about a child. Sometimes, however, the basic purpose of the conference is obscured because neither is prepared for the encounter. Rabbitt (1978) outlined the three elements of a successful conference: giving information, getting information, and finding solutions to academic and behavioral problems. When these three elements are used as a basic outline, it becomes easier for teachers to plan productive conferences. Evaluation is another important facet of the conference and should be completed by the teacher following each conference. Only by evaluating what has been successful or unsuccessful in the past can future conferences be improved.

PARENT-TEACHER CONFERENCES: TIPS FOR TEACHERS

Rathbun (1978) provides several strategies to use during parent-teacher conferences and suggests several traps to avoid. Initially she suggests that conferences be scheduled at a time when both parent and teacher can talk without interruption. She stresses the importance of putting the parent at ease and offers the following as suggestions:

1. Be friendly in greeting the parent.
2. Check the name of the parent immediately before the conference. Susie Smith's mother may have been divorced and is now Mrs. Brown. Do not assume that the child's surname is also the parent's surname.
3. Do not assume that an older parent is a grandparent.
4. Give your own name clearly, then refer to the child you intend to discuss. Some parents may have more than one conference scheduled on a particular day.

Other basic strategies suggested by Rathbun include:

1. Arrange the room so you can sit at a table beside a parent or have the conference in a conference room. Don't sit behind your desk while parents sit in student desks or on folding chairs.
2. Plan for the conference so that you have the information about the child at your fingertips.
3. Make a list of the child's grades. Otherwise, parents may wish to look at your grade book.
4. Remain flexible but have a general plan about what you want to cover at the conference.

Common traps to avoid include:

1. Speaking in generalities. Parents respond best when they are provided with specific information, e.g., "It may help increase Sue's maturity level if she is given a weekly list of chores that you see she completes." Saying "Mary is immature" provides little help to the parents.
2. Double-talk. Parents may be taken aback initially but will usually be appreciative when a teacher talks straight about the problems the child is having.
3. Attempting to be a psychiatrist when discussing the child.
4. Rudeness, whatever the provocation.

Teachers occasionally feel overwhelmed and perhaps frightened at the idea of conducting individual parent conferences. Parents may feel the same way about meeting and talking with teachers. They may be especially concerned lest they be told that their child is not doing as well as they thought or hoped. Thus, both the teacher and parent may be ill at ease at the initial meeting. Beginning the conference on a positive note can help to ease tensions. Showing the parents examples of their child's work that are especially commendable or that demonstrate progress is a good way to begin. Recounting a positive behavioral incident involving their child can also increase positive parent responses and, thus, help reduce teacher tensions. Behavior and academic areas that need improvement should be discussed. However, we suggest that the conference *begin and end on a positive note*.

Sometimes, teachers are faced with parents who are dissatisfied either with a classroom occurrence or with a school procedure. Parents can occasionally be irate. How does a teacher deal with an angry parent in order to dissipate some of the emotional aspects of the encounter and reap benefits for the child from the interaction? How does a teacher refrain from becoming angry in turn in such a situation? The following suggestions may be helpful in coping with such a crisis:

1. Refuse to conduct the conference in the classroom with students present or outside the door of the classroom during school hours. Firmly insist on arranging a conference for a later hour.
2. In conducting the conference, attempt to remain unemotional. Try not to take comments personally. Remember, the parents are probably concerned and upset over what they *perceive* is happening to their child, and their perception may or may not be correct. Try to determine how the parents perceive the incident in question and solicit their views of a solution. These views will often be expressed though unsolicited!
3. Respond to parental feelings behind the statements (e.g., "You are really concerned about..." or "...makes you very angry") rather than the content. This communicates to parents that you really understand, and reduces the likelihood of direct conflict.
4. Help the parents explore the ramifications of different solutions with the goal of providing for the best interests of the child. Attempt to work out at least a beginning solution to the problem. If possible, arrange for both you and the parents to be responsible for some aspect of implementation.
5. Arrange for continued communication. Ask the parents to call and report, positively or negatively, on what has happened since the conference. Do not be afraid to say, "I don't know," "I have tried," "I need your advice," "This may not work," "I may be wrong," or "Call me if things don't go well." Hearing teachers admit that they may not always be right can go a long way in defusing an irate parent.

Both parents and teachers would like to have students become happy, productive citizens. Parental support and cooperation are important factors in reaching this goal. Fortunately, most parents are willing to help in whatever way they can to insure that their child gets a good education. Unfortunately, they are often not consulted unless their child has broken a rule, fails to attend school regularly, or is not keeping pace academically. Few teachers remember that parents would also like to know when their child has performed especially well or has exhibited behaviors of which they can be proud. Parents appreciate knowing when a child has had a good day. They like to know when their child is making progress, even though it may be minimal. Parents can be expected to be more cooperative with the teacher and the school when they receive positive, as well as negative, feedback about their child.

We are not saying that all desirable behaviors exhibited by students can be communicated to parents. Few teachers have time to write even monthly notes. However, seeing that each child carries home a note once each grading period commending him for some appropriate behavior can do much to increase positive attitudes of parents and improve teacher-parent relationships.

Parents usually know their children well, their likes and dislikes, and can often tell a teacher what works and does not work with them. They can frequently provide information that is helpful in reducing inappropriate classroom behaviors or in increasing desired behaviors. Occasionally, students present problems that are more easily resolved through a joint effort than through either the parents or the teacher working alone.

TALKING DURING CLASS ACTIVITIES

Jimmy, an excellent student academically, often disobeyed Mrs. Sims' rule about talking to other students during class periods. Continued admonitions to pay attention and stop talking seemed to have little effect. As a last resort, Mrs. Sims contacted Jimmy's parents and asked them to come to school for a parent conference. The problems with Jimmy were carefully explained and her genuine interest in him was communicated. At this point, she admitted that she was unable to solve the problem of his talking during class activities.

Jimmy's parents, in exploring the situation with Mrs. Sims, discovered that he was invariably seated near Timmy, a neighbor and close friend. The suggestion was made that Jimmy's chair be moved in order not to be near Timmy during academic lessons. Mrs. Sims was hesitant about following this suggestion because it violated her policy of allowing students the freedom to choose their own seats and class partners for study.

Further discussion revealed that Jimmy often completed his work before many of the other students, thus providing unscheduled free time. His parents offered to send reading materials to keep him occupied during this time. This solution was helpful in reducing the chattering problem but did not eliminate the disruptive behavior completely. As a last resort, the parents' suggestion of moving Jimmy away from his friend was followed, and resulted in elimination of his disruptive behavior. Having the parents help make the decision eliminated the possibility that misunderstanding might occur when Jimmy was no longer allowed to choose his own chair.

It is our opinion that parent-teacher conferences should be scheduled at least twice each year. Some schools have experimented with the idea of providing student holidays during which time parents are scheduled for private conferences with the teacher. This approach appears to be workable as long as flexibility is included for those parents who cannot manage a conference during regular school hours. Scheduling a few conferences in the evenings to accommodate parents who work during the day is usually sufficient.

Utilize Resource Specialists

Resource specialists often have more frequent contact with some parents than do regular classroom teachers. This is generally related to the fact that resource specialists are involved with students who have problems requiring specialized services. It is important that classroom teachers work with resource teachers, school psychologists, guidance counselors, speech pathologists, and other resource persons to facilitate good relationships with parents.

Team planning conferences provide one area in which resource personnel and the regular classroom teacher can demonstrate their interest in providing the best education possible for each individual child. Planning prior to the conference should be done jointly. The contribution each professional can make toward the development of the child should be delineated and the ways the services complement each other should be outlined for the parents. It is important that all school professionals involved in the conference make an effort to help parents of exceptional children feel at ease during the planning conferences. Parents may feel overwhelmed in a team conference. Having someone to greet them, introduce them to others in the meeting, and talk with them casually about non-threatening topics before the conference begins creates more positive feelings. Resource personnel, as well as teachers, can respond to the expressed concerns of parents. As we stated earlier, problems sometimes arise due to poor communication between parents and teachers. Encouraging parents to express their concerns and making an honest attempt to resolve satisfactorily the problems, however minor, can go a long way in cementing good home-school relationships. Remember, areas which may appear insignificant to educators may be of great concern to a parent.

Resource personnel as well as regular classroom teachers can help to maintain close contact between the school and the home by sending home with the child frequent progress reports and calling occasionally to check on a child. Jointly inviting parents of exceptional children to visit the classroom and resource room can do much to allay parents' fears about whether or not a certain placement is right for their child.

Finally, although the principal is available to provide administrative guidance and support, you may occasionally wish to consult other support personnel such as the school counselor or school psychologist for specific suggestions, e.g., "What do I do if the parents totally disagree with what I have to say about Jody?" Or you may wish to discuss an incident that has happened and receive feedback concerning the appropriateness of your own behavior in the situation, not only from an administrative viewpoint regarding the outcome but also from a personal interaction viewpoint. Teachers need reinforcing too!

A SECOND OPINION

Mrs. Ruth, a ninth-grade teacher, was surprised at the vehemence of Mr. Pritney's reaction to her assessment of his son. Her intention had been to make him aware of the problems as she saw them but Mr. Pritney strongly disagreed with her and tried to prove his point with examples. She felt compelled to defend her position since she saw the boy in a different light. After much discussion and no agreement, Mrs. Ruth asked that the conference be terminated and suggested that they meet again after they had time to think about it. During the week, she made an appointment with the school counselor to discuss what had happened and to consider how to handle the conference next week. The counselor arranged a role-play session and a discussion of the implications of reacting in different ways. Through this session, Mrs. Ruth became aware that her desire to have Mr. Pritney agree with her had resulted in a failure on her part to hear or accept what he had to say. The result was an impasse. With the insight gained from working with the counselor, she was able to work out the problem with Mr. Pritney and come to a beneficial solution for his son.

About Parents

To be honest, parents sometimes intimidate teachers. The converse is also true. Often, the mutual anxiety felt by both parties has a detrimental effect on their relationship. You may find it easier to understand parents if you remember that they were once students with varying school experiences. Parents entering a classroom may face a flood of memories, both positive and negative. They may have failed in school, faced ridicule, and failed to complete school. Graduation from school may not be within the realm of their personal experience or in that of their family. Their concept of themselves as successful parents may be very low. The teacher may represent an authority figure with whom they may not agree but with whom they feel powerless to disagree. As a result, their ultimate action may be a passive one. That is, they may simply fail to act on any of the suggestions made by the teacher.

As a rule, parents have strong feelings of love for their children and the child's welfare is usually of primary concern. They will attempt to cooperate with the teacher or school authorities even though they may have misgivings about what they are asked to do. Teachers should take care to insure that the ideas they present to parents are workable and have a high probability of success for the particular child. A method for evaluating success and failure should also be given to the parents. Casual suggestions made by teachers may be taken seriously by parents and rigorously implemented. Failure to obtain success may create great anxiety if parents blame themselves for not doing things correctly while, in fact, the technique itself may be questionable. Parents should be told, "This may be helpful, but if it doesn't work, we will try something else."

"I WANT MY SON TO HAVE A BETTER LIFE"

Mr. and Mrs. Hinson, Steve's parents had not completed high school. Financially, they had difficulty making ends meet but managed to see that Steve had food, clothes, and school supplies. During a conference, they expressed to Mrs. Sams, his resource teacher, their hope that Steve could make a better living in the future than they were able to provide. Thus, they were willing to make sacrifices for his education. It was clear to Mrs. Sams that these parents were willing to do as much as they could to help Steve achieve in reading. But without concrete suggestions from her, they would be unable to do very much due to their own limited academic experiences. Mrs. Sams suggested that they might play reading games with Steve, e.g., have him find selected words in newspapers, magazines, or hidden on pieces of paper in the house. She decided to send home one suggestion, written in simple form, each week and asked that they send her a weekly note informing her of the outcome. She was careful to point out that some of the suggestions would probably be very helpful while others might fail and she counseled that they not become discouraged when this occurred. After several weeks, the notes from the parents indicated that they were beginning to think of informal ways to reinforce Steve's reading skills and they seemed very pleased with his progress and their own role in fostering his development. A positive home-school relationship had been developed.

A third fact to remember is that parents talk to other parents. When a parent is happy with the school program, teachers should expect that this satisfaction will be communicated to others. Conversely, an unhappy parent can prime others to look for the negative aspects of the school. Parents have a lot to offer. We trust that you realize the importance of making them your allies.

A Note of Caution

We do not wish to imply that all parents are model parents and have only the best interests of their child at heart. In fact, we know that some parents show little interest in their children's welfare and may neglect and abuse them. In Chapter Six we will discuss strategies that will help you identify cases of neglect and abuse as well as suggest how to meet your responsibilities in this area.

Rights of Parents

In recent years, parents have become more aware of their legal rights in the areas of student discipline, instruction, and school records. For example, parents now have the right to see all school records on their child and to challenge any record they feel is unfair or untrue. Teachers should be aware that parents do have these rights in regard to their child. The fact that this is true should generate more objectivity when compiling student records. One should be very careful about making any assumptions, and instead record only facts. Objective records not only benefit the child but also minimize disagreements when parents examine school records.

DID YOU KNOW?

A survey of all states and the District of Columbia completed by the National Committee for Citizens in Education indicated that parents have now been granted several rights in the areas of *student discipline, student instruction, student and other records,* and *other rights.* According to the NCCE survey, the following rights are granted to parents in all states as of November 1, 1977:

1. To take legal action against a school official if "excessive or unreasonable" physical force has been used in disciplining their child.
2. To appeal if their child has been suspended from school.

3. To see the instructional materials used when research programs are funded by the Department of Health, Education and Welfare and the National Science Foundation.
4. To be consulted about the evaluation and placement of their handicapped child and to have the child placed in an "appropriate" public-school program.
5. To see all of their child's records and to challenge any records they believe are untrue or unfair. A response must be made by school officials within a "reasonable" time. A hearing may be requested if parents remain dissatisfied.
6. To appeal if a school decision or policy prevents their child from expressing a controversial view that is not obscene, slanderous, or libelous and does not cause serious disruption.

Additional rights in the areas of student discipline, student instruction, student records, and other rights are granted in selected states.

One cannot assume that regulations and laws remain constant. Changes frequently occur as cases are tested in court or new problems arise. It is important that you keep abreast of the current laws in your school district. Usually, administrators are aware of changes affecting their system. In-service training should be provided to all teacher with yearly updates of changes which will directly affect them. Professional journals also attempt to keep teachers informed of developments in this area.

Summary

This chapter focused on suggestions for developing good relationships between the home and the school. The advantages of close cooperation between home and school were enumerated. Administrators, teachers, and resource personnel were provided with suggestions for dealing positively with parents. Techniques for conducting successful parent-teacher conferences were discussed. Finally, attention was given to parental feelings and the rights of parents.

You realize, of course, that one does not relate successfully to parents, or to any individual, as a result of having read a book. Surely, you must be familiar with techniques for increasing positive interpersonal interaction. But you must also recognize the feelings and worth of others. Parents are usually intelligent and can provide many valuable insights with regard to *their* child. They will probably know the child better than anyone. By applying the techniques from books such as ours *and* by approaching others as equals, we trust your relationships with parents, students, and colleagues can be enhanced.

REFERENCES

Bellanca, J. "Parent conferences: how to survive and thrive." *Instructor 88* (1978): 82ff.

Brady, E. "Home-school relations and continuity." *Theory Into Practice 16* (1977): 41-46.

Carbo, M. "A zingy parents' night all will remember." *Instructor 88* (1978): 84ff.

Johnson, E. "The home-school partnership model for follow-through." *Theory Into Practice 16* (1977): 35-40.

Mattox, B. and Rich, D. "Community involvement activities: research into action." *Theory Into Practice 16* (1977): 29-34.

National Committee for Citizens in Education. "Parents' Guide to School Rights." *Learning 7* (1978): 59.

Rabbitt, J. "The parent/teacher conference: trauma or teamwork? *Phi Delta Kappan* (1978): 471-472.

Rathban, D. "Parent-teacher talks: conferences or confrontation?" *Learning 7* (1978): 54-5 ff.

CHAPTER SIX

THEY HAVE A RIGHT: MEETING EXCEPTIONAL NEEDS

"You won't believe it when I tell you who has been assigned to my class this year. What am I going to do with these special education students?"

"I know what you mean. I don't feel that my training prepared me for teaching students who have been mainstreamed."

The impact of Public Law 94-142 is now being felt in most school systems. For the average classroom teacher, "mainstreaming" has become a common word. In this chapter, we will discuss the main provisions of PL 94-142 and the implications for teachers. Emphasis will be placed on identifying problem student behaviors that may indicate a need for specialized services. The roles of resource professionals in dealing with these special problems that may arise in the classroom will also be delineated.

Major Provisions of Public Law 94-142

"PL 94-142" is now as familiar to many educators as their own social security number. A mere mention of the numbers "94-142" results in an instant reaction, either positive or negative depending on the personal experience of these educators in attempting to implement the law. What exactly are the provisions of the Education for All Handicapped Children Act, Public Law 94-142, that has had such a far-reaching impact on the educational systems of our nation?

Appropriate Free Public Education

The basic provision of PL 94-142 stipulates that all children shall be guaranteed a free and appropriate public education. Under the law, all handicapped children between the ages of three and eighteen are entitled to educational services as of September 1, 1978, and all handicapped individuals between the ages of three and twenty-one are entitled to these services by September 1, 1980. However, a state is not required to provide a public education for the three-to-five and eighteen to twenty-one age groups if this service is not provided to all other children: a state must provide services to handicapped children when services are provided to non-handicapped children.

Least Restrictive Environment

PL 94-142 provides the handicapped child with the right to be educated in the least restrictive environment. Basically, this requirement means that, insofar as possible, the child should be educated in the "mainstream" of the school. When clearly specified in an individual educational plan, alternate placements, such as self-contained special education classes, may be made. However, an agency is required to insure that the handicapped child has the opportunity to participate with non-handicapped children in school activities where appropriate.

SECONDARY-SCHOOL MAINSTREAMING AND
THE RESOURCE ROOM

Swart (1979) described a successful mainstreaming program which involved use of a secondary-school resource room set up to reach both affective goals (e.g., increased student independence and self-confidence) and cognitive goals (e.g., increased academic achievement). Twenty or more educable mentally retarded individuals, ages twelve through nineteen, were served in the resource room for as many as four periods a day or as few as six periods a week. The remainder of the time, the students were mainstreamed into lower-track vocational and nonacademic subjects. One teacher and one teacher aide managed the resource room.

A modified open classroom gradually evolved in the resource room with each student given as much self-responsibility and flexibility as he was able to use. Affective needs were given precedence. The "core curriculum" represented the heart of the program. Teachers and parents worked with the resource teacher in establishing an individualized educational program for each child. Individual needs of the child determined the relationship between the core curriculum and the regular classroom program. One basic rule was enforced: all students had the right to work without interference from others.

Both affective and cognitive growth were seen as a result of student involvement in the program. Swart regards this model as a "truly individualized and humanistic approach" to the education of special-needs students.

Individual Education Plan

PL 94-142 requires that an individualized educational plan (I.E.P.) be developed for each child who receives special education services. The I.E.P. must be written to include: the level of functioning of the child, long- and short-term goals, services to be provided, criteria for evaluation, extent to which the child will be involved in regular classes and special education classes, initiation date, and proposed duration of the services. The I.E.P. is to be developed at a planning conference which includes the parent, child (when appropriate), teacher, someone who has recently evaluated the child, and others at the discretion of the parent. I.E.P. meetings must be held at least annually.

Access to Records

Parents of handicapped children must be allowed complete access to the educational records of their child by the agency providing the educational service. Included is the right to see all evaluations on which the child's placement was determined. Parents also have the right to amend a child's record or, in disputed cases which are ruled against the parent, to insert into the record a written statement expressing their objection to the record.

Due Process

The intent of PL 94-142 is that decisions concerning the educational placement of the handicapped child be made in the best interests of the child. To this end, parents are given the right to participate in the evaluative and decision-making process. When parents and an agency are unable to agree, either party has the right to request an impartial hearing to resolve the disagreement.

Implications for Teachers

Many teachers have had little training in techniques for working with handicapped children. With the advent of PL 94-142, those children with handicaps who can do so are now being educated in the regular classroom for all or part of the school day. Thus, all teachers need to be knowledgeable about the handicapped and be able to provide appropriate educational experiences. Positive attitudes toward the handicapped are also important. Harasymiw and Horne (1976) found that teacher opinions and attitudes toward integration of the handicapped could be modified through in-service programs, classroom experiences in working with special needs children, and the support of administrators and resource personnel. If your experience with the handicapped has been limited, you might want to request that your school arrange a special program to provide needed information and experience in this area. Colleges and universities also offer helpful courses. It is unfair to the students and the teacher to integrate special-needs children with no prior planning and no support services for the teacher.

A POSITIVE INTEGRATION EXPERIENCE

Clark (1976) reported that teachers' attitudes toward working with the handicapped in the Preschool Laboratory at California State University were changed in a positive direction as a result of integrating handicapped children into a class of normal children. Following a period of working with these special-needs children, the teachers found that:

1. Contrary to their previous belief, it was necessary to modify some classroom routines in order to accommodate these children successfully.
2. Handicapped children had more in common with the population of all children than with other handicapped children.
3. Desire and hard work were not sufficient to make the child "well."
4. Given background information on specific handicaps, they possessed the competencies for teaching most of the special-needs children.
5. The degree of handicap involvement is more important than the type of handicap in terms of successful integration into the classroom.

The major changes in teachers' attitudes occurred within the first year of the project, suggesting that brief exposure to the field of special education by those teachers who expect to work with handicapped children may result in program personnel who are more confident and competent.

Some Problems Require Referral

Identification of special-needs children is not automatic. You may be the first person to recognize the need to refer a child for special services. Although you have the primary responsibility for dealing with problems that may arise in your classroom, students may have serious problems that will not change as a result of your efforts. Some of these problems may be related to poor health; others may be tied to poor home conditions and inadequate child care. Students with serious emotional problems who cannot relate properly in the classroom may create management difficulties and may interfere with the learning of other students. At other times, normal students may engage in excessively disruptive behaviors that cannot be changed without careful planning. Success in teaching basic academic skills may well depend on whether problems such as these are remedied. Some students will require individual assistance from a specialist. Others can be dealt with in the classroom but may be more easily managed when resource consultation is obtained. Recognizing students who need specialized assistance and referring them to resource professionals should be considered part of a teacher's role.

Fortunately, teachers are realizing that being a "good" teacher does not mean that one must handle every problem alone. In fact, the idea that one is working alone can often result in loneliness and frustration. The feeling of support that can be gained from working with others and the opportunity to share ideas may very well be a major step in dealing with the problem. It is possible to be so closely involved with a situation that an objective assessment and plan cannot be made. In such cases, resource personnel may be able to provide the needed objectivity. The fact that a teacher asks for resource assistance should not be interpreted as a sign that he has failed. A team effort can pay big dividends in terms of effective classroom management.

Referrals in Perspective

Although every teacher may sometimes need to seek the assistance of resource personnel, a few teachers have mistaken expectations about referrals. They use referrals as a way of giving their problems to someone else. Actually, few students who are referred to specialists are ever completely removed from the classroom. Resource people, such as counselors and school psychologists, often work with students in the setting (e.g., the classrooms) where the students are experiencing difficulty. Furthermore, most specialists will outline a major role for the teacher in helping the student. Those teachers who expect referrals to reduce their own responsibilities or to end in the removal of a student from their classes will undoubtedly be disappointed. This line of reasoning, of course, is unproductive. Rather than viewing referrals as a way of ridding yourself of problems, we hope you will see them as a way of sharpening your own skills through cooperative efforts with other professionals. Referrals work best when the people are working together to help students.

A RESOURCE FOR THE TEACHER

Mrs. Cansler had always considered Mrs. McPeters, the resource teacher, a person to whom she could send Dawn, Tony, and Jim for two hours daily while she worked with the rest of the class. She was always glad to send these students out for a few periods since their behavior was a constant trial to her when they were in the classroom. One day, during lunch, she casually mentioned her problems to Mrs. McPeters and they began to discuss possible remedies. Tony, Dawn, and Jim were all mildly retarded but socially able to function fairly well with the other students. Mrs. McPeters made some points that Mrs. Cansler had failed to consider in working with these students. For example:

1. Mentally retarded individuals have an impaired ability to think abstractly. Therefore, it may be necessary to use concrete or tangible reinforcers in working with them. Also, complex explanations may be beyond their ability to comprehend.
2. Mentally retarded individuals do not generalize well from one situation to another. In order to help increase the probability that a learned behavior will be used in a new and appropriate setting, a variety of situations and experiences should be used in teaching behavior.
3. Mentally retarded individuals often have a short memory span. Rewards or punishments should be given immediately following the behavior or a connection between the behavior and what followed it may not be made.
4. Mentally retarded individuals often are easily distracted. Extraneous stimuli should be eliminated as much as possible and cues should be emphasized.
5. Mentally retarded individuals have the same feelings, e.g., hurt, anger, frustration, as do normal individuals. They need success

as much as we do. Programming should provide for frequent success.

Mrs. Cansler realized that she had not made allowances for these factors in her work with Tony, Dawn, and Jim. She began to see Mrs. McPeters in a new light, that of "resource" for her as well as her students.

When to Refer

While teachers must avoid transferring their problems to others, they must be willing to make needed referrals. A student should be referred to a resource specialist when he has a problem that the teacher cannot correct and that is interfering with academic achievement and personal development. It should not be assumed that someone else has already sought or will seek proper assistance. When in doubt about referrals, the teacher should always consult with resource professionals. The teacher and the resource person can then determine whether the student should be seen directly by the specialist.

Those problems that may require referral to a resource professional generally fall into seven categories: health-related, visual, hearing, learning, behavioral and emotional, speech, and home-related. We will discuss each category and indicate specific behaviors that may alert the teachers to the possibility that referral to a resource specialist is advisable.

Health Related Problems

Health-related problems represent an often unrecognized cause for poor academic achievement. Physical difficulties can impair students' performances regardless of their intellectual capacity. Health problems can also affect students' social behaviors. Very often, an irritable, inattentive, or apathetic child is labeled immature or unmotivated; the causes for his behavior are not investigated by the teacher or his parents. Health problems may occur in any classroom but are especially prevalent in school districts that serve a large proportion of students from low socioeconomic backgrounds. Behavior management techniques cannot successfully overcome problems related to poor student health.

Teachers should be aware of the more subtle behaviors that may be exhibited by students who have health-related problems. Acute medical conditions (e.g., vomiting, diarrhea) are easily recognizable and usually result in immediate action by the teacher. For example, the student may be sent to the school nurse or the parents may be notified to take the child home. Other symptoms are less easily recognized as having a medical cause and may appear to be attention-getting behaviors. We have seen children who were originally labeled as "behavior problems," but who were later diagnosed as having brain tumors or seizure disorders. Other health problems, such as inadequate nutrition, parasites, anemia, or lack of sleep, can affect a student's behavior in the classroom. Unless the cause of the problem is recognized, the behaviors may be interpreted as lack of motivation or lack of interest in learning. The latter problems are usually responsive to positive classroom management techniques. The former problems will need attention to the basic cause before the behaviors can be successfully changed.

Subtle signs that indicate a student's need for medical attention include:

1. Frequent complaints of headaches in the absence of other symptoms.
2. Lack of energy, appearing to "drag," or apathy regarding classroom activities.
3. Often falling asleep in class.
4. Irritable or hyperactive behavior.
5. Frequent stumbling or falling.
6. Sudden episodes of staring during which there is no response to classroom events.
7. Frequent absence due to illness.
8. Suspected drug abuse.

Occasionally, you may encounter students who frequently complain of being sick. A teacher cannot always tell whether a child with physical complaints is malingering or whether the symptoms are, in fact, real. A medical examination can confirm or rule out the need for medical treatment. If the problem is found to be behavioral in nature, classroom management techniques may be successful in effecting change.

Visual Problems

Students with visual problems may not pay attention or may disrupt classroom activities when board work is being completed. They may have difficulty with close work and activities that require fine visual-motor coordination. Thus, they may fail to attempt these activities seriously. Some students may have poor visual acuity, that is, they cannot see either distant or near objects clearly. Other students may have normal visual acuity, but may not be able to see objects in proper perspective. You may notice that these students have difficulty with printing and drawing activities. For example, they reverse letters and rotate designs or they confuse letters that are similar (e.g., b and d, m and w). Students with these symptoms often have visual perceptual problems. Other symptoms that may alert teachers to a student's need for an eye examination include (Willgoose, 1969):

1. Crossed, bloodshot, red, and swollen eyes. Pus and styes may be frequent.
2. Complaints of headaches, dizziness, eye pain, nausea, blurred or double vision, burning or itching lids. Some of these symptoms may also be present with serious medical disorders unrelated to eye problems.
3. Frequent stumbling or walking into objects. The student may not be able to estimate accurately the location of objects in space or may be unable to see those that are not in the direct line of vision.
4. Inability to distinguish colors. An occasional student may be colorblind.
5. Holding reading materials too close or too far away from the eyes. The student may close one eye or squint when looking at objects. Rubbing of eyes may be frequent.
6. Inability to see distant objects that can readily be seen by others. Some students may also have an undue sensitivity to light.

Vision screenings are sometimes routinely administered to all students by the school nurse or a public health nurse. An effort should be made to contact personally the parents of children whose screenings indicate the need for a more complete examination. It is not unusual for parents to postpone having the child's eyes checked because they lack the funds to pay for the examination. Teachers or school social workers can often assist the parents in locating resources that will help provide for the examination.

Hearing Problems

Teachers frequently encounter students who "tune out" or do not pay attention to class discussions. Usually the problem is behavioral in nature and is responsive to classroom management techniques. However, an occasional cause of such behavior may be poor hearing

acuity. The presence of two or more of the following symptoms suggests the need for a hearing evaluation:
1. Failure to pay attention in class.
2. Facial expression indicating lack of comprehension when oral directions are given.
3. Mispronunication of words.
4. Mouth breathing.
5. Tendency to localize sound with one ear.
6. Unnatural voice pitch.
7. Complaints of earache; frequent ear rubbing.

Hearing screenings may be routinely completed by the school speech pathologist, the school nurse, or a public health nurse. As with abnormal vision screening, an effort should be made to contact personally the parents regarding the need for a more complete examination.

TEACHERS AS HEARING SCREENING AGENTS

The role of teachers in detecting hearing problems can be important. Nador (1978), in a study involving 2231 elementary-school children and their teachers, found that teachers initially correctly identified one out of three children who were found on hearing screening to have a hearing loss. When screening and tympanometry followed by otoscopy, where indicated, were employed, teachers were able to identify almost fifty percent of the hearing loss group. Reasons given by teachers for suspecting a hearing loss included:
1. The child's behavior (51%).
2. Report from the child's parents (25%).
3. Information from the child's folder (20%).
4. Report from the child or a visible hearing aid (3%).

Nador recommended that the hearing screening team include teachers.

Learning Problems

Most teachers have no difficulty in recognizing students who do not learn as rapidly as others. Statements such as "Johnny just can't seem to catch on" or "Sue can't read even though she is in the fourth grade" are often made in response to students who fail to achieve at a level commensurate with their peers. Many of the students who fall behind academically exhibit undesirable behavior in school. They may fail to pay attention or may disrupt the class during learning activities. They may expend little effort in completing academic assignments. Some of these students may also be rejected by peers. When learning problems are present, work on social behaviors alone will be insufficient to insure that desired academic gains are made. It is possible to shape Johnny into a very obedient child, but he still may not know how to read or subtract.

Students with learning problems require a diagnostic workup to determine the major factors contributing to their poor academic performance. Some students may be found to have limited intellectual capacity. Others may have normal learning ability, but may not be achieving academically for other reasons. After the student has been evaluated, plans for remediation can be made. It is important to determine the level of functioning and the specific skills that have been mastered. Inappropriate social behaviors that occur as as result of a student's inability to achieve academically may improve when he is able to experience some success.

Behavior and Emotional Problems

Students who exhibit many inappropriate behaviors can easily tax a teacher's patience. As we discussed in Chapter Four, such children are often responding to environmental factors at home. For example, a student may be receiving peer or teacher attention for behaving inappropriately. These students usually respond well to the classroom management techniques described in earlier chapters. Sometimes, however, a student who engages in undesirable behavior may fail to respond to the classroom teacher. Consultative assistance should be requested when a teacher is unable to control the student's disruptive behavior. Students who exhibit sudden and persistent changes in learning or behavior patterns may require an evaluation before a plan can be made to change the behavior.

Sometimes a student may exhibit clearly inappropriate or even bizarre behaviors. Such a student requires individual assistance from a specialist. Presence of the following behaviors should alert the teacher to the need for a referral:

1. Appears to be "out of contact." The student may be zombie-like in appearance or engrossed in a fantasy world.
2. Irrelevant or bizarre talk. A rare student may be echolalic. Speech may be infantile.
3. Apparent aversion to people. The student may withdraw, isolate himself, and fail to communicate with others.
4. Self-mutilation. For example, the student may continually pick and scratch at himself until he bleeds.
5. Continual rocking, finger wiggling, and extreme fascination with spinning objects.

6. Perseverative behavior. The student exhibits the same behaviors over and over again.
7. Extremely aggressive or violent behavior.
8. Antisocial behavior, such as lying or stealing.
9. Inability to concentrate or to remain still for more than a few seconds at a time.
10. Excessively fearful or suspicious behavior.

Speech Problems

Students who are unable to pronounce words clearly or who stutter are sometimes mimicked and teased by their peers. Other students may have communication problems that are not as readily apparent but that interfere with their academic performance. For example, they may be unable to remember names of objects or to put events in a logical order. Referral to a specialist should be considered when the student exhibits the following difficulties in communicating (Zaslow, 1974):

1. Frequent misarticulation of words. The student may be difficult to understand.
2. Stuttering.
3. Abnormal voice quality. The student may have a very nasal or hoarse voice.
4. Inability to remember common words. The student may gesture and say "thing" or "stuff" in place of common words.
5. Tangential or irrelevant conversation.
6. Inability to follow oral directions.
7. Difficulty with tasks, such as sequencing problems or stories.
8. Frequent grammatical errors incommensurate with age.
9. Difficulty in remembering what to say after raising hand in class. The student may appear to understand a process and then forget it or be unable to apply it to a different situation.

Home-Related Problems

All children do not live in an adequate home environment. Many are deprived, both economically and emotionally. Some children are the victims of intentional neglect. In other cases, the parents may simply be unable to provide for their children. As a result, a student may be unkempt, improperly clothed, malnourished, and constantly sick. Lack of heat or irregular meals may be reported. Frequent absences from school are common. Children who are neglected or deprived are usually unable to perform at their potential level in school. A resource professional, such as a social worker, must often intervene and assist the family in obtaining needed resources and in improving the home environment.

In addition to living in a deprived environment, some children are the victims of abuse. This fact is a reality which should be recognized by all educators. Child abuse may involve physical maltreatment, emotional maltreatment, sexual abuse, and neglect. The incidence of child abuse is not restricted to any socioeconomic level; it occurs in all social classes. All states have now passed laws that require the reporting of abuse or suspected abuse. In some states, failure to report can result in legal action against the person who has knowledge of or suspects abuse. Immunity from lawsuits is provided to professionals when suspected abuse cases are reported in good faith (Leaman, 1979).

One should take seriously a child's report that he/she has been maltreated. Teachers are in a position to develop relationships which allow a child to confide the secrets they may be carrying as a burden. One form of abuse, sexual abuse, is not immediately discernible and may sometimes be confided to an understanding adult such as a teacher or school counselor. Nothing can be done by child protective services to rectify the situation for the child until the matter has been reported.

All teachers should familiarize themselves with the law and the reporting procedures of the state in which they are teaching. Mitchell (1977) suggests that the following procedures may be helpful in developing reporting procedures for a school:

1. One person should be delegated to make the formal report. This could be the principal, assistant principal, or school counselor.
2. All school personnel should be provided with specific instruction regarding reporting procedures.
3. Abuse or suspected abuse should be reported immediately. Twenty-four hours is suggested as a time frame.
4. A standard form should be prepared and used for all reports to insure that all necessary information is collected and recorded.
5. Abuse should be reported to the proper authorities. Attempts should not be made to handle the problem through the school.

It is important to remember that one does not have to have absolute proof of abuse. If abuse is suspected, it should be reported. The agency handling abuse in your state will make the investigation to determine whether further intervention is warranted. If you hesitate to become involved, you should know that teachers are rarely called to court (Mitchell, 1977). Some states provide for confidentiality regarding the source of the report. Failure to report immediately an incident of child abuse may endanger the child's life and will delay needed professional assistance to the parents. What child can perform well in school or develop emotionally in a normal fashion when exposed to such conditions?

SIGNS TO WATCH FOR

A child's appearance, his reports of inhuman treatment, and his behavior may all signal that he is being maltreated by caretakers. Teachers should be alert to the following indicators that the child may need help.

Physical Appearance

Does the child have bruises or abrasions, suspicious burns, cigarette-burns, bite marks? Are the injuries repeated, located on unlikely parts of the body, or inadequately explained?

Does the child show evidence of medical neglect? Does he need dental care, glasses, or treatment for a medical condition such as impetigo?

Is the child malnourished? Does he come to school without breakfast or go without lunch?

Does the child wear adequate clothing for the weather? Is the clothing well cared for? Is the child dirty?

Does the child appear listless or tired or does the child fall asleep in class?

Behavior

Does the child display aggressive, disruptive, or destructive behavior in school?

Does the child display withdrawn, passive, or excessively compliant behavior? Does he have a low self-image?

Does the child habitually come to school much too early or hang around after school?

Does the child frequently fail to come to school or exhibit chronic tardiness?

Making Referrals for Resource Services

Most schools have a procedure to follow in making referrals for specialized services. Teachers should use the process that is recommended at their school. When planning conferences are scheduled following the referral, teachers should participate in these conferences in order to provide input and help insure that the most appropriate plan is made. During the conference, the teacher can emphasize that the student is the major focus of concern. Occasionally, parents may state a feeling that the teacher would like to "get rid of the child" or that the teacher should know how to deal with the problem. It may be helpful to reiterate how other specialists can be of benefit to the child. Teachers can express a willingness to work with resource specialists on recommendations, thus indicating to parents that they are not abandoning the student to others.

Directly related to the above procedures for making a referral is the uncertainty about where to refer certain types of problems. For example, teachers may notice that a student appears malnourished, has learning problems, and is frequently absent from school. Should the teacher consult the school nurse, the school psychologist, or the school social worker? If possible, it would be appropriate to arrange a joint consultation with all these professionals, but referral to any one of them would be appropriate. One should not be unduly concerned about referring to the wrong person. In addition to being trained in their respective fields, resource professionals have also been taught to recognize problems that should be dealt with by other specialists. Most professionals are quick to admit the limits of their own competencies and can direct a problem student to the appropriate specialist. If the resource person cannot arrange the proper consultation directly, the teacher will be notified of the need for a different referral. Now let us take a close look at school resource personnel.

School Resource Specialists

With the emphasis on providing services for children with special needs, it is important that teachers develop professional working relationships with resource specialists in the schools. These specialists include school counselors, school psychologists, school nurses, speech pathologists, and school social workers. In working with these specialists, it is helpful to be familiar with the role each of these experts can play in assisting students who have been referred

"Before we settle for a simple Oedipus complex, Mr. Merrill, I feel obliged to mention that Daddy is a male nurse and Mommy drives an oil rig for a petroleum company."

for services. In addition, these professionals can provide needed support services to the teacher who deals with the special-needs students for most of the day.

School Counselor

Originally, counselors were assigned primarily to secondary schools. Now many elementary schools also have them. Counselors are trained to work with emotionally and socially maladjusted students and with normal students who are engaged in decision-making. At the secondary level, aptitude testing, educational placement, vocational guidance, and educational guidance may be part of their role. At both the elementary and secondary levels, counselors may provide consultative services for classroom management techniques.

Counselors often have heavy caseloads that prohibit them from working intensively with large numbers of students on an individual basis. Thus, group counseling sessions may be arranged for students who are experiencing similar problems. In addition to being more economical of the counselor's time, group counseling allows participants to help one another. At the elementary-school level, counselors may work with entire classes by conducting class meetings. During these meetings, students have the opportunity to bring up problems of concern (or the counselor may propose a problem) and to discuss them as a group. Meetings are structured to minimize generalized complaining. One problem is usually dealt with at a time, and alternatives for solving the problem are suggested. When several consecutive meetings are held, students have the opportunity to try out proposed solutions and discuss the results in subsequent class meetings.

THE CASE OF THE DISAPPEARING ARTICLES

Mrs. Meadows, a fifth-grade teacher, became concerned after several children reported that many of their personal articles, such as money or pencils, had disappeared. She suspected who might be taking the articles, but had no conclusive proof. After giving the matter some thought, she decided to consult the school counselor, Mr. Brown. He arranged to visit the classroom and conduct a series of class meetings in which the problem of the disappearing personal articles was raised. Students were encouraged to express how they perceived the situation and to propose solutions. One student suggested that perhaps the offending person did not realize how others felt when their personal things were taken. Another student suggested that the stolen goods be returned anonymously: no questions asked and no accusations. The class agreed that this might be a good solution. A meeting was set for the following week in order to assess the effectiveness of the solution and to propose alternatives if needed. No further actions were required.

Anandem and Williams (1971) propose a model for counseling services that differs from the traditional individual and group counseling model. They suggest that the counselor serve as a consultant to assist teachers in devising and carrying out behavior management plans in the classroom. The goal of this model is to change environmental conditions that may be affecting the student's behavior. Counselors using this approach may observe in the classroom, assist in setting up a classroom management plan, monitor the effectiveness of the plan, and suggest modifications when necessary. The consultative approach can be especially productive when a teacher desires assistance in dealing with problems of disruptive behavior. A joint effort between counselor and teacher is necessary, however, to insure success. Even though a teacher may be experiencing serious classroom management problems, most counselors would be hesitant to offer services unless the request is initiated by the teacher.

Individual and group counseling often work best when the referral is initiated by the student. Tesh (1974) recommends that teachers play a role in increasing the number of self-initiated referrals and in making the counselor more "visible" to the students by : (1) providing opportunities for student-counselor contact by inviting the counselor into the classroom to present information; and (2) making positive comments to students about the work of the counselor. Together, the teacher and counselor can become a strong team in maximizing all aspects of a student's development. Why don't you make an effort to get to know and use the counselor in your school? If you are still preparing to teach, you might ask one of your college professors to invite a counselor to be a guest speaker at an appropriate point in your studies.

THE COUNSELOR AND PL 94-142

PL 94-142 will have a far-reaching effect on all professionals working in the educational system. Sproles, Panther, and Lanier (1978) discussed the implications, challenges, and responses needed by counselors as a result of this new legislation. Implications specifically related to the local school system included the necessity of achieving a number of new tasks such as mainstreaming, parent involvement, detailed record-keeping, and monitoring of the I.E.P. An important role of the counselor was defined as helping modify attitudes in a positive direction in order to increase the probability that the tasks would be successfully achieved.

PL 94-142 was seen to represent a challenge to counselors whereby the basic goals of social equality and human development might be realized. Necessary responses from counselors included:

1. Becoming cognizant of the law, its intent and its potential.
2. Assessing their own abilities to determine which ones could be used to make the law work and which need further developing.
3. Actively using available skills and knowledge to help implement the law and seeking training in the deficient areas.

School Psychologist

The school psychologist specializes in working with children and adolescents and is trained to work in educational settings. The role of the school psychologist has traditionally been to evaluate children with problems in order to provide a basis for making improvements (Cowen & Lorion, 1976).This role has now been expanded to include other services. Fairchild (1974) analyzed the services performed by a school psychologist and found that school psychological services could be divided into four categories: assessment (testing and other activities related to diagnosis), intervention, evaluation of psychological services, and adminis-tration. In this study, a large proportion of the psychologist's time (39.7%) was found to be devoted to diagnostic activities, with consultation also consuming a large share of time. Granger and Campbell (1977) report that school psychologists are often asked to provide systemwide program evaluation. However, administrators generally continue to rate traditional child study and diagnosis as the most important function of the school psychologist (Kaplan, Clancy & Chrin, 1977). Gilmore and Chandy (1973) rated the following groups as the most likely candidates for referrals to the school psychologist: children with apparent emotional problems, children who present behavior problems in the classroom, children who are intellectually retarded, and bright children who are low achievers.

TEACHERS' VIEWPOINTS:
SCHOOL PSYCHOLOGISTS' RESPONSIBILITIES

What do teachers think school psychologists do? Medway (1977) sought to answer this question by comparing the time fifteen school psychologists devoted to seven professional activities to the time teachers perceived that the school psychologists devoted to these activities. Teachers were divided into two groups: high contact with the psychologists and low contact with the psychologists.

An analysis of the results indicated no marked differences in accuracy of teachers' perception of school psychologist responsibilities between the high and low contact teacher groups. However, differences did occur between teachers' perceptions and reports of actual work done by the psychologists. Specifically, teachers saw teacher consultation, diagnostic interviewing, and student counseling as occurring most frequently while testing, report writing, and principal consultation were least frequent. Psychologists reported that most of their time was spent in test administration and report writing and that the least time was spent in diagnostic interviewing and teacher consultation.

It appeared that neither high nor low contact teachers had a good idea of school psychologists' responsibilities in general.

After receiving a referral, many school psychologists prefer to begin their services by observing the child in the classroom and on the playground. The observational period allows the psychologist to gain a picture of how the child functions in a natural setting. Through observation, environmental factors that may be influencing the child's behavior may also be detected. Many students are then scheduled for individual testing. The testing procedure allows the psychologist to sample the child's behavior under controlled conditions. Typically, assessment includes evaluation of intellectual functioning level, coordination skills, academic achievement, personality factors, and speech development. At the secondary level, interest and aptitude tests may also be administered. Students with learning problems may be given special tests designed to suggest channels through which learning may occur more easily. Test results and interpretations along with recommendations are usually reported in written form.

RETARDATION OR LEARNING DISABILITY?

By the time he reached seventh grade, Joe was seriously behind his peers in ability to read. As a result, he was experiencing difficulty in all academic areas and was falling farther and farther below grade level. Mrs. Green, his teacher, decided that Joe would be more appropriately placed in a special education class for the intellectually limited than in a regular seventh-grade class where he could not keep up with other students. It was evident that his efforts were resulting in much frustration, and she felt that he was beginning to have emotional problems.

A referral to Mr. Blackwell, the school psychologist, was initiated and he arranged to see and evaluate Joe. The results of the evaluation indicated that Joe's intellectual ability was normal. Mr. Blackwell arranged for more extensive evaluation to help determine the cause of Joe's learning disability and to assist in planning remedial learning activities. Joe was not appropriate for placement in a class for the intellectually limited. However, assistance from a learning resource teacher was arranged.

School psychologists generally confer with both parents and teachers on recommendations for students who have been referred for psychological services. They may also provide consultative assistance in implementation of the recommendations in the home or the classroom. The school psychologist also arranges for referral to other appropriate specialists in the school or in the community. The need for psychologists to be alert to problems other than the referring problem was well documented by Chrin (1974). Four cases were cited from his personal experience in which students with learning or behavior problems were subsequently found to have serious medical problems.

If teachers are to make effective use of psychological services in the schools, they must be cognizant of the types of services the psychologist can render. School psychologists are usually willing to organize in-service training programs that focus on available services and on ways the services can be utilized. They may also conduct workshops on topics such as child management techniques or how to individualize instruction. Most school psychologists are interested in providing services that help prevent the occurrence of serious problems. Intervention before a child becomes unmanageable or fails completely can be most effective. The consultative approach, in which teachers are assisted in identifying and dealing with problems as they occur, appears to be a step in this direction.

School Nurse

Many school systems now employ school nurses. Students who display symptoms suggesting a health-related problem are appropriate to refer for school health services. In general, the function of the school nurse may include the following activities (a joint statement of the American Nurses' Association and the American School Health Association, 1973):

1. Participation in obtaining a health history.
2. Performing a physical appraisal.
3. Evaluating developmental status.
4. Advising and counseling children, parents, and others.
5. Helping in the management of technologic, economic, and social influences affecting child health.
6. Participating in appropriate routine immunization programs.
7. Assessing and treating certain minor illnesses and accidents of children.
8. Planning to meet the health needs of children in cooperation with physicians and other members of the health team.

Emphasis is now being placed on expanding the scope and training of the school nurse from the traditional model to that of the school nurse-practitioner. The professional role of the nurse-practitioner is significantly increased beyond that of the traditional school nurse and allows more responsibility in securing student health care in the schools. A study evaluating the impact of school nurse-practitioners (Lewis, Lorimer, Lindeman, Palmer & Lewis, 1974) found considerable enthusiasm by teachers and principals for increasing the scope and amount of nursing services available.

COPING WITH A MEDICAL PROBLEM

Mary Jane was a normal ninth grader who did well academically and generally got along well with other students in her classes. However, she was a victim of epilepsy, which could not be completely controlled by medication. As a result, she occasionally had a seizure that resulted in loss of consciousness. When this happened in class, other students became frightened. Following the seizures, they questioned her about what had happened. Mr. James, her homeroom teacher, referred Mary Jane to the school nurse, Mrs. Mason. Following the consultation, Mrs. Mason offered to talk with Mary Jane's classmates about seizure disorders, what happens during a seizure, and what should be done for someone who is having a seizure. Many students became very interested in the topic and were especially intrigued at the idea of electrical activity in the brain. The next time a seizure occurred in a classroom, they were able to react calmly and no longer treated Mary Jane with curiosity.

School nurses can take part in solving classroom management problems only when students are referred for their services. In addition to handling minor illnesses and accidents, they may serve as consultants to parents, teachers, and administrators in identifying resources for community health care. When warranted, they may make home visits and consult with parents regarding the health of their child. They can consult with teachers as an aide to insuring that the best adjustment is made by disabled children who have been mainstreamed. Often, they can fill the role of interpreter and advocate for the disabled child at school (Miller & Janosik, 1978). Additional ways in which school nurses can assist teachers were suggested by Parker (1974):

1. Attending staffing conferences with other specialists and providing a diagnosis and plan for action on the referred child.
2. Assisting orthopedically or physically handicapped children by making special arrangements, such as transportation, seating, remedial physical education, adjustment of orthopedic devices, etc.
3. Making special arrangements for children with chronic impairments, such as diabetes or epilepsy, and providing teacher education regarding these conditions.
4. Serving as a resource teacher to educate pupils regarding impairments that classmate may have.
5. Serving as a resource teacher of health.
6. Serving as a health counselor and source of referral for diagnosis of VD and drug abuse.
7. Serving as a resource teacher in home and family living classes and in programs serving pregnant teenagers.

Speech Pathologists

It is not unusual for students with communication disorders to present classroom management problems by withdrawing or by becoming disruptive. The undesirable behaviors may, at times, represent an attempt to compensate for an inability to function satisfactorily in the classroom. Speech pathologists and speech therapists work with such students in overcoming these problems. These resource professionals are familiar to most teachers. You probably have one in your school.

IMPROVING ARTICULATION ABILITY

Louis was unable to pronounce the "r" and "l" sounds correctly. As a result, he said "wabbit" for "rabbit" and "wets" for "lets". Other students in the class began to mimic his speech patterns and to refer to him as "Wouis". As a result, he gradually refused to participate in classroom discussions and began to withdraw from interactions with other students in the class. From his behavior, he could be described as a very shy and unhappy child.

Mr. Johnson, his teacher, consulted Mrs. Taylor, the speech pathologist, about Louis's speech problem and his behavior. Louis was scheduled for an evaluation and subsequent speech therapy. As his speech improved, he became more outgoing with other students and began to participate actively in class discussions.

Students with suspected problems in speech and language should be referred to the school speech pathologist (or therapist) for evaluation and remediation when indicated. In addition to working with students who cannot pronounce words plainly, speech specialists can assist teachers in dealing effectively with students who have limited hearing, who stutter, who have an abnormal voice quality, or who have delays in receptive or expressive language.

As with other referrals, the teacher should be specific when identifying suspected problems for a speech specialist. This information allows the screening or evaluation to be tailored to assess the suspected problem, and insures that some of the more subtle language difficulties are not overlooked.

Following the evaluation by a speech specialist, arrangements can be made for those students who require individual or group therapy. Any suggested remedial procedures are greatly enhanced when the teacher works with the speech specialist in stressing and reinforcing the development of the deficient language skills. For example, the speech pathologist may provide instructions for simple remedial exercises that can be used in the classroom, and may advise about other school activities for further assisting the child. Some communication disorders can be handled by the teacher through consultation with the speech pathologist. Severe problems usually require direct intervention by a specialist.

School Social Worker

Teachers expect to encounter few problems in working with middle- and upper-income parents. These parents are, for the most part, extremely interested in their children, and view education as a vehicle for "making it" in society. They tend to respond to requests for conferences and most of them attempt to do their part in working out problem situations. A few parents, however, do not respond to a teacher's notes or calls requesting consultation on their child. Lack of parental response is especially frequent in inner city and ghetto areas, but is not limited to these districts. Lack of parental involvement can be encountered in any school. A school social worker can be especially helpful in dealing with situations in which the parents make no voluntary contact with the schools.

HELPING PARENTS UNDERSTAND REASONS FOR A REFERRAL

Mrs. Greenlee was concerned because Linda was failing in class and appeared to have emotional problems. She decided that Linda should be seen by the school psychologist. As was school procedure, she sent home the standard permission form for Linda's parents to sign. The parents did not return the form, and refused to respond to any subsequent notes.

Mrs. Greenlee discussed the problem with Mrs. North, the school social worker, who arranged to visit Linda's parents in their home. At first, the parents were hostile and repeatedly stated that their daughter "was not crazy." It became clear that the basic problem was the parents' lack of understanding regarding the purpose of the recommended psychological evaluation. The parents further assumed that only "crazy" people went to see psychologists. Mrs. North was able to explain the role of the school psychologist and to allay their fears that the teacher felt Linda was crazy. Mrs. North specifically stressed how the evaluation could be of benefit to Linda.

Following the visit of the social worker, Linda's parents signed a permission form to allow the testing to be completed. They also agreed to talk with the psychologist, teacher, and social worker following the evaluation in order to discuss findings and recommendations.

School social work originated early in the twentieth century when "compulsory attendance" laws were passed. The duty of the social worker was to improve children's attendance and, thus, preclude delinquency and ignorance (Cowen & Lorion, 1976). In the past, social workers employed by school systems were usually assigned the duty of dealing with truants, earning reputations as "truant officers" of sorts. The focus of school social work changed during the 1930s and 1940s to a casework model that deals with adjustment problems of children (Anderson, 1974). School social workers are the professionals in the schools most likely to work intensively with home- and community-related problems. Many social workers now serve as members of a school multidisciplinary team. This team usually includes the school psychologist, the speech pathologist, the school nurse, the counselor, the teacher, and perhaps the principal.

Specifically, what services can a school social worker offer to teachers? (1) Social workers are trained to make assessments of family functioning. They can often provide information on students' home environment that is useful in explaining behaviors that occur in the classroom. For example, it may be found that some students do not have a stable home environment. One or both of the parents may be alcoholic, and the child may be shifted from relative to relative. These children may fail to learn and may appear apathetic or withdrawn, or may be aggressive toward other students. The social worker can perform an important function in establishing rapport with the family and in assisting them in obtaining the aid needed to provide adequately for the physical and emotional needs of their children. (2) A social worker can help the teacher by communicating positive aspects of the child's experience to the family. In getting to know and work with the family, he may be able to improve communication between teacher and parents. (3) Due to training emphasis on working with families and communities, a school social worker can usually offer expertise in dealing with problems of truancy. (4) Social workers can assist other school professionals and students to change conditions in the school that may serve as contributing factors to students' problems (Nieberl, 1974). Students who are interested in exploring and making changes in school procedures may receive a helping hand from the school social worker.

Teachers should attempt to maintain regular communication with parents; social workers should not be expected to fill this role. However, when communication problems are encountered, the social worker may be able to serve as a liaison between home and school in effecting the needed changes.

Summary

The focus of this chapter has been cooperation with resource professionals to maximize the development of children with special needs. The main provisions of PL 94-142 and implications for teachers were discussed. It was also pointed out that teachers should become cognizant of the types of specialized services available in the schools and should refer students with special problems for assistance. Indicators for referral were provided for health-related, hearing, visual, learning, behavior, emotional, speech, and home-related problems. The types of services provided by counselors, school psychologists, speech pathologists, school nurses, and school social workers were discussed.

Resource specialists can contribute a great deal to the development of students who require their services. Alertness in detecting serious problems is important. However, it should be stressed that few children in a classroom need specialized assistance. Every child who misbehaves is not an appropriate referral for a specialist. The techniques described in Chapter Three and Four remain appropriate for dealing with most of the problems that you will encounter in daily teaching.

REFERENCES

American Humane Society. *Guidelines for Schools.* 1971.

Anandam, K. and Williams, R.L. "A model for consultation with classroom teachers on behavior management." *The School Counselor 18* (1971): 253-259.

Anderson, R. "School social work: The promise of a team model." *Child Welfare 53* (1974): 524-530.

Chrin, M.J. "The school psychologist." *Today's Education 63* (1974): 23-24.

Clark, A.E. "Teacher attitudes toward integration of children with handicaps." *Education and Training of the Mentally Retarded 11* (1976): 333-335.

Conti, A.P. "A follow-up investigation of families referred to outside agencies." *Journal of School Psychology 11* (1973): 215-223 .

Cowen, E.L. and Lorin, R.P. "Changing roles for the school mental health professional." *Journal of School Psychology 14* (1976): 131-138.

Ethical principles in the conduct of research with human paticipants. Washington, D .C.: American Psychological Association, 1973.

Fairchild, T.N. "An analysis of the services performed by a school psychologist in an urban area: implications for training programs." *Psychology in the Schools 11* (1974): 274-281.

Gilmore, G.E. and Chandy, J. "Teachers' perceptions of school psychological services." *Journal of School Psychology 11* (1973): 139-147.

Granger, R.C. and Campbell, P.B. "The school psychologist as program evaluator." *Journal of School Psychology 15* (1977): 174-183.

Harasymiw, S.J. and Horne, M.D. "Teacher attitudes toward handicapped children and regular class integration." *The Journal of Special Education 10* (1976): 393-399.

Kaplan, M.S., Clancy, B., and Chrin, M. "Priority roles for school psychologists as seen by superintendents." *Journal of School Psychology 15* (1977): 75-80.

Leafman, K. "Recognizing and helping the abused child." *Nursing* (1979): 64-66.

Lewis, C.E., Lorimer, A., Lindeman, C., Palmer, B.B., and Lewis, M.A. "An evaluation of the impact of school nurse practitioners." *The Journal of School Health 44* (1974): 331-335.

Medway, F.J. "Teacher knowledge of school psychologists' responsibilities." *Journal of School Psychology 15* (1977): 301-307.

Miller, J. and Janosik, E. "The nurse." *The Exceptional Parent 8* (1978): 62-68.

Mitchell, K.L. "What you can do about child abuse." *Early Years 8* (1977): 40-41ff.

Nador, R.H. "Teacher identification of elementary school children with hearing loss." *Language, Speech and Hearing Services in Schools 9* (1978): 24-28.

Nieberl, H.R. "The school social worker." *Today's Education 63* (1974): 25-26.

Parker, N. "The school nurse." *Today's Education 63* (1974): 30-31.

Powell, T.H. "Educating all disabled children: a practical guide to P.L. 94-142." *The Exceptional Parent 8* (1978): 13-16.

"Recommendations on educational preparation and definition of the expanded role and functions of the school nurse practitioner." American Nurses' Association and American School Health Association, *Journal of School Health 43* (1973): 594-597.

Sapir, S. and Wilson, B. "*A Professional's Guide to Working With the Learning Disabled Child.* New York: Brunner/Mazel, Inc., 1978.

Schaar, K. "Handicapped law beset with problems." *APA* (American Psychological Association) *Monitor 10* (1979): 11.

Shanas, B. "Child abuse: A killer teachers can help control." *Phi Delta Kappan 56* (1975): 479-482.

Sproles, A.H., Panther, E.E., and Lanier, J.E. "PL 94-142 and its impact on the counselor's role." *Personnel and Guidance Journal 55* (1978): 210-212.

Swart, R. "A secondary school resource room makes mainstreaming work." *Teaching Exceptional Children 11* (1979): 77-79.

Tesh, B.D. "The counselor." *Today's Education 63* (1974): 20-22. *United States Code, Vol. 5.* 1976 Edition. Washington: United States Government Printing Office, 1977.

Willgoose, C.E. *Health Education in the Elementary School.* Phildelphia: W.B. Saunders Company, 1969.

Zaslow, E.L. "The speech pathologist." *Today's Education 63* (1974): 27-29.

CHAPTER SEVEN

I'D RATHER DO IT MYSELF: GUIDING STUDENTS TOWARD SELF-MANAGEMENT

"Did you observe how nicely Bobby behaved in the cafeteria today? I'm trying out a different behavior change strategy—self-management."

"Well, it certainly seems to be working for Bobby. If you have some time later, I'd like to talk with you about how to go about using the technique."

All of the preceding chapters have emphasized things *teachers* can do to manage students. While there is considerable merit in the teacher's management of student behaviors, a number of important reasons exist for teaching students how to manage themselves effectively. First, teachers may actually have a broader, more significant influence by teaching students to govern themselves. If teachers indefinitely assume responsibility for student actions, students may become overly dependent. They may behave appropriately only when the teacher is present to offer reinforcement or punishment. Absence of the teacher could produce frustration and inappropriate private behavior. Second, students may perform better both socially and academically when given opportunities to manage themselves. Recent research (Arlin & Whitley, 1978) relating to perceived opportunities for self-managed learning and perceived academic locus of control has suggested that students are likely to accept responsibility for academic successes *and* failures if they perceive the classroom as a place where they can play a part in managing their own instruction. Many students express resentment over having all decisions made by others. Third, students are often the only ones in a position to know what changes are needed. Teachers can never hope to know all the inner thoughts of students, nor can they expect to see everything that happens in and out of the classroom. Fourth, and closely related to the previous point, students may know better than the teacher what is reinforcing and punishing. Desired changes are possible only when meaningful consequences are applied for designated behavior. Finally, many of the ethical and legal problems involved in the use of various rewards and punishers can be avoided when students take part in decision-making processes. Too often, teachers get themselves into difficulty by making all decisions regarding the behavior of others.

Many benefits are obviously associated with the development of self-management skills. Of course, self-management never completely frees a student of all dependence on others. Support, encouragement, and feedback from teachers and other significant persons will always be needed. An ultimate goal of education has always been to help youngsters achieve enough independence to live happy, productive lives. This chapter is aimed at just that goal by emphasizing ways in which self-management can be attained, focusing specifically on the origins of self-management, techniques for achieving self-management, and major concerns related to self-management.

Origins of Self-Management

In order for teachers to help youngsters become more self-directive, they must have a clear conception of how individuals develop self-management skills. Some teachers have the idea that self-control or self-management (we will use the terms inter-changeably) is a matter of personal desire. They contend that if students really "want to," they can overcome bad habits and develop new skills. They often exhort students to "set your mind to it," "show a little initiative," and "come in here with a better attitude." All responsbility for change is, thus, attributed to some internal reservoir of strength. Students who fail to change may be regarded as lacking "what it takes." Certainly, no one would deny that desire is an indispensable ingredient in self-management, but desire alone is hardly a sufficient condition for the development of self-control. Students must also know *how* to produce wanted changes (Williams & Long, 1979).[1] Desire by itself in no way provides the knowledge that is essential for developing new behaviors.

1. For a more comprehensive discussion of the philosophical foundations of self-management as well as specific details for its developing in various social and academic areas, see R.L. Williams and J.D. Long. *Toward a Self-Managed Life Style.* Boston: Houghton Mifflin, 1979.

Even when desire is recognized as an essential part of self-management, the origin of desire remains a question. Does it come solely from within the person, or is it influenced by environmental factors? We believe the latter gives students the impetus to want to improve. Social contacts at school, encouragement from the teachers, success experiences, a setting conducive to self-improvement, and a host of other environmental events can influence how much desire a student displays. Students who receive reinforcement for their efforts in self-management are undoubtedly going to exhibit more interest in it than students who are mostly overlooked and punished for their failures. The kind of feedback that students receive can also influence what students "want" to do. Highly specific feedback, for example, can convey necessary information about how a person can change, whereas global feedback may only discourage by leaving too much doubt about how change can be accomplished. Similarly, the example set by the teacher can influence the amount of desire shown by students. Teachers who are self-confident will probably imbue others with confidence in themselves. Our point is this: teachers can create desire. There is no longer any reason to assume that students either do or do not have it.

Just as teachers can help increase students' desire to improve, they can also help students develop the knowledge required to produce wanted changes. Students do not come into the world knowing how to study more effectively, improve interpersonal relationships, or break a distasteful habit. They must learn to manage these areas of their lives in much the same way that they learn any academic skill. Of course, students sometimes accidentally discover how to manage a specific behavior without the help of others. But such changes are of minimal benefit when the individual cannot deliberately sustain desired changes. Even when students can sustain a behavioral change in one area, they may be unable to manage other dimensions of their lives. Effective self-management exists only when students learn to produce deliberate, long-lasting outcomes in whatever areas they choose. We believe that effective self-management can be best achieved when students are taught specific self-management strategies. In this way, the teacher can also avoid the frustrations and chaos that could result from the assumption that students know how to control themselves if only given the chance. With that in mind, let us take a look at a few of the strategies that can help students gain better control over their own behaviors.

Techniques of Self-Management

The techniques discussed in earlier chapters clearly represent ways that teachers can manage student behaviors, but many of the same techniques can be used by students to change their own behaviors and achieve self-control. In this section, we will discuss the most prevalent techniques for self-management: self-recording, control of setting events, managing consequences, self-verbalization, and behavioral contracting. Although we will discuss each technique separately, they can be used in combination. Most students will probably benefit by learning all the strategies, and then selecting what seems most natural and effective.

Self-Recording

Students are often unaware of how they actually behave. Some of their behavior may occur so automatically that it completely escapes their attention. Other behavior by itself may seem too unimportant to notice. However, by recording their own actions, students can become more aware of how they appear to others. That feedback alone may be all that is required to produce a change in behavior.

BILL LEARNS SOMETHING ABOUT HIMSELF

Bill was a seventh grader who seemed to be complaining constantly. He complained about his classmates, his assignments, the weather, the school. Mrs. Vandiford, his teacher, was worried about the effect his complaining was having on his relationships with others. Finally, Mrs. Vandiford asked him if he knew how he appeared to others. Bill remarked that he seldom complained and was generally regarded as a likeable person. Mrs. Vandiford then asked him if he would be willing to keep a record of the times he expressed dissatisfaction to others. Together, Bill and Mrs. Vandiford made a list of his frequent complaints. He was to check any of the items that he complained about during the day and discuss them daily with Mrs. Vandiford at the close of school.

Something remarkable happened when Bill began self-recording. His behavior improved immediately. Maybe he was trying to avoid complaining to prove something to Mrs. Vandiford or perhaps he was learning something about himself that he did not like. In any case, Bill was a changed person. Mrs. Vandiford felt so differently about him that she began praising him more for his cooperative behaviors. Within three weeks he asked to discontinue self-recording, but he continued to complain less throughout the term.

While the results obtained in the preceding illustration may be more dramatic than can normally be expected, research does support the theory that self-recording can result in greater self-control. For example, Broden, Hall, and Mitts (1971) found that self-recording was effective in increasing attention to classroom lesson activities of an eighth-grade girl. In a second experiment, Broden and her colleagues found that self-recording also reduced talking without permission by an eighth-grade boy, but in this case, self-recording eventually lost much of its effectiveness. The researchers suggested that external support might be needed to sustain the behavior changes intitiated through self-recording. They commented that "perhaps the most promising feature of self-recording will be to use it as a procedure for initiating desirable levels of appropriate behavior to a point where the teacher can more easily reinforce the desired behavior with attention, praise, grades, or other reinforcers available in the classroom." Of course, when desirable behavior changes become habitual, self-recording and reinforcement could be gradually reduced.

Other researchers have reached similar conclusions. Sagotsky, Patterson, and Lepper (1978), for instance, found self-recording was effective among a group of fifth- and sixth-graders for increasing the amount of study time and rate of progress through an individualized mathematics program. In the self-recording phase of that study, the students periodically marked a + or a- on grids to indicate whether they were actually studying math. The procedure reminded students to continue study. Still other researchers have found that self-recording can even be effective with special-education students. Long and Williams (1976), for example, employed self-recording with a group of retarded adolescents. Each student had to maintain a point sheet on which he recorded points for appropriate responses. The students logged points for being ready to start lessons, having appropriate materials, completing assignments, working quietly for specified time periods, and similar activities. Recording of points increased levels of appropriate responding for the group by approximately ten percent during spelling and by approximately fifteen percent during reading.

In case you're worrying about how accurate students are in self-recording, don't be overly concerned. Studies suggest (e.g., Nelson, Lipinski & Black, 1976; Zegiob, Klukas & Junginer, 1978) that positive changes occur with self-monitoring even when self-recording is inaccurate.

"It's called a self-instructional activity. That means you've gotta get a certain amount of it done before the teacher gets back or she gets mad."

Although self-recording may prove beneficial for many students, several research studies (Bolstad & Johnson, 1972; Long & Williams, 1976 ; Mahoney, Moura, & Wade, 1973) reveal that it can be more effective when combined with other techniques. Teachers can use self-recording with external reinforcements they provide, with other self-management techniques, or with both. We will discuss a number of possible combinations in the remainder of the chapter. Teachers should also recognize that self-recording is not foolproof. It may work best for those students who seek help and who are already highly motivated to change. Because many students may be unfamiliar with the alternative methods of self-recording, let us turn briefly to a discussion of them.

Methods of recording. The methods selected for record-keeping will depend largely upon the behaviors themselves. Behaviors that have a discrete beginning and end lend themselves to a *frequency count.* This involves nothing more than counting the number of times the behavior occurs. Number of positive and negative comments, questions asked or answered, times late for class, and similar behaviors can be subjected to a frequency-count assessment. Paper and pencil or a mechanical counter (e.g., a golf counter) can be used by students in making frequency counts. Some behaviors that occur over extended time periods do not readily lend themselves to the frequency count. Time spent studying, working on special projects, sleeping, being off the task, and other continuing kinds of behavior can best be subjected to *time assessment*. The simplest way to measure this type of behavior is with a stopwatch. Rather than making a continuous frequency count or an assessment of all the time spent at a specific behavior, a student could be assisted in *sampling* a behavior at designated intervals. Sampling can provide valuable information if a behavior occurs frequently enough so that periodic measures are representative of the student's total behavior pattern.

Students will probably want to devise their own record-keeping system. However, a form similiar to Table 7-1 could be used for recording most classroom behaviors. Students need only to (1) make tally marks in the appropriate block every time the behavior in question occurs, or (2) record the amount of time spent on the task. Although separate tables would be required for each behavior, students generally would be recording only one or two behaviors. The effort in trying to record a host of different behaviors could be counterproductive. It is better to begin by gaining control over one behavior than by trying to change everything simultaneously.

Irrespective of the method used for recording behaviors, students will probably find it helpful to graph their behavior on a daily basis. Sometimes a student feels that no progress is being made and graphing will permit him to make a quick assessment. Even seeing that slight improvements are occurring can be extremely helpful in maintaining self-management efforts.

A form similar to Figure 7-1 could be used for graphing specified behaviors. In constructing such a graph, the ordinate (vertical line) can be used to indicate the frequency of a given behavior or the amount of time spent on a behavior, and the abscissa (horizontal line), the days. The student only plots the level (frequency, or amount of time) of the behavior on the appropriate day. Drawing a line connecting the plots on the various days will yield a picture of the behavior.

In establishing a record-keeping system, students should consider measuring not only their behavior but also the events that precede and follow behavior. Recording these events may provide clues as to why the behavior occurs and what needs to be done to change it. For

TABLE 7-1
BEHAVIOR RECORD SHEET

TIME or CLASS	M	T	W	Th	F	M	T	W	Th	F
8:00—8:55 Math										
9:00—9:55 English										
10:00—10:55 History										
11:00—11:55 Study Hall										
12:00—12:55 Lunch										
1:00—1:55 French										
2:00—2:55 Science										
TOTALS										

BEHAVIOR _____

FIGURE 7-1
DAILY BEHAVIOR GRAPH

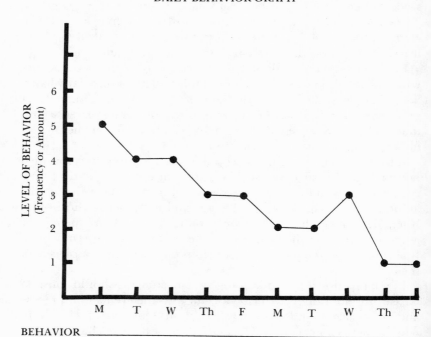

BEHAVIOR _____

example, behavior is often associated with particular times of the day, persons, and settings. A student, whose friends support him after every misdeed, may want to ask that their reinforcement be directed at other behaviors. Students who fail to take into account the events that make them angry, happy, critical, cooperative, and so on, possess only limited potential for producing worthwhile changes in themselves.

Control of Setting Events

An effective self-management technique alluded to in the previous section as well as in Chapter Four is the control of setting events. Many students have never consciously considered how setting events influence their behaviors. Thus, teachers will have to encourage students to think about the factors that influence behavior: the amount of time taken on a task, the order in which activities are undertaken, how other people, places, the composition of a group, and other environmental stimuli affect their behavior. Students will usually recognize immediately that their behavior does not occur in a vacuum. The most important point for them to learn, though, is not *why* they behave as they do, but that something can be done to change their behavior.

MANAGING STUDY BEHAVIOR

Joe, a tenth grader at Central High School, was taking his first course in French. He had never studied hard because most things came easily for him. French was different. Joe was falling farther behind each day. He tried to make himself study, but usually little got accomplished. Joe really wanted to do better so he asked his teacher, Mr. Pharr, for help. Together they discussed Joe's behavior. Joe explained that frequently he tried to study in the school library, but that he generally wound up talking with other students or looking at girls. Mr. Pharr and Joe concluded that, for Joe, the library was a stimulus for socializing, not study. Joe also indicated that he sometimes tried to study in the afternoon, immediately after school, but this was ordinarily a time when he played tag football or just goofed-off with his friends. Because the afternoon hours were associated with other acts, Mr. Pharr and Joe reasoned that time was also triggering nonstudy behaviors.

To remedy the situation, Mr. Pharr and Joe devised a plan that would help Joe control setting events. He set aside one hour after dinner for study. Although he decided to begin by studying fifteen minutes each day and gradually build up to the full hour, no other activity was planned during the study hour. He thought a gradual process would be better than a radical change. Joe also decided to set aside a portion of his room for study, and cleared his personal desk of all pictures, magazines, and materials that might conflict with anything other than school work. Mr. Pharr and Joe agreed that controlling setting events was at least a step toward greater self-management of study.

Generally, controlling setting events involves either: (1) reducing the stimuli that trigger unwanted behavior, or (2) increasing the stimuli that foster desired behaviors. Students who refuse to bring nonacademic materials to class (unless requested to do so) reduce the range of stimuli that could generate unwanted behavior. Similarly, students who elect not to sit beside friends who encourage inappropriate talking, who limit the distractions occurring during their study time, or who avoid associating with peers who insist on misbehaving are reducing the probability of misbehaving. Since students cannot always avoid troublesome situations, they may have to concentrate on increasing the stimuli that foster desired behaviors. Strenghtening desired behavior, of course, will also invariably reduce unwanted behavior. Shy students who associate with persons who encourage socializing increase the probability of overcoming their shyness. Likewise, students who bring appropriate texts and materials to class and who develop a schedule for their daily activities increase the stimuli that can cue appropriate behavior. With the teacher's help, they can probably think of numerous other stimuli that can be altered for better control of their own behavior.

Managing Consequences

Although self-recording and control of setting events alone may produce changes in behavior, these techniques are often most helpful when combined with the management of behavioral consequences. It is the events that occur after an individual has emitted a behavior that largely determine whether the behavior will occur again. To maintain desired changes that result from self-recording, control of setting events, or other techniques, teachers should help students manage the consequences of their own behavior. In fact, several studies have found self-management of reinforcers to be superior to teacher-management of reinforcers. Lovitt and Curtiss (1969), for example, found that the academic response rate of a twelve-year-old student was higher when the student specified the requirements for reinforcement than when only the teacher specified the requirements. Similarly, Bolstad and Johnson (1972) revealed that self-regulation of reinforcers (self-recording and self-dispensing of reinforcers) was more effective in reducing disruptiveness among the most disruptive students in ten first- and second-grade classrooms than was teacher regulation of reinforcers. Other studies (Ballard & Glynn, 1970; Long & Williams, 1976) attest to the potential usefulness of self-rewards. More studies (e.g., Arwood, Williams & Long, 1974; Dickinson, 1968; Williams, Long & Yoakley, 1973) suggest that students' input into the management of punishers can improve their behaviors. In fact, Grusec and Kuczynski (1977) found that children can be taught to punish themselves. Other researchers (Pease & Tyler, 1979) found that self-management of time-out duration is as effective as teacher-management in reducing the rate of disruptive behavior.

SELF-REGULATION OF TIME-OUT BEHAVIOR

The effects of teacher-determined versus self-determined time-out duration on the rate of disruptive behaviors and amount of time spent in time out was investigated by Pease and Tyler (1979). Subjects were fifteen students, ages seven to fourteen, from a rural elementary classroom. Five phases of ten days each were involved in the experiment and all students participated in each phase. All data were recorded by teachers who had been trained to observe and record.

Baseline data were taken during *Phase I* of the experiment. During this phase, a time-out procedure that had been in operation for four months prior to the study remained in effect. Time-out duration was five minutes during this period. During *Phase II*, the use of time out was discontinued. Instead, teachers recorded occasions when they felt students deserved time out and commented to the student that he was misbehaving. *Phase III* involved a return to baseline conditions. When disruptive behavior was noted, the student was sent to the time-out area for five minutes. During *Phase IV*, students were told to go to the time-out area but the amount of time spent in the area was determined by the student. Data were recorded on the number of times each child went to the area and the amount of time spent there. During *Phase V* of the study, the teacher specified the time-out duration with the amount actually duplicating the amount the student chose in *Phase IV*.

An analysis of the data indicated that student-determined time-out duration was as effective as teacher-imposed time-out duration in reducing disruptive behavior. In this classroom, self-imposed duration was also found to be easier to operate than teacher-imposed duration.

Teachers who are interested in having students manage behavioral consequences need to consider a number of factors related to the effective control of consequences:

1. Since accurate management of reinforcers and punishers necessitates record-keeping, students may need assistance in developing adequate record-keeping systems. The previous discussion on self-recording should be helpful in this respect.

2. Research (Kanfer & Duerfeldt, 1967) suggests that individuals reinforce themselves in much the same way as they have been reinforced by others. Thus, teachers may find that they can increase student success with self-reinforcement by first successfully reinforcing desired student behaviors. Teachers who find that students are either too lenient or too stringent with rewards and punishers may want to consider how they themselves are responding to the students.

3. Students may need assistance in identifying appropriate reinforcers and punishers. Atkins and Williams (1972) found that students often have difficulty identifying stimuli that actually serve as reinforcers. Perhaps this is a result of limited exposure to a variety of potential reinforcers. In any case, students must realize that something is reinforcing only if it will maintain or strengthen behavior for them. Teachers may find that by having the entire class make a list of potential reinforcers, the likelihood that each student identifies appropriate reinforcers will be increased. Likewise, students may require assistance in identifying potential punishers. Many students probably think that punishment constitutes a paddling, a trip to the principal's office, or suspension. They may never have considered the possibility of withholding a privilege, overcorrection, or other type 2 punishers.

4. If students are to manage behavior consequences, they should receive instructions in the use of effective rewards and punishers. The same principles that were discussed in earlier chapters of teachers' use of rewards and punishers should apply when students themselves control the consequences. For example, applying reinforcers contingent on desired behavior, applying them immediately, and using a variety of reinforcers are just as applicable when self-applied as when externally controlled. Students can achieve success with self-management of consequences only to the extent that they know how to control those consequences properly.

KAY MAKES A DECISION

Kay was a ninth-grade general math student who spent too much time reading paperbacks when she was supposed to be working math problems. Kay frequently got into trouble with her math teacher, Mr. Carson, because of her reading. Mr. Carson did not really mind if Kay spent some time reading as long as she paid attention to explanations and completed the assignments. One day, during a conversation with Kay, Mr. Carson suggested that she try doing math first and afterward rewarding herself with reading. Mr. Carson explained that his suggestion was based on the Premack principle, which asserts that a highly probable activity (e.g., reading) could be used to reinforce a less probable activity (e.g., math). Kay simply would need to do the less probable activity first. Since Mr. Carson was primarily interested in seeing that Kay completed her assignments, he suggested that she monitor her own behavior and reward herself whenever she did complete them. Kay felt that Mr. Carson was being very fair and decided to follow his suggestion.

Self-Verbalization

From time to time, most persons instruct themselves vocally or subvocally on what they should and should not do in given situations. Athletes, for example, often tell themselves, "Watch the ball," "Wait for the signal before starting," "Keep your head down." Similarly, some motorists, when caught in a line of traffic, remind themselves to "be patient," "remain calm," or "try to be courteous to other drivers." There are also occasions in the classroom when self-verbalization could help students achieve better self-control. They can verbalize to themselves to control anger, reduce anxiety associated with giving a speech, and be more positive in the comments they make to others. Unfortunately, some students, especially those who are impulsive, act before they think. As with other self-management techniques, however, students can learn to self-verbalize.

An interesting study by Meichenbaum and Goodman (1971) demonstrated that a group of second graders who were exhibiting hyperactive and impulsive behaviors could be trained to talk to themselves as a means of developing self-control. They were trained on a variety of tasks, such as copying line patterns and coloring figures within boundaries. During the training sessions, students individually observed the experimenter perform the task while giving himself instructions aloud. The following is an example of the experimenter's self-verbalizations:

Okay, what is it I have to do? You want me to copy the picture with the different lines. I have to go slowly and be careful. Okay, draw the lines down, down, good; then to the right, that's it; now down some more and to the left. Good, I'm doing fine so far. Remember, go slowly. Now back up again. No, I was supposed to go down. That's okay. Just erase the line carefully. . . . Good. Even if I make an error I can go on slowly and carefully. Okay, I have to go down now. Finished. I did it.

After observing the experimenter, each student performed the task while instructing himself aloud. Next, he performed the task while whispering instructions. Finally, he performed the task silently (without lip movements). The idea was to help him internalize self-instructions. The students who received training in self-verbalization subsequently performed significantly better on psychometric tests which measured cognitive impulsivity, performance I.Q., and motor ability than did control students who were exposed to the training tasks, but were not trained to self-verbalize.

O'Leary (1969) has also demonstrated the utility of teaching students to self-verbalize. In his experiment, first-grade boys received a marble for pressing a telegraph key. The marbles could be exchanged for prizes; the more marbles a boy earned, the more valuable a prize he could purchase. But the boys were supposed to press the key only when a certain stimulus was flashed on a screen. Eventually, the boys were left alone to perform the task while the experimenter observed through a one-way mirror. Boys who were trained to verbalize aloud what they could and could not do were less likely to "cheat" on the experimental task than boys who were simply told what was right and wrong. You can probably think of similar classroom situations in which students might be trained to verbalize rules out loud. Asking students to tell themselves what they have done correctly on academic and social tasks might also cue further appropriate behavior. In the following illustration, at least one student used self-verbalization to control his temper.

TOM HAS A TEMPER

Tom was a sixth grader who had never learned to control his temper. If someone said something that Tom did not like, he generally wanted to fight. Sometimes he cursed and threw things. Everybody seemed afraid to say anything to him. Tom's problem reached a critical level one day when he cursed the teacher. The teacher sent for the principal, and Tom was threatened with expulsion unless he could learn to control his temper. He was later given an opportunity to talk with the school counselor. They discussed the possibility of self-verbalization. The counselor suggested that Tom start subvocalizing the things that could happen to him if he continued to lose his temper and Tom made a list of them. Thoughts like, "You could hurt someone or get hurt," "How must you look to others," "How would you feel if someone reacted that way toward you," and "Try saying something nice and see how ... will respond" were included on Tom's list. He even thought about counting to ten when he got mad before he would make any response. The counselor had Tom visualize different problem situations and verbalize what he would say to himself when those situations arose.

Behavioral Contracting

Behavioral contracting is a technique that appears to be widely used with students of vastly different backgrounds. Researchers have found contracting to be effective in improving classroom behaviors of inner-city blacks (Sapp, 1971), disadvantaged white students (Arwood, Williams & Long, 1974), and economically advantaged students (Williams, Long & Yoakley, 1973). Others have found contracts to be useful with students adjudged potential school dropouts (Homme, 1966) and in treating problems ranging from hyperaggressivity and stealing to under-achievement and school phobia (Cantrell, Cantrell, Huddleston & Woolridge, 1969). In all of these studies, school personnel got more of what they wanted (e.g., improved academic and social behaviors from students) by reaching agreements with students on how they could earn existing reinforcers (e.g., free time, grades).

The real value of contracting, however, does not lie in its potential to alter problem behaviors, but in its provisions of means by which students can progress from external control of their lives by others toward greater degrees of self-management. Contracting enables teachers and students to reach *mutual agreements* in which students can assume more control as they demonstrate greater personal responsibility. Clark (1978), in a study involving 150 adolescent students, found that most students considered the contracts used in the study fair and worthwhile and that they preferred them to other teaching methods. Students gave the following reasons (ranked by frequency) for enjoying the contracts: (1) allow individuals to work at their own pace without being nagged, (2) provide knowledge as to what is expected of students, (3) allow students to improve their course grade, (4) allow independent work, (5) provide an opportunity to earn free time by completing work, (6) allow students to receive individual teacher attention, and (7) allow students the opportunity to choose from a variety of activities.

One of the most practical plans for using contracting to help students achieve greater self-control has been developed by Homme, Csanyi, Gonzales, and Rechs (1970). Their plan embodies five stages. The first is labeled manager-controlled contracting—an adult manager (e.g., a teacher) determines the task to be performed and the amount of reinforcement to be given for completion of the task. Upon acceptance of the contract by the child and completion of the assigned task, the manager delivers the reinforcer. In the second stage the child may be given joint control of the task or of the reinforcer. If the child assumes partial control of the task, the manager maintains complete control of the reinforcer . If the child jointly controls the reinforcer, the manager determines the task. You will notice that at this stage greater control is still maintained by the adult manager. The third stage, however, allows equal control by the manager and the child. The child can: (1) jointly control the task and the amount of reinforcement, (2) completely control the task, while the manager controls the amount of reinforcement, or (3) control the amount of reinforcement, while the manager controls the task. The fourth stage shifts even more control to the child. The child can take complete control of the task while jointly sharing control over the reinforcer, or he can take complete control over the reinforcer while sharing control of the task. In the fifth and final stage, labeled child-controlled contracting, the child has control over both the task and the reinforcer. Homme and his colleagues suggest that students achieve success with each stage and with each possible type of control before advancing to the next stage. We think their plan has considerable merit because it allows a gradual transition to self-control as students demonstrate ability to assume new responsibilities. Of course, you and your students alone must judge whether you want to use contracts and, if so, how those contracts will be managed.

A GOOD-BEHAVIOR CONTRACT

White-Blackburn, Semb, and Semb (1977) used a good behavior contract to alter on-task behavior, disruptive behavior, completion of daily assignments and weekly grades of four sixth graders in a public school classroom. The contract involved a list of goals for good conduct and assignment completion and a list of disruptive behaviors coupled with a list of rewards and penalties. The teacher negotiated the good-behavior contract with each experimental subject at the beginning of each morning work period. Student self-management was emphasized during negotiations and each student was encouraged to earn a reward by achieving the good-conduct goals and completing assignments. The students were allowed to leave their desks and work in an isolated area for a fixed period of fifteen minutes. Following the work period, the teacher determined a reward or penalty commensurate with completion of assignments and observed behavior. Throughout the study, student agreement with the teacher's choices was high. Results of the study showed that on-task behavior and assignment completion increased, weekly grades were higher, and disruptive behavior decreased while the contract was in effect. During the contract period, the performance of the contract students compared favorably with selected model students who were not exposed to the contract but who consistently produced acceptable assignments and did not engage in high rates of off-task or disruptive behavior.

At this point, you realize that both teachers and students can exercise varying amounts of control in contracting, but you may still be wondering about some of the mechanics of implementing a contract: whether it should be positive or negative, whether it should be used with individuals or groups, and how to obtain student participation. First, although contracting can consist of agreements to do or not to do certain things, we believe that it should emphasize positive behaviors. This does not mean that rewards should never be withdrawn for engaging in inappropriate acts, but contracts that clearly identify appropriate behaviors and the payoffs for engaging in those behavoirs should be far more acceptable to teachers and students. The contracting process can be greatly simplified by remembering that the same principles of reinforcement discussed in Chapter Three and mentioned in this chapter (managing behavioral consequences) should be followed, no matter who controls the contract. Second, our own experiences suggest that contracts can be effective whether they are used with individuals, small groups, or large classes. You will probably find that using the same format for an entire class is less demanding on you than developing unique instruments for each student. Of course, the tasks that students perform and the reinforcers they select can vary without having different contracts. Students can simply be given a choice of rewards once they have completed their assigned task. Finally, to involve students, we have found a straightforward approach to be best. We ask them to define appropriate and inappropriate classroom behaviors and what the consequences (rewards and punishers) should be for those behaviors. Students can also be involved in the wording of written contracts, in maintaining records, in providing feedback on the success of the contracting, and in making recommendations for new ways of using contracts. Besalel-Azrin, Azrin, and Armstrong (1977) found that a program which maximized student responsibility resulted in fewer classroom problems as reported by students, teachers, and independent observers. Students at all ages will have ideas to share if their teacher is willing to solicit and reinforce student input. Possibly the most important consideration in implementing a contract is the teacher's willingness to involve students. After all, contracting connotes cooperation.

Although you and your students could devise many different types of contracts, an illustration of a behavioral contract negotiated between an eighth-grade teacher and her students follows. Perhaps you and your students would be interested in trying a similar contract in your class.

CONTRACT FOR CLASSWORK

I agree to abide by the following conditions and consequences during Math 101. I understand this agreement will be renegotiated after a trial period of three weeks or before that time if a majority of students or the teacher feels another agreement would be more desirable.

Conditions
1. To be seated and ready to begin work before the tardy bell rings.
2. To bring pencil, paper, and appropriate books to class.
3. To avoid engaging in loud talking, noise making, and other behaviors that could interfere with others' learning.
4. To complete class assignments each day and correct all errors on previous day's assignments.

Consequences
Free time will be available for approximately ten minutes at the end of each class period for those who have met all the preceding conditions for that day. During free time, eligible persons may read comics, draw, listen to radio (if earplugs are used), play math games provided, work on other assignments, or engage in other relaxing activities that do not disturb others. Those who do not meet the

conditions or those who disturb others during free time must begin their homework assignment or proceed with other assigned tasks.

Signed: _____

(Student)

_____

(Teacher)

Concerns About Self-Management

As with most other strategies, the proposed use of self-management raises a number of important concerns for teachers. They may hesitate over the suitability of self-management techniques for some students: "Aren't elementary students a little too young for self-management?" "Can *this* work with retarded students?" "Don't some students have to be directed by others?" These are legitimate questions for which absolute answers are difficult, if not impossible. However, we believe that most students are capable of far more self-control than they presently exert. Even nursery-school children can be given opportunities at self-management. While this may involve only a simple choice between two activities, making choices is a step toward greater self-management. Retarded students, too, are probably more capable of demonstrating personal responsibility than many persons think. Of course, some students may require more direction than others. But self-control begins with proper control of the environment by someone else. Students who have been exposed to a setting in which others have failed to recognize and reward desired changes may initially need a great deal of direction. Once they receive consistent, predictable responses from important people, they can move to higher levels of self-management. Certainly, you will agree that students can develop self-management skills only when people in authority provide the opportunities for learning those skills.

Another concern of teachers is the trustworthiness of students who are given chances to govern themselves. Teachers tell us that a few students cannot be trusted to make accurate self-reports while others reportedly give themselves reinforcers they have not earned. Admittedly, the accuracy of self-reports may vary from student to student. However, "cheating" can be reduced through teacher surveillance. Students can also be "caught" keeping accurate records and properly reinforcing themselves. Remember, those behaviors that get rewarded by the teacher will undoubtedly increase in frequency.

The long-range effects of self-management are also a matter of concern. Teachers rightfully wonder if students who enthusiastically undertake self-management will continue with those efforts. Workman and Hector (1978), in reviewing the literature on behavioral self-control, found little evidence that the procedures are effective over a long period. However, these authors pointed out that the procedures did appear to be equal in effectiveness to external contingencies with three classes of behavior: on-task, disruptive, and academic. Despite the lack of followup data, they concluded that the effectiveness of behavioral self-control procedures in the classroom should warrant more widespread implementation, particularly in those situations in which teacher-administered or teacher-determined external contingencies are not feasible or are undesirable.

Perseverance in self-management efforts is probably affected by the goal an individual sets and the motivation to reach that goal. Teachers can help with both. They can caution students against setting unrealistic goals that are apt to create frustration and failure. Teachers can also praise students as they progress toward their goals. Few things are more motivating than positive responses from significant adults. Initial enthusiasm can be sustained, but teacher support may be required for some time. No one is suggesting that students can be turned loose and expected to perform indefinitely without any assistance.

Occasionally, teachers also express concern over the amount of teacher involvement that is required to teach self-management. Any teacher who has ever involved students in classroom management knows that a great deal of teacher time and effort is required. We do not deny it. No worthwhile procedure can be implemented without expending some energy. And although self-management tactics may initially require a lot from the teacher, we think a savings will be the long-term result. Teachers who are eventually freed from continuous monitoring and reinforcement of every student's behavior, for example, can devote more time to those who need more individual assistance. In addition, students who learn to assess their own behaviors, set appropriate tasks for themselves, and provide their own rewards are on the way to becoming responsible citizens. And that is what the business of education is all about.

Summary

In this chapter, we have pointed out that the ultimate goal of all education is successful management by students of their own behaviors. We have suggested that students do not learn self-responsibility by having others continuously manage their affairs or by having total control thrust upon them. Instead, the chapter stressed that students learn self-management in the same way any other task is learned. It was posited that teachers must help students become aware of alternative ways for achieving self-control, as well as provide opportunities for students to use those techniques. Self-recording, control of setting events, management of rewards and punishers, self-verbalization, and contracting were discussed as the principal techniques of self-control. A number of important concerns that teachers raise about self-control were also discussed. While the chapter has revealed the broad potential of self-management, teachers surely recognize that it does not free one from dependence on others. Concern, encouragement, and positive responses from others will always be needed. Coupled with external support, the learning of self-management skills is unlimited in value.

REFERENCES

Arwood, B.,Williams, R. L., and Long, J. D. "The effects of behavior contracts and behavior proclamations on social conduct and academic achievement in a ninth grade English class." *Adolescence 9* (1974): 425-436.

Atkins, J. W. and Williams, R. L. "The utility of self-report in determining reinforcement priorities of primary school children." *Journal of Educational Research 65* (1972): 324-328.

Arlin, M. and Whitley, W. "Perceptions of self-managed learning opportunities and academic locus of control: a causal interpretation." *Journal of Educational Psychology 70* (1978): 988-992.

Ballard, K. D. and Glynn, T. "Behavioral self-management in story writing with elementary school children." *Journal of Applied Behavior Analysis 8* (1975): 387-398.

Besalel-Azrin, B., Azrin, N. H., and Armstrong, P. M. "The student-oriented classroom: a method of improving student conduct and satisfaction." *Behavior Therapy 8* (1977): 193-204.

Bolstad, O.D. and Johnson, S. M. "Self-regulation in the modification of disruptive classroom behavior." *Journal of Applied Behavior Analysis 4* (1972): 443-454

Broden, M., Hall, R. V., and Mitts, B. "The effect of self-recording on the classroom behavior of two eighth-grade students." *Journal of Applied Behavior Analysis 4* (1971): 191-199.

Cantrell, R. P., Cantrell, M. L., Huddleston, C. M., and Woolridge, R. L. "Contingency contracting with school problems." *Journal of Applied Behavior Analysis 2* (1969): 215-220.

Clark, L. N. "Let's make a deal: contingency contracting with adolescents." *American Secondary Education 8* (1978): 12-23.

Dickinson, D. J., "Changing behavioral techniques." *Journal of School Psychology 6* (1968): 278-283.

Glynn, E. L., "Changing applications of self-determined reinforcement." *Journal of Applied Behavior Analysis 3* (1970): 123-132.

Grusec, J. E. and Kuczynski, L. "Teaching children to punish themselves and effects on subsequent compliance." *Child Development 48* (1977): 1296-1300.

Homme, L. "Human motivation and the environment." *In* N. Haring and R. Whelan, eds. *The Learning Environment: Relationship to Behavior Modification and Implications for Special Education.* Lawrence: University Press of Kansas, 1966.

——————, Csanyi, A. P., Gonzales, M. A., and Rechs, J. R. *How to Use Contingency Contracting in the Classroom.* Champaign, Illinois: Research Press, 1970.

Johnson, S. M. and White, G. "Self-observation as an agent of behavioral change." *Behavior Therapy 2* (1971): 488-497.

Kanfer, F. H. and Duerfeldt, P. H. "Motivational properties of self-reinforcement." *Perceptual and Motor Skills 25* (1967): 237-246.

Long, J. D., and Williams, R. L. "The utility of self-management procedures in modifying the classroom behaviors of mentally retarded adolescents." *Adolescence 41* (1976): 29-38.

Lovitt, T. C. and Curtiss, K. A. "Academic response rate as a function of teacher- and self-imposed contingencies." *Journal of Applied Behavior Analysis 2* (1969): 49-53.

Mahoney, M. J., Moura, N. G. M., and Wade, T. C. "The relative efficacy of self-reward, self-punishment, and self-monitoring techniques for weight loss." *Journal of Consulting and Clinical Psychology 40* (1973): 404-407.

Michenbaum, D. H. and Goodman, J. "Training impulsive children to talk to themselves: A means of developing self-control." *Journal of Abnormal Psychology 77* (1971): 115-126.

Nelson, R. O., Lipinski, D. P., and Black, J. L. "The reactivity of adult retardates' self-monitoring: a comparison among behaviors of different valences, and a comparison with token reinforcement." *The Psychological Record 26* (1976): 189-201.

O'Leary, K. D. "The effects of self-instruction on immoral behavior." *Journal of Experimental Child Psychology 6* (1968): 297-301.

Pease, G. A. and Tyler, V. O. "Self-regulation of time-out duration in the modification of disruptive classroom behavior." *Psychology in the Schools 16* (1978): 101-105.

Sagotsky, G., Patterson, C. J., and Lepper, M. R. "Training children's self-control: a field experiment in self-monitoring and goal-setting in the classroom." *Journal of Experimental Child Psychology 25* (1978): 242-253.

Sapp, G. L. "The application of contingency management systems to the classroom behavior of Negro adolescents." Paper presented at the meeting of the American Personnel and Guidance Association, Atlantic City, N.J., April, 1971.

White-Blackburn, G., Semb, S., and Semb, G. "The effects of a good-behavior contract on the classroom behaviors of sixth-grade students." *Journal of Applied Behavior Analysis 10* (1977): 312.

Williams, R. L. and Long, J. D. *Toward a Self-Managed Life Style.* Boston: Houghton Mifflin, 1979.

————, and Yoakley, R. W. "The utility of behavior contracts and behavior proclamations with advantaged senior high school students." *Journal of School Psychology 10* (1972): 329-338.

Workman, E. A. and Hector, M. A. "Behavioral self-control in classroom settings: a review of the literature." *Journal of School Psychology 16* (1978): 227-236.

Zegiob, L., Klukas, N., and Junginger, J. "Reactivity of self-monitoring procedures with retarded adolescents." *American Journal of Mental Deficiency 83* (1978): 156-163.

CHAPTER EIGHT

RIGHT AND WRONG: ETHICAL AND LEGAL PROBLEMS OF CLASSROOM MANAGEMENT

"Did you see yesterday's paper? One of the teachers at P.S. 21 has been sued for negligence."

"Oh, dear. With all of the lawsuits, I'm almost afraid to go into my classroom. Who knows what may happen next?"

The classroom management strategies described in the previous chapters share a common purpose: behavior change. In most classrooms, techniques such as these are used to bring student behavior into conformity with a teacher's concept of desirable or appropriate behavior. Many decisions pertaining to classroom management rest entirely on a teacher's sense of right and wrong. Ethical and legal questions may, thus, arise concerning the goals of behavior change and the techniques that are used to reach them. Teachers are unlikely to use methods that are regarded as immoral, and rightly so. Similarly, few teachers use techniques that are clearly in violation of the law. Unfortunately, decisions must sometimes be made in haste and may be based on misconceptions of the appropriateness of various behavior change techniques. Often, the laws pertaining to school affairs are learned after a costly mistake has been made.

In this chapter, we will examine some of the ethical and legal aspects of classroom control. Each teacher must decide for himself which behaviors are to be changed in the classroom and the techniques that will be used to make the change. Critical study of the issues can facilitate the decision-making process, and may clarify previous misconceptions. Careful deliberation of the issues should assist you in making your own decisions in the classroom.

Ethical Issues: Goals of Behavior Change

The accepted goal of the educational process is to change behavior. Six-year-olds entering first grade have few academic skills, and their social behaviors are immature. At the end of their public school training, however, society expects them to exhibit advanced academic skills and mature and independent functioning. The entire schooling process, then, from grades one through twelve is directed toward this goal.

In recent years, new techniques have been developed that increase the probability of desired behavior changes and, as a result, questions pertaining to the goals of behavior change have become more crucial. Several issues have been raised and debated in the professional literature, for example: are behavior management techniques being used merely to induce conformity; who should make the decisions in regard to which behaviors should be changed; does one stifle creativity when students are required to conform to the expectations of the teacher?

In addition to issues pertaining to the goals of behavior change, questions have been raised about behavior change methodology. Is it ethical to use extrinsic or tangible rewards? When rewards are made contingent on desired behavior, is the process equal to bribery? Does a reward system teach undesirable values, for example, that desired aims can be bought? What are the long-range effects of providing tangible rewards? Other issues revolve around the use of negative behavior control techniques. Is it ethical to use criticism or corporal punishment to control students' behavior? What are the problems in using response cost or time out? Should aversive methods be used in the classroom? These questions and others may arise in any consideration of classroom control. Your resolution of these issues will be reflected in the goals you set in the classroom and the methods you use to reach them.

Purpose of Behavior Change

Traditionally, teachers have been considered successful when they are able to maintain a classroom in which students sit quietly, refrain from talking to their neighbors, and raise their hand for permission to speak. The emphasis in recent years on informal education and open classrooms has changed this situation for some teachers. However, many principals still expect to see a quiet, well-controlled group of students when they patrol the halls or walk into a classroom.

In reviewing behavior management studies that appeared in the *Journal of Applied Behavior Analysis* from 1968 to 1970, Winett and Winkler (1972) concluded that children in these studies were not allowed to be children, but, rather, were required to be docile, quiet, and obedient "young adults." Suggesting that such a situation might be destructive, these authors proposed that a freer classroom atmosphere can also be conducive to learning. Further, they contended that behavior modification techniques are often used to maintain the status quo in the schools.

Certainly, the question of whether behavior change techniques should be used to induce conformity of this type must be taken seriously. We would agree with most educators that academic skills cannot be taught successfully when the classroom climate is utter chaos. There is a need to maintain a classroom environment that enables students to hear class discussions and to finish assigned seatwork without constant interruption; on the other hand, maintaining a quiet classroom sometimes becomes the primary goal. Students' mastery of academic and independent thinking skills becomes secondary to their demeanor in the classroom. Sophistication in the area of behavior control techniques has increased the probability that teachers will attain whatever goals are set in the classroom. Consequently, the goals of behavior change become critically important.

Personal Versus Institutional Goals. McIntire (1974) contends that many schools propose to provide students with the requisite skills necessary for attainment of personal goals that will increase happiness and effectiveness. However, schools may have a number of other goals, such as "keeper of parental morality, daytime babysitter, organizer of the PTA, and depository of young potential workers in order to keep the job market clear" (p. 409). Further, McIntire believes that schools often set convenient goals regardless of students' needs. For example, talking may be prohibited, even though social and verbal skills are important. Conformity may be required, not only in regard to clothes and conduct but also in the intellectual area. Discussions of controversial issues may, therefore, be avoided.

The definition of personal versus institutional goals is often skirted by educators. In considering your own school policies and procedures, you may find that certain rules effectively stifle individual goal-setting and independent thinking. However, most educators would deny that such a situation may also occur in the classroom. For example, do you tend to steer away from controversial discussion topics? Do you fail to solicit students' input regarding classroom rules and topics to be discussed? Have you ever asked students what they would like to accomplish during the school year? Reducing the conflict between institutional and individual goals may result in increased goal attainment for all.

Guidelines for Goal Setting. There is controversy over who should set educational and behavioral goals for students. Traditionally, adults have set the goals, and adults, unless they are incapacitated or otherwise incapable, have been allowed to make the decisions about what to do with their own lives. It has generally been accepted that individuals will be adequately able to set personal goals when they reach adulthood, but this assumption may be erroneous for many individuals. McIntire presents the thesis that goals are best set after individuals have been taught how to set goals. Skills necessary for the self-selection of goals include: recognition and evaluation of alternatives, anticipation of future consequences, and accurate assessment of one's current behaviors. We also believe that pinpointing desired behaviors, teaching, and modeling goal-setting behavior are crucial elements in helping students learn to set appropriate goals, and, as the chapter on self-management explains, we believe most students are capable of much more self-direction than has previously been thought possible. If you allow students the freedom to determine some of their own goals and manage their own lives, it should reduce the likelihood that behavior management techniques will be used merely to enforce nonmeaningful goals and conformity.

STUDENTS MAKE THEIR OWN RULES

Elardo (1978), in a study incorporating a token reward system, found that the older children (ages 9-11) were able to assume much responsibility for developing and supervising a token program. In this study, a token reward system was planned by a consultant and staff members and initiated in an entire inner-city school (grades 1-5) at the beginning of the 1972-1973 school year. Students were allowed to earn tokens for acceptable behavior and academic work. Penalties in the form of tickets were issued for misbehavior at lunch and recess. Tokens were deposited in the token bank daily and were exchangeable for various activities. Students who failed to earn enough tokens to allow their participation in an activity were required to spend the Thursday or Friday activity period in a quiet "helping" room.

In order to prevent students from building up reserve stocks of tokens and then misbehaving until more tokens were needed, the program was changed in November to require that bank balances be returned to zero each week. The change upset the fifth-grade students who asked for some involvement in the decision-making process. These students were asked to plan their own rules in consultation with their teacher. In January, the entire student body developed a uniform set of rules for all classes. Following this change, the program was implemented harmoniously and without the use of corporal punishment for the remainder of the academic year.

Elardo's article describing school wide behavior modification programs illustrates the need for educators to know more about how to successfully implement behavior modification techniques in school settings. In particular, Elardo notes a need to find out how to better design school justice systems. What is your opinion?

Conformity Versus Creativity. The issue of student conformity versus independent behavior has not been satisfactorily resolved for many educators. Is a student being molded into a conforming adult when he is expected to sit quietly and follow class rules, but is also encouraged to think independently on controversial issues and to pursue research related to his areas of interest? We believe that stimulating ideas can be presented and independent thinking skills can be established at the same time students are conforming to classroom rules. Few students who sit quietly in class behave in the same manner in other settings, such as at home or at play. In fact, similar behavior would be expected to occur only to the extent that the non-classroom setting resembled the classroom and to the extent that the same types of behavior were reinforced.

We are not saying that students should be shaped into docile beings who accept any rule without protest. We feel that students should be taught to discriminate between appropriate or inappropriate behaviors for a particular setting. The primary emphasis in the classroom should be on learning and thinking. Behavior requirements should be developed in accordance with the type of skill being taught. Rules for rules' sake should be avoided.

Another issue in changing behavior is the shy, withdrawn child. Most teachers feel that shyness is an undesirable state and that the child should be helped to overcome it. Other teachers argue that many creative individuals are shy and withdrawn and, thus, one should never attempt to change this behavior. The question becomes, does the use of behavior management techniques to induce outgoing behavior in shy individuals stifle creativity?

Although many creative individuals tend to be shy and reclusive, there are also scores of shy people who will never become creative geniuses, who show, by their demeanor, that they are desperately unhappy. Through use of positive behavior management techniques, a shy child may be helped to experience success in social relationships and become a "happier" individual. We do not believe that it is necessary for a child to be unhappy and withdrawn to be creative. Furthermore, if solitary behavior is more satisfying to a child than interacting with others, he will probably fail to respond to attempts at behavior change.

Ethical Issues: Behavior Change Methodology

Ethical considerations related to classroom management often involve the methodology employed to effect the change. Both positive and negative techniques have been questioned. These questions are important and deserve serious consideration in any discussion of behavior change methodology. A teacher who has ethical reservations about a particular behavior change technique will probably not apply it. We will discuss some of the issues that have been raised. A careful perusal of these issues should aid you in deciding which methodology you are willing to use in your classroom.

Ethical Considerations Related to Positive Behavior Change Techniques

Positive behavior management techniques include those methods discussed in detail in Chapter Three. Essentially, the process provides a reward or payoff, which may be social, tangible, or an activity, when a student exhibits desired behavior. What is necessary is that the student perform the desired behavior in order to earn the reward. The application of tangible reinforcers has raised an ethical question. Can the use of tangible rewards to change or maintain behavior be equated with bribery?

O'Leary, Poulos, and Devine (1972) discuss in detail eleven major objections that have been raised against the use of tangible reinforcers to change behavior. These include concerns about whether a child will be taught to be bad because he is rewarded when he is good, whether receiving tangible rewards teaches recipients to use tangibles to control others, and whether reward systems teach self-doubt by implying through "if-then" statements that one doubts the ability of the individual to perform the behavior. Further concerns have been expressed about the dispenser of token reinforcement—will he come to rely on this form of behavior control and fail to develop other methods—and on individuals who are not rewarded for displaying a particular behavior. Will people who observe others being rewarded for behaving appropriately behave inappropriately in order to be offered rewards for desirable behavior? Additional questions relate to the duration of behavior change achieved via tangible reinforcement and to the effect of rewarding certain behaviors on other behaviors that are not rewarded. A final objection suggests that tangible reinforcement may interfere with learning.

Reinforcement Versus Bribery. In considering this question, it becomes apparent that different standards are applied to children than to adults. For example, as employed adults, we are presently receiving a payoff for performing the duties outlined in our job description. Most of us would be highly unlikely to continue if financial remuneration were suddenly discontinued. Are our employers bribing us to work? Or, to ask a more personal question, are you being bribed to teach? Most of us would answer a resounding "No"! We feel that we are making honest and important contributions through our work. On the other hand, outlining desired behaviors for a child (e.g., making a bed, picking up toys, completing homework, bringing books to class), and providing a tangible reward contingent on the desired behaviors is often regarded as bribery. Expectations for children are sometimes higher than for adults. Just as work is usually not intrinsically rewarding enough for us to continue when external support (i.e., the paycheck) is withdrawn, so certain behaviors required of children may not be inherently reinforcing. External support may be required until the behavior is well-established and is being maintained by intrinsic reinforcement.

Apparently, the concept of bribery remains unclear for many people. The primary definition of a bribe agrees with the view of rewarded behavior only to the extent that an individual in a position of trust is induced to commit illegal or corrupt acts. Careful study of the classroom research using tangible reinforcers indicates that the procedure has been used to induce appropriate academic and social behavior in the research subjects. No studies can be found in which illegal and corrupt acts receive a payoff. Thus, tangible rewards for appropriate behavior cannot be considered bribes in the primary sense of the word. The secondary definition of a bribe, "something that serves to induce or influence," is more consistent with the use of tangible rewards in the home or classroom. Using the term in this very general sense also means that most of us are bribed daily.

Effects of Tangible Rewards on Recipients. The effects of receiving tangible rewards contingent on performing a specified behavior can be considerable. On the positive side, the receiver will probably emit the desired behaviors, and, thus, may be able to learn new skills and to improve his functioning in the environment. On the negative side, greed may inadvertantly be taught and the receiver may imitate the dispenser in attempting to control others through this method. Some receivers may attempt to manipulate the dispenser by demanding rewards for the performance of additional behaviors. For these reasons, tangible reinforcers should be used only when social or activity rewards are ineffective. In such a case, they should be paired with intangibles (e.g., praise) in an attempt to develop other reinforcing events which will gradually induce a more naturalistic system. Fortunately, as people learn to perform new skills, the new behaviors often become reinforcing in their own right, and extrinsic rewards are no longer required for the maintenance of the behavior.

The possibility that a person will be taught to be bad by being rewarded for being good increases when rewards are not offered until he engages in undesirable behavior.

AN UNEXPECTED RESULT

Susie, a fourth grader, liked to walk about the room and talk to her peers. Whenever she did this, her teacher, Mrs. Brewster, responded by saying, "Sit down, Susie, and I'll let you . . . ." The offending behavior invariably ceased at that time. However, Susie was observed to get up more and more frequently. At one point, she asked Mr. Brewster, "If I don't talk to Brenda, will you let me . . . ?"

Mrs. Brewster was aghast at Susie's presumptiveness. Then she realized that her method of applying positive reinforcement might be teaching Susie to behave badly in order to receive additional privileges. She, therefore, spelled out the contingencies in advance for all the children and refrained from offering a special reward when a child was observed to be misbehaving. With the contingencies made clear and with consistency in implementing the program, no other problems were encountered.

In such situations as the one described above, if-then statements ("If you'll stop talking, then you may have some bubble gum") contribute to the problem. O'Leary, Poulos, and Devine contend that continued use of if-then statements, even for the development of positive skills, may be aversive to the recipient, and suggest that the use of these statements be minimized as much as possible.

Effects of Tangible Rewards on Dispensers. The successful use of tangible reinforcement may also have an effect on the dispenser of the rewards. Certainly, finding that one can control another person's behavior through use of these procedures is potentially reinforcing. It is important, then, that individuals who administer behavior change programs gradually diminish tangible rewards in favor of social reinforcement. Perhaps teachers should think of tangible rewards only as a temporary tool, and, perhaps, they should consider a self-monitoring program to determine the extent to which their classroom behavior change program continues to rely on tangible reinforcement. No teacher wants to fall into the trap of using tangible rewards simply because he is getting reinforced by the system. As with all classroom management systems, the ultimate aim is to help the students.

Effects of Tangible Rewards on Non-Rewarded Individuals. The effects of giving tangible rewards to one person and not to others must also be considered. When children who are not rewarded see one or more of their peers receiving rewards for performing a particular behavior, they may feel that the situation is unfair.

REINFORCING NEAT BEHAVIOR

Jerry was a chronically messy student. Mr. Delano decided to use a token program to increase neat behavior. Thus, he instituted a desk check three times a day, and awarded tokens when Jerry's desk met his criteria for neatness. The tokens were exchangeable for money to operate a coke machine. Jerry's messy behavior improved rapidly, and he became very proud of his neat desk. To Mr. Delano's surprise, however, other students began to complain bitterly about not receiving tokens for their clean desks. In two weeks, messy desks began to proliferate in the classroom. What appeared to be a successful behavior change program had degenerated into an unworkable situation.

We would be in much the same situation as the above if we worked overtime without pay only to discover that one of our colleagues received pay for the same service. Williams and Anandam (1973) suggest that this type of problem can be circumvented in the classroom by contracting with all of the students. Under a contract, students may be allowed to pursue independent alternatives and still receive a reward. Thus, one individual is not singled out for special attention.

Effects of Non-Natural Rewards. In general, behaviors supported by reinforcers that are unnatural to the situation (e.g., tokens) may extinguish when the external support is withdrawn. A teacher who proposes the use of tangible reinforcement must make an effort to develop more natural reinforcers (e.g., social attention) if the behavior change is to be of long duration. O'Leary, Poulos, and Devine suggest that the use of tokens may be inadvisable if the program is short-term, because tokens may come to represent a distraction which interferes with learning. This effect is not felt to hold when the program continues for a long period of time.

Ethical Considerations Related to Negative Behavior Change Techniques

Ethical questions also arise out of the use of negative techniques for change. Two negative means, in particular, have traditionally been accepted and used frequently to control behavior in the classroom: criticism and corporal punishment. During the past ten years, two additional methods have been employed with increasing frequency: time out and response cost. We have already discussed the use of these strategies in Chapter Four, but we want to reconsider them in this chapter, primarily in light of the ethical and legal questions they pose for teachers. The major ethical issue related to negative means of behavior change is whether they should be employed at all. Is it wrong to punish a child? The answer to this question involves a value judgement that we cannot make for you. However, we will discuss some of the ethical issues that should be taken into account when negative means of behavior change are considered for use in the classroom.

Corporal Punishment

The roots of corporal punishment go back to the Puritan settlement in the Massachusetts Bay Colony (Piele, 1978). Use of this technique for behavior control continues to represent a well-established means of discipline in the schools. Yet, the question of who will decide what behaviors should be changed is seldom asked when it is considered. Perhaps the relatively short-term effectiveness of this technique has resulted in complacency. Further, corporal punishment is often employed without prior planning. Regardless of the frequency of application, the question pertaining to the purpose of behavior change should apply here. A teacher who paddles a child for talking during class periods is communicating his values loudly and clearly. A teacher who spanks a child who talks back is publishing a belief that children should show respect for those in authority.

Educators in school districts that allow corporal punishment must ask whether an individual has a right to inflict pain on another human being. Certainly, most of us refrain from doing so on an adult. In the case of a child, however, physical pain is often inflicted with the verbal justification that the child will "learn to do better" or that the whipping is administered for the "good of the child." As pointed out in Chapter Four, it is known that the punisher is modeling aggressive behavior for the child, and children tend to imitate aggressive behavior that they have seen modeled. Children who are abused by their parents often grow up to abuse their own children. Furthermore, the use of corporal punishment may engender strong emotional reactions in the recipient. The possibility thus arises that children who are repeatedly physically punished may suffer emotional problems. When one is made to feel inconsequential, one's self-esteem cannot help but be lowered.

As we just mentioned, adults tend to refrain from physically striking adults. However, inflicting pain on others seems to continue in a different form. Criticism, sarcasm, and verbal downgrading of others results in emotional pain for the recipient. Is it possible that the negative events that are suffered in childhood are imitated, in perhaps a different and more acceptable form, in adulthood?

Additional questions related to the use of corporal punishment in school districts where it is legally sanctioned included the following: is this child entitled to the same rights as adults; what am I teaching this child by spanking him; will the child refrain from performing the deviant behavior, or will he learn that one can do as one pleases when big enough to exert power over others; emotionally, how will this child react to paddling; will he develop a dislike for the teacher; more serious, how can we be sure that emotional behaviors that are engendered by physical punishment will not generalize to the school itself; will the child begin to dislike coming to school. Behavior theory postulates that repeated pairing of physical punishment and school could result in such a reaction. No conscientious teacher can say that this situation would be desirable.

Criticism. Criticism represents a commonly used method for changing behavior, but one seldom hears ethical questions raised about it. Nevertheless, not all teachers and parents are constructive in their approach. For example, criticism may be employed without thought given to the overall effect it can have on the recipient. It is not unusual to hear a teacher say, "John is a lazy child. He could do better if he tried," or "Mary, you are a sloppy writer. You must learn to be neater." Most individuals who attempt to change behavior through criticism are quick to point out that only "constructive" criticism is used. The term "constructive criticism," however, is often used to cover any criticism they might employ.

Ginott (1965) defined constructive criticism as criticism that is confined to the target behavior and that omits negative remarks about personality. For example, a teacher might say, "Mary, papers are easier to read when they are neatly copied." Such a statement provides information regarding the task to be completed, and it casts no aspersions on the recipient. Or, perhaps, a teacher might say, "John, in order to complete your arithmetic assignments on time, it will be necessary for you to work during study time rather than look at a comic book." This statement tells John what is necessary, but does not imply that he is lazy. In particular, one should refrain from using derogatory adjectives when pointing out the shortcomings of others. According to Ginott, when parents call their child clumsy or stupid, the result is a chain of reactions that makes both the child and the parents miserable. When a child is repeatedly described in derogatory terms, he begins to believe these things about himself, and begins to behave in a manner that is consistent with these beliefs. In order to use criticsim in a constructive manner, teachers should focus on the task to be done, avoid attacking the personality of the recipient, and avoid derogatory comments. And teachers should give criticism quietly, limit it to the situation at hand, and be brief with their remarks. Our opinion is that destructive criticism is always unethical and unnecessary. How do you view such criticism?

Time Out. Time out, as you will recall from Chapter Four, is a behavior control technique that involves removing an individual from a reinforcing situation and placing him in a situation that does not provide rewards. Unfortunately, it is sometimes used with abandon, thus taking on the characteristics of an aversive technique. Situations have been described in which children or adults were isolated for hours or placed in dark or locked rooms. When time out is applied in a harsh fashion, individuals may be deprived not only of basic social contact but also of basic human needs for long periods of time. In addition, the person's legal rights may be violated. Intense frustration and other emotional reactions may be associated with the process. As with any negative behavior control technique, care must be taken that an inhumane approach is not used. Time out should be employed only when one has a basic understanding of the method and its application. Arrangements should be made for continual monitoring of any behavior change program incorporating time out in order to insure that the method is not abused.

Response Cost. You will remember from earlier discussions that the classroom use of response costs usually involves the loss of a privilege or points toward a grade. The technique appears to be a reasonable method for controlling behavior when used properly. For example, care should be taken that minor infractions of the rules do not result in extreme penalties. Failure to turn in homework on Tuesday should not result in loss of enough points to fail a student for the week. The fine or cost should be appropriate to the "crime." Earning an excessive fine on Monday would, no doubt, remove incentive for completing assignments for the remainder of the week. On the other hand, a very minor fine may result in no behavior change. Thus, a teacher must attempt to set an optimal and fair penalty when using this technique.

It is especially important that the cost of misbehaving be specified in advance. The technique should not suddenly be applied at the whim of a teacher. If students are to learn to control their own behavior, they must learn to appreciate in advance the consequences of performing specified behaviors. Erratic application of behavior control techniques does not always afford them this opportunity.

The response-cost technique can be applied on a group basis as well as on an individual basis. Some teachers choose to use the procedure with entire classes.

FAIR OR UNFAIR?

Mr. Bluefield, a ninth-grade shop teacher, continually had a problem with tardiness to his sixth-period class. He decided that the problem would be solved only if he imposed a stiff penalty. Accordingly, he announced that each time a student was late, the entire class would be denied the privilege of being dismissed five minutes earlier to board school buses. Since the problem was confined to two or three students who were chronically late, the rest of the students complained bitterly about the contingencies. As expected, group pressure was applied to the boys, and the situation improved somewhat. However, tardiness was not completely eliminated, and the class a a whole continued to lose occasionally the special privilege of boarding the bus early. It was circulated through the student grapevine that Mr. Bluefield was an unfair teacher.

The application of the response-cost technique on a group contingent basis raises questions of an ethical nature. Is it fair to penalize several children for the misbehavior of one child? Should group pressure be applied in changing an individual student's behavior? The group contingent response-cost technique is generally a powerful one for changing behavior. However, we believe that response cost for an entire group should be considered a supplementary means of behavior control, to be used only when the behavior of several students needs to be changed at the same time. Further, group contingent programs should be of short duration. Ultimately, each student should be required to deal with the consequences of his own behavior. Is it right to ask a student to accept indefinitely the consequences of peers' behaviors?

GUIDELINES FOR EDUCATORS

The ethical implications of behavior modification remain a legitimate concern. The public at large has become more aware of this method of behavior change and the approach has been attacked by the press and politicians. Most guidelines covering ethical use of these techniques were developed using behavioral procedures on clinical patients in a closed setting. Harris and Kapche (1978) propose that the following issues be addressed in the use of behavior modification procedures in a school setting:

1. Is the child who has been referred for special services a legitimate target for a behavior modification program? Does initial observation reveal that the problem behavior is exhibited more frequently than normal?
2. How would changing the target behavior benefit the child or group of children? Whose values are represented in determining the behaviors to be changed? Does the change focus on positive goals (what he should be doing) rather than negative goals (what he should *not* be doing).
3. How is data to be collected and maintained? How is accountability to be demonstrated?
4. How will confidentiality of records be maintained?
5. Have the basic procedures been determined prior to implementation of the program?
6. Have behavioral change procedures been selected on the basis of: demonstrated effectiveness, appropriateness relative to behaviors,

rapidity of effect on behavior, fewest possible adverse side effects?
7. Is the behavior modifier well-trained in the ethics and implementation of behavior modification techniques?

Legal Issues: Students' Rights

In the past, teachers and principals considered it their job to maintain discipline and to teach in the way they saw fit. Little attention was given to the rights of students or to the techniques used to maintain classroom control. This situation has changed in recent years. School personnel must now be aware of the legal implications of techniques used in the classroom. In fact, many teachers consider it prudent to carry some type of malpractice insurance in the event that legal problems arise over something that has happened in the classroom. Students' rights and due process are terms that have been added to the vocabulary of most educators. Parents and students now realize that there are definite limits to the authority that teachers and principals can exercise. We will discuss some of the issues now facing teachers with regard to legal aspects of behavior control. It is important to be aware of the current status of these issues. It is equally important to be aware that legal interpretations may change and that new issues may arise, which can have legal implications for teachers.

Due Process

The Fifth Amendment to the Constitution provides in part that "No person shall be ... deprived of life, liberty, or property, without due process of law." The Fourteenth Amendment further states, "Nor shall any State deprive any person of life, liberty, or property, without due process of law; nor deny to any person within its jurisdiction the equal protection of the laws." Basically, due process has been interpreted to require that prior notice of prohibited behavior be provided. In addition, notification of when the penalty is to be applied for some suspected reason must also be given (Martin, 1975). In the past, students have not always been accorded the privilege of due process, with the result that many have been expelled without adequate hearing, or have been required to accept severe and unfair treatment. Court decisions (Gault, 1967; Goss & Lopez, 1975) within the past decade have provided new guidelines for interpreting these clauses as they apply to children. Basically, the Gault case made it clear that the rights guaranteed by the

"The Bill of Rights he knows—the Bill of wrongs he forgets!"

Constitution are not for adults alone. The Goss and Lopez case held that students facing suspensions from school are entitled to due process under the law. The court further held that students have a right to know the charges against them and be given an opportunity to respond to them. Thus, the idea that children have basic rights has now been made clear by the courts. Teachers and school administrators can no longer overlook this aspect of law when making decisions pertaining to behavior control. Ritchie (1973) suggested the following guidelines that still remain appropriate: (1) rules and procedures for dealing with conflicts between school and student should be nonadversary in nature and design; and (2) procedures relating to serious student-school conflicts that could result in suspension or expulsion of a student should include due process exemplified by prior knowledge of the behavior that is required or prohibited, prior notification that the proposed penalty is to be imposed and the specific reason for imposing the penalty, opportunity for a hearing regarding the charges, and a fair decision.

Equal Protection

Individuals are not only entitled to due process of law but also to equal protection by the law. Martin (1975) interprets equal protection to mean that "a state agency cannot treat one group substantially differently from other groups entitled to the same treatment!"

EDUCATION: A RIGHT OF ALL CITIZENS

Marian, a girl of normal intelligence, was a victim of cerebral palsy, which limited her ability to engage in all the activities of children her age. In order for her to be successful in school, special arrangements were necessary. At times, she had seizures that required attention from her caretaker. Thus, very early in her school career, teachers suggested to her parents that she did not fit in and that it would be best if she were not sent to school. Her parents were unwilling to accept this suggestion, feeling that their daughter was entitled to the same basic education as were nonhandicapped children. However, they were unsuccessful in obtaining educational training for Marian. Now, twenty years later, their dream for their daughter has become a reality for many other handicapped children.

Fortunately, the equal protection clause covers the handicapped. In addition, identifiable groups (e.g., blacks, Spanish-speaking, females) cannot be singled out for treatment different from that received by other students. Martin suggests that one should examine a chosen intervention strategy to determine whether it incorporates different treatment for one discernible group. If so, it should be changed. In addition, one should make sure that any discernible group of people is not excluded from the treatment without justification.

Freedom of Speech and the Press

The First Amendment guarantee concerning freedom of speech and of the press also applies to the student press. Thus, schools cannot prohibit freedom of expression as long as the rights of others, either students or nonstudents, are not violated (Gibbs, 1978). The protection applies whether or not a student newspaper is school sponsored (Flygare, 1977). School authorities may exercise prior restraint through reasonable regulation on student expression only when evidence is available that "substantial disruption of, or material interference with, school activities and appropriate discipline in the operation of the school or interference with the rights of others" (Gibbs, 1978) will occur. Fear or apprehension concerning the outcome of specific student expressions is insufficient to allow administrators to impose regulations. Therefore, you should be aware that you cannot censure the student press according to your own ideas about what should or should not be printed.

DO YOU KNOW YOUR RIGHTS (AND WRONGS)?

Blackman, Broussard, and Mundt (1978) devised a study to determine whether high school principals, faculty advisors, and students editors were knowledgeable about students' rights of expression. A questionnaire containing ten sets of "facts" (each set contained a First Amendment question that had been presented to the judgement of a court) were submitted to each principal, advisor, and editor at 126 randomly selected high schools from thirty-one states. Three hundred seventy-eight subjects were surveyed. In order that the answers be based on principles of law rather than on recognizable cases, the questionnaire contained hypothetical cases that had been suggested by actual court decisions.

Results of the study suggested that principals, advisors, and editors do not have adequate knowledge of First Amendment precedents involving the student press. Judgments were made by these individuals based on self-interest rather than the law. With one exception, in cases involving some form of principal-student confrontation, more student editors than did principals sided with the student position. The advisors tended to occupy a middle position.

Blackmon, Broussard, and Mundt's introduction to the study provides a summation for educators: "The law is clear enough: student publications enjoy First Amendment rights in pretty much the same manner and degree as their adult counterparts."

Legal Issues: Behavior Change Techniques

Behavior change techniques should be scrutinized to detect legal implications that may be related to their use or misuse. Improperly applied, some techniques may result in curtailment of basic student rights. Due process and equal protection may not be afforded when the technique is used. This can happen with positive reward systems as well as with negative, such as corporal punishment and time out.

Positive Reward Systems

Positive behavior management techniques have been fully described in previous chapters, and ethical aspects related to reward systems have been discussed in this chapter. An additional consideration pertaining to positive rewards may have legal implications. Basically, one should insure that students are not deprived of items to which they are entitled as a right. For example, John may certainly be motivated to earn the privilege of eating his lunch. However, the right to eat is basic, and manipulation of a right such as this can have legal implications. It is better that he be allowed to earn a bag of potato chips as an extra treat and that his basic meal be noncontingent on a specific behavior. To quote Martin (p. 126), "If the program leads to a severe change in status or if personal property is taken away and used as a reward to be earned, it may violate the Fifth Amendment." Therefore, teachers should question the frequent practice of confiscating student property that is to be returned when the student has met a certain behavioral or academic standard.

Time Out

As we stated earlier, time out has often been used inappropriately. Martin, in discussing this technique, points out the importance of providing for due process (e.g., notice of intent to discipline, allowance of a period of time to prepare a defense, and a hearing) when isolation is imposed for disciplinary reasons. Fortunately, very few teachers consider long periods of isolation to be necessary motivators of student behavior. But what of short periods in a time-out room? Martin (p. 86) suggests that if one can assure that "any administration of time out as a motivating technique will not stretch to an hour or otherwise represent a substantial deprivation of liberty, then it might be used. If you cannot make that guarantee, then it should not even be attempted." Any educator who proposes to use time out should be aware of the legal ramifications pertaining to its use. Certainly, if the technique cannot be applied appropriately, it should not be used at all.

Corporal Punishment

The use of physical punishment raises not only ethical questions; legal implications may also arise from its use or misuse. The Supreme Court ruling in *Baker vs. Owen* (1975) upheld a lower court opinion that schools have a right to use corporal punishment, under state law, even though the parents may object. In accordance with this ruling, procedural safeguards are: giving prior warning that certain behaviors will result in corporal punishment; arranging for another school official to witness the punishment; telling the witness, beforehand and in the student's presence, the reason for the punishment; and providing parents who request an explanation a written statement detailing the reasons for the punishment and the name of the witness. A more recent Supreme Court ruling (*Ingraham vs. Wright*, 1977) held that the cruel and unusual punishments clause of the Eighth amendment does not apply to corporal punishment which is used as a disciplinary measure in the public schools. The Court further held that the due process clause of the Fourteenth Amendment does not require that notice and hearing be given prior to the imposition of corporal punishment as that practice is limited and authorized by common law (Englander, 1978).

Do not assume from the above-mentioned cases that all teachers have a right to use corporal punishment. At least three states—Maine, Massachusetts, and New Jersey—presently prohibit it while Maryland permits it only in some counties (Lines, 1978). Even in states where corporal punishment is not explicitly prohibited by state law, local ordinances may prohibit its use. Remember, too, that although you may be permitted to use physical punishment, you cannot apply it indiscriminately. You should be aware that it is becoming increasingly common for parents to turn to the courts for redress in cases where they feel their child has been wronged or has been administered cruel and unusual punishment.

CORPORAL PUNISHMENT: A NEW RULING

The use of corporal punishment as a disciplinary measure in the public schools remains a controversial issue. It was again brought to the attention of the courts when Ingraham, Adams, and other students at Drew Junior High School, Dade County, Florida, charged they had been the victims of beatings which resulted in injuries ranging from a bleeding hematoma to a badly disfigured hand. A class-action claim was also included seeking relief against the use of corporal punishment in the Dade County School System. Following appeals through the lower courts, the case was heard by the United States Supreme Court in 1977. The Court held in *Ingraham vs. Wright* that the Eighth Amendment cruel-and-unusual-punishment clause was not applicable to the disciplinary process in the schools. Likewise, the Court held that the Fourteenth Amendment due process clause was not applicable in this case.

In writing the majority opinion, Justice Powell noted that schools are essentially open institutions where the support of family and friends is available. Therefore, he reasoned that the student has little need of the protection offered by the Eighth Amendment. Justice Powell further noted that students' interests are adequately protected by state law. The first type of safeguard is prescribed by Florida Statute and requires that the teacher confer with the principal before using corporal punishment on any student. The second safeguard results from the teacher's liability for civil damages in tort when corporal punishment that is unreasonable under the circumstances is used, and the third, the teacher's liability for the crime of assault and battery if a child is physically harmed.

The issue of corporal punishment remains controversial. The court ruling was a close one (5-4) with the minority opinion taking issue with the arguments offered in the majority opinion.

Flygare reports that the *Ingraham vs. Wright* decision will have no immediate impact on current policies related to the use of corporal punishment in the schools. States that ban corporal punishment will not be required to change while states and localities that permit such punishment may continue to do so. The debate on the use of corporal punishment is not ended with the *Ingraham vs. Wright* decision.

Legal Issues: Caution for Teachers

The vulnerability of teachers to liability for actions in the classroom is an increasing area of concern. Many teachers now consider it prudent to carry liability insurance to protect themselves in case litigation is brought against them. Most teachers are now aware of the legal ramifications of employing disciplinary measures such as corporal punishment. In using this behavior control technique, a teacher could be held liable for an intentional act. Not all teachers are aware that they can also be held liable for negligent conduct. According to Ripps (1975), the same principles and rules of law which apply to negligence when a teacher acts in a private capacity also apply to a teacher in the classroom, i.e., one must provide the same standard of care as would a reasonable and prudent person who is acting under the same circumstances. If a breach of duty causes damage or injury, the teacher can be held liable.

Intentional action for which teachers may be held liable is primarily interference with the person of the student. Assault and battery arising out of disciplinary acts of the teacher have comprised the majority of court suits. Teachers should take care to consider their actions carefully. Attempting to enforce one's "will upon a student without the authority of at least written rules and regulations is acting foolishly" (Ripps, 1975). A teacher cannot always rely on the institution for support.

Most court actions involving the supervisory role of teachers have been taken against teachers who are absent from the classroom when a student is injured. Therefore, you should always arrange for adequate supervision when you find it necessary to leave the classroom. To help provide protection in the legal sense, evidence of a well-developed plan for adequate supervision should be maintained at all times. Risks are particularly high in gym and laboratory classes. Teachers must supervise properly *and* prevent injury. It is extremely important that instructions be given regarding basic procedures with equipment and other potential dangers. Failure to provide necessary safety equipment, e.g., guard rails, can result in liability. However, the availability of the equipment alone is not enough to protect the teacher. It must be maintained (Ripps, 1975).

The influence of the courts on the conduct of teachers and administrators cannot be predicted at this time. Issues continue to arise which may eventually be settled by the courts. Teachers should keep abreast of new developments and the ramifications of these developments on their own actions in the classroom.

TEACHERS AND PRIVATE EXPRESSION

In 1968, the Supreme Court, in a landmark decision (*Pickering vs. Board of Education*) held that Pickering, a high school teacher, had as great a constitutional right as any other citizen to public expression on political issues. Other court decisions, *Perry vs. Sindermann (1972)* and *M. Healthy vs. Doyle* (1977), have further upheld teachers' rights to public expression. A recent Supreme Court ruling in *Givhan vs. Western Line Consolidated School District* (1977) held that teachers also have a constitutional right to private expression as guaranteed under the First Amendment. In this case, Givhan had sued following her failure to be recommended for reappointment based in part on the principal's report that she interferred with his job by making "petty and unreasonable demands." Based on the ruling in this case, Flygare reports that the protection afforded private expression may be somewhat different from that afforded public expression. Basically, teachers who choose to express their views privately must do so in a manner that does not interfere with the "regular operation of the schools." Otherwise, teachers' expressions may be restrained or punished, possibly by dismissal.

Legal Issues: Accountability

Undoubtedly, teachers and other school personnel will eventually have to become accountable for making changes in behavior. Unfortunately, the goals of many schools and teachers are so elusive as to make accountability impossible. For example, how does one measure whether a second grader has learned to become a good citizen? Cox (1977) argued that teachers are unable to control outcomes of teaching and, therefore, it is unfair to hold them accountable. For example, he feels that "school-ability", a student trait composed of several elements such as intelligence, attitudes toward school, self and others, language ability, and social class has more influence on the outcomes of instruction than the teacher's teaching methods. In his view, holding teachers accountable would foster a lower quality of education since he feels that teachers would be likely to set lower-level goals that would be most likely to be achievable. Raybin (1979) avoided the controversy over teachers' accountability for outcomes of instruction by suggesting that educators be held accountable for developing and implementing basic instructional programs in the various subject areas. Under his plan, a program of minimum essentials, by semester and grade level (or course title), would be developed by a responsible person in order to provide students with a certain amount of knowledge in the field. These minimum essentials would be agreed upon by teachers in the subject areas and would require only forty to fifty percent of class time for mastery by the average student. The plan would allow significant time for other teaching activities by each individual teacher. Since there is no guarantee that students would eventually learn the material, accountability under Raybin's plan is seen to rest upon implementation rather than outcomes of the program.

Regardless of the controversy among educators concerning accountability, it is conceivable that the public will more and more hold educators accountable for making specific changes in students' behavior. Setting precise goals and documenting students' progress will not only assist in teaching but can also provide information for accountability. While higher order goals may be more difficult to specify, one can subdivide these goals into component parts. The standards for judging achievement of any level goal rest on observable behavior. The task of the teacher becomes that of defining what the student will be doing when he has mastered the goal.

Summary

This chapter focused on ethical and legal implications related to the use of behavior management techniques in the classroom, and guidelines related to the ethical use of these techniques were presented. Specific ethical questions concerned with behavior change include: should behavior management techniques be used to induce conformity, who should make the decisions regarding the behaviors to be changed, and does changing shy, withdrawn behavior stifle creativity. Questions pertaining to positive behavior change methodology include: is it ethical to use tangible rewards, does a reward procedure teach desirable values, and is tangible reinforcement equal to bribery. Ethical questions arising from the use of negative behavior change techniques were seen to revolve around corporal punishment, criticism, time out, and response cost. Problems related to the use of these techniques were discussed.

The discussion of legal implications related to the use of behavior management techniques stressed the importance of educators' awareness of new developments in this area. Due process, equal protection under the law, and accountability represent concepts that should be meaningful to every educator. Specific problems that could be encountered with the use of reward systems and time out were delineated, as were actions for which a teacher might be held liable. The 1975 and 1977 Supreme Court decisions pertaining to corporal punishment were discussed and educators were cautioned to set school policies that are harmonious with existing laws and court rulings. Diligence in complying with these policies was also stressed.

REFERENCES

Blackmon, R. C., Broussard, E. J., and Mundt, W. R. "Before you judge your next student press First Amendment case." *Phi Delta Kappan 60* (1978): 105-107.

Cox, B. C. "Responsibility, Culpability, and the cult of accountability in education." *Phi Delta Kappan 59* (1977): 761-766.

Elardo, R. "Behavior modification in an elementary school: problems and issues." *Phi Delta Kappan 59* (1978): 334-338.

Englander, M. E. "The Court's corporal punishment mandate to parents, local authorities, and the profession." *Phi Delta Kappan 59* (1978): 529-532.

Flygare, T. J. "Ingraham v. Wright: the return of Old Jack Seaver." *Inequality in Education 23* (1978): 29-36.

————. "School-sponsored student newspapers are entitled to First Amendment protection." *Phi Delta Kappan 58* (1977): 768-769.

————. "Teachers' private expression: constitutionally protected, but with a limitation." *Phi Delta Kappan* (1979): 602-603.

————. The free speech rights of teachers: public v. private expression." *Phi Delta Kappan 60* (1978): 242-243.

————. "The Supreme Court approves corporal punishment." *Phi Delta Kappan 59* (1978): 347-348.

Gibbs, A. "The student press: institutional prerogatives versus individual rights." *Journal of College Student Personnel 19* (1978): 16-20.

Ginott, H. G. *Between Parent and Child.* New York: The Macmillan Company, 1965.

Harris, A. and Kapche, R. "Behavior modification in schools: ethical issues and suggested guidelines." *Journal of School Psychology 16* (1978): 25-33.

Lines, P. M. "Corporal punishment after Ingraham: looking to state law." *Inequality in Education 23* (1978): 37-51.

Martin, R. "Legal challenges to behavior modification." Champaign, Illinois: Research Press, 1975.

McIntire, R. W. "Guidelines for using behavior modification in education." *In* R. Ulrich, T. Stachnik, and J. Mabry, eds. *Control of Human Behavior.* Glenview, Illinois: Scott, Foresman Company, 1974.

O'Leary, K. D., Poulos, R. W., and Devine, V. T. "Tangible reinforcers, bonuses or bribes?" *Journal of Consulting and Clinical Psychology 38* (1972): 1-8.

Piele, P. K. "Neither corporal punishment cruel nor due process due: the United States Supreme Court's decision in Ingraham v. Wright." *Journal of Law and Education 7* (1978): 1-19.

Raybin, R. "Minimum essentials and accountability." *Phi Delta Kappan 60* (1979): 374-375.

Ripps, S. R. "The tort liability of the classroom teacher." *Akron Law Review 9* (1975): 19-33.

Ritchie, R. M. "Due process and the principal." *Phi Delta Kappan 54* (1973): 697-698.

Williams, R. L. and Anandam, K. *Cooperative classroom management.* Columbus, Ohio: Charles E. Merrill Publishing Company, 1973.

Winnett, R. A., and Winkler, R. C., "Current behavior modification in the classroom: be still, be quiet, be docile." *Journal of Applied Behavior Analysis 5* (1972): 499-504.

CHAPTER NINE

ALPHA BUT NOT OMEGA: PUTTING IT ALL TOGETHER

As the preceding chapters have indicated, establishing effective classroom discipline is no simple matter. Many variables operate in every classroom, making it impossible to provide a single answer that can be universally applied. Furthermore, effective classroom management seldom results from making just *one* change in the classroom. The successful approach requires the careful orchestration of many factors. Of course, knowledge of and competency in applying specific disciplinary techniques are important, but equally so is the ability to "put it all together." The effective teacher is one who is able to see each situation objectively and to change as many aspects of the situation as required to establish and maintain an optimal learning environment. In this chapter, we want to look at the way suggestions in the previous chapters can be integrated to help with the establishment of effective classroom management. We will apply our suggestions to the solution of two common classroom problems. Then we will give you the opportunity to see how well you can do with specific problems.

General Review

The opening theme of the text defined classroom management: influencing students' behavior in a positive direction (Chapter One). Attention was then directed to the way in which teacher attitudes can substantially alter the students' awareness of a classroom environment as positive or negative (Chapter Two). We pointed out that the attitudes a teacher holds toward students as well as toward himself affect his perception of classroom incidents, and largely determine if they are viewed as troublesome or trivial. We noted that the ability of teachers to have a favorable and lasting influence on students is enhanced to the extent that they empathize, accept, and display genuine feelings toward others. Being able to admit mistakes, listening to what students have to say, looking for positive qualities in students, and responding positively to students were recognized as procedures that could go a long way in increasing genuine communication. Positive feelings about oneself were also recognized as being representative of positive attitudes toward others.

While we recognized the value of positive attitudes toward students and oneself, we stressed that attitudes *alone* cannot be expected to prevent or solve all classroom management problems. The way teachers organize the classroom was seen as having a profound effect on classroom behaviors. We cautioned that desired student behaviors often must be prompted and reinforced (Chapter Three) because many students simply do not bring all desired academic and social skills into the classroom. In brief, students have deficits. We emphasized that students should be told what is expected of them since rules cannot be followed if they have only been assumed by the teacher and have never been made explicit for the students. We also stressed that instructions should be given in a clear and simple manner; a setting that is conducive to learning should be provided; appropriate materials should be used; and critical behaviors should be modeled for the students.

After stressing the importance of prompting desired behaviors, attention was directed to the significance of properly managing the consequences of student behavior. We indicated that in order to establish and maintain effective classroom control, teachers must arrange to make desired behavior pay. Social rewards (e.g., teacher praise) were discussed as potential payoffs for most students. However, the necessity for providing a variety of rewards to meet the needs of every student was also recognized. You will remember that all payoffs must be rewarding to the recipient, not just to the dispenser of the reward. Although a number of specific suggestions were offered for proper control of consequences, the overall theme was: focusing on the positive, rather than the negative, aspects of student behaviors can exert a strong influence on the emotional climate and productivity of a classroom.

As noted earlier, exhibiting positive attitudes combined with prompting and reinforcing desired behaviors prevent many problems that teachers encounter. In fact, one of the best ways to avert problems is to increase desired student behaviors. But, as you would suspect, increases in appropriate student behaviors is not the total answer to classroom management. Teachers need strategies for dealing with excessive behaviors (Chapter Four). Altenative strategies identified for handling such problems were: altering setting events, reinforcing behaviors incompatible with inappropriate behaviors, using appropriate peer models, and extinction. Mildly punitive techniques such as soft reprimands, time out, response cost, and overcorrection were also discussed.

We suggested that classroom problems are frequently influenced by factors outside the classroom. The need for greater cooperative efforts between the school and the home was emphasized and practical ways of achieving better home-school relationships were examined in Chapter Five. We also noted in Chapter Six that virtually every teacher will face difficulties that transcend his level of ability. We asked that a working relationship be established with resource persons in the school in order to meet the needs of exceptional students. Throughout Chapters Five and Six the implication was that no one can solve all problems alone. We have always felt that seeking needed assistance from parents and colleagues is a sign of maturity—not of weakness.

We recommended that student involvement, too, play a major role in effective classroom management (Chapter Seven). The desire of most students for independence becomes especially acute as they grow older. Students, like most of us, like to feel they have a measure of control over what happens to them in daily life. What is more, students are expected to manage their own lives after they finish school. So we discussed a number of techniques that are frequently used to help others achieve a greater degree of self-control: self-recording, control of setting events, management of consequences, self-verbalizations, and behavioral contracting. The emphasis was on a planned program that gives students more responsibility for directing their lives as they demonstrate greater self-management abilities.

Finally, attention was given to the ethical and legal problems of classroom management (Chapter Eight). While specific classroom management techniques may be combined to produce changes in student behaviors, we realized that teachers often use different techniques because of their beliefs about right and wrong. Therefore, we asked that a careful examination of all classroom management practices be made to determine if those techniques could meet the highest ethical standards, as well as correspond to all legal requirements. The special attention to ethical and legal issues underscored our own belief that only classroom control that recognizes the rights and dignity of every person can ultimately accomplish the high goal of enriching the lives of students and teachers.

Approaching Actual Problems

We believe effective classroom management entails some elements from each of the preceding chapters. Indeed, Chapters Two through Eight constitute a model for managing most classroom problems. This is not to say that our format is the only one to follow. Far from it. But few problems can be permanently resolved without some plan. Our plan includes:

1. Assessing teacher attitudes.
2. Selecting a classroom strategy for altering deficit or excess student behavior.
3. Working with the home.
4. Working with school resource personnel in managing children with special needs.
5. Moving students toward higher degrees of self-responsibility.
6. Maintaining the highest ethical and legal practices.

Naturally, some problems will involve greater emphasis on one or more of the above points than others. For example, if you have determined that the problem represents a deficit in a given behavior, you would rely heavily upon prompting and reinforcing desired actions. You would avoid punishments, because punishment would lead to further suppression of behavior. Of course, you would still examine your own attitudes, perhaps involve the parents or others, try to move the student toward self-management of his own behavior, and insure that you did not violate your own conceptions of right and wrong or break any laws. Similarly, if the problem is excessive behavior, you would be just as thorough in applying each of the above procedures. But you might also legitimately rely on certain forms of punishment to suppress the unwanted actions. With the preceding format as our model, let us now look at a way of solving two different problems—one representing a deficit behavior and one an excessive behavior. We will make a number of suggestions from each chapter. You can use those suggestions that seem most appropriate for you and your students.

Motivating Students to Complete Assignments

Mrs. Wilson, a fifth-grade teacher, told us that one of her major problems was "motivating" students to complete assignments. She said that TV, sports, and other competing student interests ranked higher on students' hierarchy than school work. She said it was getting harder every year to get students to do homework. Mrs. Wilson also confided that students frequently did not complete class assignments. "They seem busy, but too many fail to complete their classwork" is how she described her class. What do you think can be done?

Assessing teacher attitudes. In assessing how attitudes affect student behaviors, one should consider how his own feelings are communicated to the students. It is the manifestations of feelings, not the inward thoughts themselves, which influence others. In thinking about Mrs. Wilson, we asked ourselves what she might be communicating to her students. Is she telling them through verbal and nonverbal messages that outside activities are *always* less important than homework? Does she consider *special* events when she gives assignments? Does the way she personally relates to extracurricular events influence how the students perceive her? Is it possible that Mrs. Wilson is indirectly indicating to her students that they are not as *good* as former students? Could an increased interest by Mrs. Wilson in a hobby or nonschool activity improve her classroom management skills? Of course, we have no absolute answers. However, by asking herself these and similar questions, Mrs. Wilson might come up with some ideas which would be helpful.

Managing deficit behaviors. Since the problem of motivating students to complete assignments represents something teachers want students to *do* rather than *not do*, the emphasis should be on prompting and reinforcing desired actions as opposed to punishment. While there are many plausible explanations for the behavior of Mrs. Wilson's students, we wondered if the students could actually do the work that was being assigned. Could some of her students have been assigned inappropriate books? Does she need to simplify her instructions? Does she need to link some of her assignments to outside student activities? You could probably think of other questions for Mrs. Wilson that might suggest how to prompt more of what she wants from her students.

Although this was never stated in her explanation of the problem, we hypothesize that Mrs. Wilson's students find little reason for completing assignments. Yes, they may fail for not doing them. But so what. A good grade for performing or the threat of a poor one for nonperforming may be insufficient to motivate many students. There must be a *meaningful* reward for everyone. Mrs. Wilson must get just as enthusiastic about the completion of assignments as she does about noncompletion, perhaps even more so. She has to recognize and reward improvement. We are not implying that Mrs. Wilson is the sole problem. The problem is finding appropriate ways of cuing student performance and insuring that students get reinforced for their efforts. Then, the students will *want* to perform. They will have a good reason for doing so.

Working with the home. Failure of students to complete homework assignments immediately suggests a need to increase the involvement of parents. Mrs. Wilson might be able to use some of her parents as tutors, aides, or resource persons. Or, she might wish to develop a cooperative program with some parents to provide reinforcement to students at home for work completed at school. Judicious use of the telephone, "Happy Grams" (positive notes to parents about a student's performance), and home visits might improve the school situation. Certainly, all of these suggestions take time. But the alternative is the continuation of the problem. Often the initial expenditure of a little time eventually results in a savings.

Working with school resource personnel. Through use of the techniques described in earlier chapters, Mrs. Wilson can probably increase homework completion without outside consultation. However, school specialists such as the school psychologist or counselor can provide assistance in this matter. Possibly Mrs. Wilson could use assistance in establishing a reinforcement program for her class. Perhaps she could benefit by discussing "what's new" in classroom management with colleagues or others. (Maybe one of them has read the latest edition of *Making It Till Friday*.) After all, Mrs. Wilson did say that things were getting worse each year. Maybe someone else can re-spark the old interests that led her into teaching.

Teaching self-responsibility. Students performing work assignments without being prodded is an important goal in education. Unfortunately, some students will always require more nudging than others, but most are capable of achieving fairly high degrees of self-responsibility. (Of course no one ever becomes *totally* independent of others.) Many teachers find contracting to be an effective way of moving away from a teacher-dominated to a student-teacher controlled environment. In schoolwork contracts, students can share in specifying assignments and the payoffs for performance and nonperformance. Another relevant strategy is self-recording. By logging the time they spend studying, watching TV, and engaging in other activities, students often realize the need for changing their behaviors. Still another approach is to increase student input in class discussions. Maybe Mrs. Wilson is too much the center of the class. Many students have the attitude that when someone else makes all the decisions, that person can also do all the work. Perhaps you have other thoughts on moving students toward greater self-responsibility.

Maintaining high ethical and legal practices. Ethical and legal issues must be considered when using any classroom management strategy. Mrs. Wilson has a continuing responsibility to examine the means by which she achieves desired ends. If external rewards are being used, she should have a plan for phasing out those rewards. Long-term use of any extrinsic, artificial reward system can diminish the value of doing a task for the joy of learning. Students ought to be asked what personal pleasure they receive from a task well done. They should be helped to assess their pride in achievement and not be asked to do something indefinitely because it makes the teacher proud. Mrs. Wilson should also consider personal accountability. If students do not complete the required assignments, will they be able to attain an adequate mastery of the subject matter?

Student Defiance

Mr. Johnson, a first-year teacher, had been experiencing increasing difficulties with a number of his general math students. Early in the year, he seemed to get along well with them and they worked hard for him. They appeared eager to please him. As time passed, he noticed that many of the boys were becoming less compliant with his requests. They would murmur among themselves, laugh at his requests, and take their own time about doing what he asked. Sometimes students would ignore him, acting as though they could not hear what he said. Mr. Johnson initially avoided taking any action, hoping the situation would improve. He feared getting a reputation for not being able to handle his classes. However, he realized something had to be done when one of his students made an obscene gesture after being asked to stop talking. Assume you are the teacher. What can be done?

Assessing teacher attitudes. Regardless of whether the problem is one of getting students to perform a desired act or to refrain from performing an undesirable one, you will want to assess your own attitudes to determine if they may be contributing to the problem. This step is especially critical when the problem involves disagreements between you and a student. Perhaps a change in your behavior can steer student-teacher relationships in a positive direction. Consideration of the following questions may help you to clarify teacher attitudes toward student defiance:

1. *Attitudes toward others.* Has the student done something in the past to make you more "watchful" of him? Could you be expecting the worst as far as the student is concerned? Do you believe that a teacher should show students who is boss? As a result, do you dare students to defy you? Have you, perhaps unconsciously, built situations that will increase the probability of confrontative behavior?

2. *Attitudes toward self.* How does it make you feel when a student refuses to comply with your requests? Are you afraid of appearing weak if compromise is allowed? Do you feel that respect for a teacher will be lower if he admits to making a mistake? How do you think other people will view you if they find out that a student has successfully defied you?

After examining your own attitudes, you may find that the problem is being prompted or exaggerated by your own actions. If so, perhaps you might choose to implement one or more of the following suggestions:

1. Demonstrate a willingness to admit mistakes. Your credibility will be increased, and it is more likely that students will consider your requests worthy of compliance.

2. Use an indirect approach when dealing with defiant students. Respond to the feelings behind their overt behavior. (Remember our comments on listening to others.)

3. Attempt to establish a personal relationship with your students. Knowing and communicating something good about each student can demonstrate that you care about each person in your class. Direct defiance of your authority is less likely if students feel you are interested in them.

4. Put misbehavior in perspective. Students who defy your authority may have little against you personally. Realizing this, you may respond more calmly.

5. Treat all students equally. Do not require compliance from some students while other students are not required to comply with the same request or rules.

Managing excessive behaviors. As we mentioned previously, the management of excessive behaviors may involve nonpunitive as well as punitive techniques. Nonpunitive strategies typically include procedures designed to increase behaviors incompatible with undesirable behaviors. In Mr. Johnson's class it would seem highly desirable to increase cooperative student behaviors. Any strategies designed to reinforce cooperation, model desired actions, and change setting events in such a way that the unwanted defiance is prevented would seem appropriate. Negative intervention techniques might also be used to deal temporarily with the worst acts of defiance. Mr. Johnson could select a combination of the following management strategies to better his situation:

1. Make an effort to notice when students cooperate, and verbally praise this behavior.
2. Make sure students understand that praise and rewards are tied to cooperative behavior. Reward immediately following acts of cooperation.
3. When a student seldom cooperates fully, shape cooperative behavior by rewarding behaviors that approximate the goal of full cooperation.
4. Model the behaviors you expect. That is, tell students why you are following certain policies yourself and demonstrate how you comply. You should also avoid behaving in aggressive ways.
5. Closely related to modeling appropriate behavior is the need to avoid giving commands that you have no authority to enforce or that you would be unable to enforce if confronted. It is better to ask students to do something than to tell them what they are going to do.
6. Try to deal with the inappropriate behavior in private (a change in setting events). Little can be accomplished when opposing individuals are forced into a confrontation while other individuals are watching. If the student complies with your request to accompany you out of the room, try to find a place where he can sit quietly and "cool off" before you attempt to discuss the problem. This time will also allow you to make arrangements for your other students.
7. While withholding all attention for defiance is probably an unrealistic request, attention can be directed at the student's feelings and reasons for defiance rather than at the overt behavior itself. For example, you might say, "You believe I

should not have asked you to stop talking at this particular moment," "You feel I have been unfair with you today." If the student responds in any way positively to your empathy, the door may be open for talking out the problem. In effect, you have started an extinction process by withholding attention for inappropriate behavior while reinforcing appropriate expressions.

8. When a teacher's authority is challenged, the problem is usually not confined to one student and the teacher. Other students in the class may also become emotionally involved even though they do not overtly act out. To avoid having students take sides and possibly reinforce defiance by directing attention to the problem, we suggest that student attention be focused on assignments. To say, "We have work to do; this is between ... and me," will usually suffice. You might also consider having a group meeting at a later time to discuss how peer attention influences class behavior.

9. If a student is obstinate about staying in the class and is threatening you, it may be necessary to ask for assistance from the school administrator. However, the basic problem cannot be solved by the principal or vice-principal. The problem remains between you and the student. The principal may be required to remove the student for a temporary period (time out), but you should personally work out the problem with the student after a cooling off period has been allowed.

10. Avoid using harsh punishment or suggesting to the principal that the student be suspended. A positive approach incorporating some curtailment of privileges, but allowing the student to overcome the incident without extreme action, seems preferable. Suspension may be viewed by the disinterested student as a holiday, rather than punishment. Thus, the intended effect may not result.

Working with parents. Any time a problem with a student appears to be escalating, it would be wise to consider talking with the parents. You could indicate that you and their child are having difficulties. You could also get their suggestions for dealing with their child. Talking with parents can avert subsequent disagreements over why they have not been advised earlier, should the necessity for punishment arise. Mr. Johnson's problems might never have occurred had he established a good relationship with his students' parents. Students are more likely to cooperate when you are on positive speaking terms with their parents. In any case, Mr.

Johnson's situation is such that a talk with some of his parents is essential. Chances are the parents will come to him if he waits much longer.

Working with school personnel. One possible aid when confronted with a defiant student is consultation with the school counselor or school psychologist. If the problem has been going on for some time without resolution, you may need objective analysis from another professional. You might ask the counselor, for example, to observe your interactions with the students and give you suggestions for possible changes. In the problem before us, we suspect that Mr. Johnson does, indeed, need to consider the manner in which he makes requests as well as the demands he is placing on students.

Teaching self-responsibility. No teacher can eliminate defiance without the cooperation of the students. Frequently, defiant students wish they had never challenged others, but they lack the knowledge for achieving greater self-control. At other times, students may become defiant simply because they have been excluded from decision-making processes. We suggest that the students be given the opportunity to:

1. Examine the setting events and reinforcers that may be precipitating and controlling their behaviors.
2. Consider the merits of self-verbalizations. (This tactic seems extremely appropriate for helping students practice more acceptable ways of expressing themselves.)
3. Develop behavioral contracts for appropriate classroom behaviors.

Maintaining high ethical and legal practices. Chapter Eight implied that many classroom management problems could be averted if teachers would carefully consider the ethical and legal implications of their actions. Indeed, much student defiance could be a direct result of their feeling that they are not being treated as they should be. In considering the problem of defiance, we recommend that you ask yourself:

1. Is the defiance a result of attempts to create unnecessary conformity? Do I give the students ample opportunity to question classroom goals?
2. Have the techniques (either positive or negative) I am using generated defiance? Would an alternative approach be just as acceptable without creating a similar problem?
3. Have I recognized the rights of the students? Are they being treated as I would treat adults? Have any basic privileges to

which students are entitled by right been withheld?

4. Are some students being treated "more equally" than others?

From the discussion of the preceding problems, it is amply clear that no simple solution exists for managing classroom difficulties. Still, you may wonder which specific techniques should be applied when several options are available for remedying one of the factors. For instance, if immediate action is needed, which technique should be used: a soft reprimand, time out, response cost, or overcorrection? The answer depends on your setting, your students, and your own preferences. Some school administrators may ask that certain techniques be avoided. The age of your students might preclude frequent use of certain techniques. Also, your experiences with a student may reveal that one technique will work for him while another technique does not. And you may prefer one strategy over another. Probably, however, you will use most of the techniques with different students at different times.

We think you ought to be familiar with as many alternatives for changing behavior as possible. We also think you should be prepared to deal with a variety of problems so you are not caught without any idea of what is happening when misbehavior occurs. For that reason, we are offering a number of simulated classroom problems to allow you to practice working through different incidents before facing them in class. Imagine yourself as the classroom teacher who must deal with each of these common problems. Just as we did on the problem of defiance, we suggest that you peruse Chapters Two through Eight, selecting the techniques you believe most appropriate for each problem. Remember to: (1) assess your personal attitudes, (2) select your classroom strategies dependent upon whether the problem represents a deficit or excess of student behavior, (3) work cooperatively with the home, (4) use all available resources in your school, (5) work toward helping students achieve self-responsibility for their behaviors, and (6) maintain the highest ethical and legal practices in classroom management.

1. Marie is an attractive, first-year high school physical education and health teacher. Frequently, she comes from a physical education class to a health class in gym shorts because she doesn't want to change clothes three to four times each day. Several of the mature boys in class have been making remarks about her legs and her good looks. She is afraid things are going a little too far. What can she do?

2. Christy is a very quiet, shy, and withdrawn fifth grader. You

observe that she is a loner in class and that she does not approach other students. In addition, she is not approached by them. She seems to be an unhappy child. As her teacher, you are concerned about her inability to interact with her peers. What can you do to help her?

3. You notice that your eighth-grade students are apathetic during history class. Very seldom do they comment and then only in response to your direct questions. You question the desirability of this situation. What can you do?

4. Scott tends to assume a threatening posture and is often verbally aggressive to other seventh graders. In particular, he engages in name-calling, and brags about beating up other boys if they bother him. How can this problem be resolved?

5. Andrea and Deborah are close friends. During class periods, they continually whisper and pass notes. Some of the other students complain that they cannot work because the whispering disturbs them. How can you deal with students who talk during class activities?

6. Several of your fourth-grade boys are loud and boisterous during the lunch period. Their table manners are usually poor, and some days worse than others. For example, they throw bread and swap food, sometimes overloading their plates. The behavior of the students disrupts your own lunch periods. How can you create a calmer, more enjoyable lunch period for all?

7. Mary and Susan run to tell you that two of your fifth-grade boys are fighting on the playground. This is not the first time that your boys have become involved in fights during the recess period. You do not wish to have the fights occur again. What can you do to deal immediately with the behavior at hand, and how can you prevent fights in the future?

8. Leroy appears to have good intentions about doing his school work. However, he seldom completes an assignment. You realize that something should be done to change his behavior. Analyze and provide suggestions for this common problem.

9. You enter your room on Friday to find desks overturned, walls decorated with writing, and papers strewn over the floor. You are distressed at the wreckage, but must continue the day as usual. You feel, however, that something should be done about the vandalism problem. What are some things that you as a teacher might do?

10. Two of your tenth-grade girls are consistently tardy to history class. They give one excuse and then another for being late. You want to give them the benefit of the doubt, but you are convinced that their excuses are invalid. What can you do to reduce their tardy behavior?

11. Your fourth-grade students tend to run in the school halls unless directly supervised. In addition to being unsafe, this behavior is disruptive for other classes. You certainly do not wish to have it continue. What can you do to eliminate the problem of your students' running in the halls?

12. Several of your students are reported to create disturbances on the school bus. In particular, they push and shove and refuse to share seats with others. Is there anything you can do to reduce this behavior, even though you do not ride the bus?

13. Several students report that their school supplies and personal clothes have been "ripped off" at school. Problems with stealing appear to be increasing. What are some ways you might approach student theft?

14. It is becoming increasingly apparent that drugs and alcohol are problems for some of the students in your class. The problem obviously cannot be extinguished by ignoring it. What are some constructive ways of approaching it?

15. You have been given a teaching assignment as a twelfth-grade English teacher in an inner city school. You find that students tend to group together with no interaction taking place among the various racial groups in your classroom. How would you approach this problem?

16. You have been asked to supervise a fifth-period high school study hall class. You know that several big, boisterous boys have been assigned to this class. Therefore, you are concerned that you will be unable to maintain order and to deal with problems that may arise. However, you have no choice but to carry out this assignment. What are some ways that you might approach the study hall in order to minimize problems?

17. Bob, a young teacher, is having difficulties with several of his eighth-grade girls. They follow him around, want to talk with him in private, pass notes to him, and in general let him know that they like him a lot. Bob wants to be friendly, but he realizes that he must do something to establish the *proper* relationship with these girls. What can he do?

18. One of your ninth graders, Jay, is absent from school more

frequently than he is present. You are concerned about his truant behavior. What can you do to help keep Jay in school.

Concluding Remarks

Classroom management problems have always existed and, at least to some extent, always will. No one is suggesting that teachers can prevent every problem. Some problems are simply the result of normal interpersonal interactions. We are not sure life would be enjoyable if we never experienced any problems. Some of our most worthwhile achievments have come from gaining better understanding of ourselves as a result of working through a problem situation. Similarly, we have experienced much joy in helping others overcome difficulties and move toward greater self-control.

However, it is one thing to face an occasional problem and another to live a life inundated with problems. Too many teachers tell us the latter situation characterizes life in today's classrooms. No one deserves such a fate. We think teachers can improve circumstances by becoming more aware of the techniques now available for improving most classrooms. But awareness alone will not make a good teacher. One must have the courage to apply what is known. There is a big difference between knowing and doing. We hope our book has helped increase your knowledge. If so, only the task of application remains. Only you can make the application.

INDEX

Absenteeism, *see* Truancy
Abuse, child, 131-132
Academic materials
    programmed, 42
    teacher developed, 42-43
    variety of, 43-44
Acceptance, 20
Accountability, *see* Legal issues
Administrators, working with,
    106-109
Anxiety, teacher, 1-2
Approval
    rules for using, 56-57
    teacher, 55-57
Attention
    seeking, 75-76
    teacher, 55-57
    withholding teacher, 74-76
Attitudes
    critical teacher, 18-23
    impact of teacher, 16-18,
      199, 201-202

Behavior change, *see also*
    Classroom management
    ethical issues of, 171-184
    guidelines for, 183-184
    legal issues of, 187-190
    model, 198
    purposes of, 171-175
    teacher, 23-30
Behavior problems, 129-130, *see*
    also Classroom

    management problems
Bribery, 176-177

Class meeting, 34-35
Classroom management, 10-11
Classroom management
    problems
    behavior and emotional,
      129-130
    causes of, 4-5
    defined, 10
    hearing related, 127-128
    home related, 130-132
    learning disability, 128-129,
      138
    reading, 41
    speech related, 130, 141
    vision related, 126-127
Conformity, 174-175
Contracting, 7, 161-165
Corporal punishment
    as a change strategy, 80-81
    ethical problems of, 179-180
    legal aspects of, 188-190
Creativity, 174-175
Criticism, 180-181, *see also*
    Reprimands

Defiance of authority, 201
Discipline, 2, *see also* Classroom
    management
Disruptiveness
    creating, 4

examples of, 67
treatment of, 67-93
Due process, 184-186

Emotional problems, 129-130,
    see also Classroom
    management problems
Empathy, 20-21
Epilepsy, 140
Equal protection, 186-187
Extinction
    applications of, 74-78
    defined, 74

Fading, 62

Genuineness, 19-20
Goals
    behavior change, 171-175
    guidelines for setting,
        173-174
    institutional, 172-173
    personal, 172-173
Group alerting, 45
Groupings, classroom, 43-44

Happy grams, 106
Health problems, 125-126, see
    also Classroom
    management problems
Hearing problems, 127-128, see
    also Classroom
    management problems
Home problems, 130-132, see
    also Classroom
    management problems
Hope, teacher, 2-9
Hyperactive child, 63

I.E.P., 121, see also Public law
    94-142
Impulsiveness, 160
Instructions, giving clear, 37-38
Interests
    student, 44
    teacher, 28-29

Learning disability, 128-129, 138
Legal issues
    accountability, teacher, 192

cautions, 190-191
in behavior change
    techniques, 187-190
student rights, 184-187
Listening, 26
Locus of control, 4

Mainstreaming, 120, 122, 124,
    see also Public law
    94-142
Mistakes, admitting, 30
Modeling
    crucial variables, 47-48
    defined, 45
    uses, 45-46
Models
    peers, 72-74
    teacher, 45-48
Motivation, 32-65, 199-200

Overcorrection
    applications of, 90-92
    defined, 82

Parents
    as teachers, 104-105
    cooperating with, 103-117,
        142, 200
    night, 108
    rights of, 116-117
Payoffs, 52-58, see also
    Reinforcers
Public law 94-142
    explanation of, 119-120
    implications of, 121-122
Prompting behavior, 33-48,
    50-51
Punishment
    alternatives to, 67-78
    ethical problems of, 179-180
    guidelines for using, 83-84,
        94-95
    legal issues, 188-190
    types of, 80-82

Questions, 49

Realness, 19-20
Record keeping
    methods, 152-153

sheets, 154
Referrals, 123-125, 142
Reinforcement
    ethical problems of 175-179
    of incompatible behaviors,
        69-72, 78-79
    legal issues, 188
    positive, 48-49
    self, 156-159
    techniques, 58-60
Reinforcers
    defined, 48-49
    selection of, 52-55
    types of, 53, 58-60, 106
Reprimands
    harsh, 80
    soft, 84-86
Response cost
    applications of, 88-90
    defined, 82
    ethical problems of, 182-183
Resource specialists, 113-114,
        133-144
Rewards,see Reinforcers
Rules
    classroom, 34-36, 173-174
    guides for establishing,
        35-36
    schoolwide, 36-37

School counselor, 134-136
School nurse, 139-140
School psychologist, 136-139
School social worker, 142
Self-esteem, teacher, 23-26
Self-management
    concerns about, 165-166
    origins of, 148-149
    teaching, 200-201, 205
    techniques of, 150-166
Self-recording, 150-155
Self-verbalization, 159-160
Sensitivity, teacher, 17-18
Setting events

cues for appropriate
    behavior, 39-40
managing disruptive
    behavior, 68-70
self-control, 155-156
Shaping, 61
Shyness, 62-63
Skill levels, 41-42
Speech pathologist, 141-142
Speech problems, 130, 141, see
    also Classroom
    management problems
Stealing, 89-90, 135
Student rights, see Due process
    and Equal protection
Study behavior, 155-156
Successive approximations, see
    Shaping

Talkativeness
    student, 112
    teacher, 26
Tangible rewards
    effects of non-natural
        rewards, 179
    effects on dispensers, 178
    effects on non-rewarded
        individuals, 178-179
    effects on recipients, 177-178
    types of, 53
Tantrums, 160-161
Tardiness, 60
Time out
    applications, 86-88, 157
    defined, 82
    ethical problems of, 181-182
    legal problems of, 188
Truancy, 60
Vandalism, 93-98
Violence, 93-98
Vision problems, 126-127, see
    also Classroom
    management problems

A comprehensive coverage of the techniques that help teachers instill desirable social skills and weaken undesirable behaviors so that the ultimate goal will be realized: to facilitate learning. Both prospective and in-service teachers will find many practical ideas they can apply.

"Teaching isn't a fun-thing anymore."

Princeton Book Company, Publishers
P.O. Box 109, Princeton, New Jersey 08540